The Advance of the Weird Tale

THE ADVANCE OF THE WEIRD TALE

S. T. Joshi

Sarnath Press • Seattle

Contents

I. Some Overviews

Weird Fiction and Ordinary People

I have just emerged from a reading of the complete works of Stephen King, a horrific experience (and not in the way King intended) that I would not wish upon anyone. But this experience has forced me to come to grips with the whole notion of how, and why, modern (i.e., post-Lovecraftian) weird fiction seems so different *in kind* from weird fiction of the era of Machen, Blackwood, Dunsany, and Lovecraft. Oddly enough, my thoughts on this matter have received an impetus from a recent debate in the letter column of *Weird Tales*. In the Spring 1992 issue, Pete Miller wrote that he found the lengthy character descriptions in the work of Stephen King and Dean R. Koontz tiresome and irrelevant, noting that this sort of thing is not to be found in earlier weird writing. "Take, for example, the work of our greatest writers in the genre, Edgar Allan Poe and H. P. Lovecraft. Neither of them ever developed a 'believable character' in his best work, yet they are still fascinating readers of all ages while the work of our current 'giants' (King and Koontz) is forgotten shortly after it is read. How do you explain that?"

Weird Tales editor Darrell Schweitzer pooh-poohed this, but his arguments do not convince. He first says, pontifically, that "Stories are about people" (a generalisation so broad as to be meaningless) and then notes that there are believable characters in Poe and Lovecraft; but there is not much to be said for this, for what we find in these latter writers are either very penetrating studies of abnormal psychology (Poe) or rather bland characters whose sole significance lies in serving as a sort of prism through which the reader experiences the weird events of the tale (Lovecraft). This whole notion of human characters and their role in weird fiction needs to be considered in detail, for I think it really is at the heart of the very fundamental difference between modern and older weird writing.

Let us start with a statement made by Lovecraft in 1921:

I could not write about "ordinary people" because I am not in the least interested in them. Without interest there can be no art. Man's relations to man do not captivate my fancy. It is man's relation to the cosmos—to the unknown—which alone arouses in me the spark of creative imagination. The humanocentric pose is impossible to me, for I cannot acquire the primitive myopia which magnifies the earth and ignores the background.

Lovecraft no doubt used this dictum to justify his idea of "cosmic" weird fiction, in which the entire human race is regarded as an insignificant blot on the back door of the cosmos; but I think his words have a broader implication. What has been happening in weird fiction since Lovecraft is a vast reorientation of focus: ordinary people are somehow regarded as intrinsically *important*, and the weird phenomena are, very broadly, seen as threats to their middle-class stability. Stefan Dziemianowicz has labelled this tendency the "banalisation" of horror, although he did not intend the term pejoratively but merely descriptively. What he meant was the increasing concern by weird writers to depict the minute details of the mundane lives of mundane people, both in an attempt to win the reader's sympathy (we all like to read about ourselves) and so as to lay the groundwork for the intrusion of the weird into a familiar realm. There is no question, of course, that this sort of thing has been an important factor in the popular success of the modern weird tale, especially amongst readers who are not otherwise attracted to weird fiction; but whether there has been a corresponding literary advance is another matter. Stephen King has stated that "my idea of what a horror story should be [is that] the monster shouldn't be in a graveyard in decadent old Europe, but in the house down the street." King maintains, correctly, that this notion was evolving in the generation just prior to his, with such writers as Ray Bradbury, Shirley Jackson, and Richard Matheson; but it can serve as a very clear formulation of what modern weird fiction purports to be, and a supposed justification for putting ordinary people at the forefront of a weird situation.

But I do not think that weird fiction should be about ordinary people. Even if one does not adopt the cosmic attitude of Lovecraft, even if one wishes to depict the insidious incursion of the weird into the ordinary, the emphasis should be on the weird and not the ordinary. It is because so many weird writers emphasise the latter rather than the former that their work seems to me thin and poorly conceived: amidst all the effort spent upon portraying "realistic" human figures, not enough attention is devoted to what is presumably the raison d'être of the work itself, the weird phenomenon. I do not think this is merely a personal prejudice: if weird fiction is to be a distinct mode of writing, then it should not feel the need to ape so many of the conventions that make mainstream fiction a distinct mode of writing. There is scarcely a single "normal" character in all Thomas Ligotti's work, and this is what gives it much of its effectiveness. I am not saying that weird fiction should simply deal with odd people; but the overall *scenario* should be odd and strange, with the human figures subordinate to the general weird conception. Stephen King may fancy himself the modern-day Theodore Dreiser, just as Peter Straub imagines that he is our contemporary Henry James; but a ploughing through even a single one of their gargantuan tomes full of superficial portrayals of boring people and their boring problems that have nothing to do with the weird phenomenon is enough to make one despair for the future of all weird writing. It is only the exceptionally talented writer—a Shirley Jackson or a Robert Aickman—who has the insight to depict human relationships in all their complexity and the skill to incorporate these relationships into the very fabric of the weird situation.

Let us consider some specific examples. Stephen King's novel *It* (1986) may be one of the most spectacular fiascos in modern literature. This grotesquely bloated novel—1150 pages long—is so crippled by inessential and superficial character description that the actual horrific scenario has no chance to develop. We encounter seven children, six boys and one girl, in the Maine town of Derry in 1958. Aside from having to escape frequent pummelings from the school bully, Henry Bowers, they each find themselves facing some loathsome entity which they can only label "It." After about 700 pages pass, we finally learn that this entity is a manitou or shapeshifter, which has the convenient capacity of presenting itself in the form most terrifying to its observer. Years pass; the children grow up to become entirely undistinguished adults (one of whom, Bill Denbrough, is another in a long line of Stephen King stand-ins, being a bestselling horror writer). It transpires that It reawakens in Derry every twenty-seven years or so to murder children or, indeed, anyone who has the misfortune to cross its path. The children had taken a vow to return to Derry if It ever showed its face again, so sure enough they come marching back from all across the country to battle the evil thing and, naturally, to conquer it. This entire scenario allows King to go on at appalling length about both the youthful and the adult lives of his utterly unremarkable characters; but, in the actual manifestation of the manitou, he faces the same difficulty that Peter Straub encountered in *Ghost Story* (1979), from which the central weird phenomenon was surely derived: the manitou is a virtually eternal entity, so how is one to dispatch it? But in some fashion or other that remains entirely unclear, our courageous band manages to do so. What has happened in this novel is that King is under the misguided conception that we are reading his book for the sake of the characters and not for the sake of the weird phenomenon; so he puts all his effort into the former, and tosses off the latter with such little attention to logic and plausibility that the novel collapses of its own absurdity.

Let us now turn to another novel of King's that has been received far more favourably—*Pet Sematary* (1976). In my mind there are many serious problems with this novel, but its true failing is an utterly maudlin and dripping sentimentalism. This problem dogs nearly all King's work, but here it is worse than usual. King wants us to be intimately concerned with the fate of a nice, wholesome, middle-class family—husband, wife, young daughter, and infant son—as they move into an anomalous region in Maine; but who aside from other nice, wholesome, middle-class people could possibly care about what happens to them? Consider the wife's reaction when her son dies in a car accident:

> "I moved the couch while you were in Bangor . . . I thought running the vacuum around would take my mind off . . . off things . . . and I found four of his little Matchbox cars under there . . . as if they were waiting for him to come back and . . . you know, play with them . . ." Her voice, already wavering, now broke. Tears spilled down her cheeks. "And that's when I took the second Valium because I started crying again, the way I'm crying now . . . oh what a fucking soap opera all of this is . . . hold me, Lou, will you hold me?"

Can one imagine Robert Aickman writing something like this? If King's self-proclaimed virtue lies in bringing horror down to the level of ordinary people, then things like this are the best possible argument for believing that horror has no business with ordinary people.

I fear that even Ramsey Campbell, surely the leading weird writer of our generation, occasionally falls into this trap. It seems to me as if, in most of his novels—*The Face That Must Die* (1977) and *The Count of Eleven* (1991) are the obvious exceptions—Campbell has made a conscious decision to make his vision less intense than in his short stories and more in conformity with middle-class values. Although *Midnight Sun* (1990) is easily one of his best novels, this attitude of regarding the ordinary lives of ordinary people as somehow having intrinsic significance cripples the book at its conclusion. Throughout the novel Ben Sterling senses that he is on the brink of some vast revelation, which is somehow connected with the dense forest behind his ancestral home ("It seemed to him that the silent luminous dance was constantly about to form a pattern in the air—that if he could only distinguish the pattern, unimaginable revelations might follow"; "he felt as though an inspiration or a vision larger than he could imagine was hovering just out of reach"). Finally the revelation comes. Ben's great-grandfather Edward Sterling was found dead of exposure in the icy forest, and Ben realises that "Edward Sterling's death had been only the beginning. The forest concealed what his death had liberated—what had accompanied him beyond the restraint of the midnight sun." In other words, there is some vast ice-entity waiting for release in the forest. Now Ben feels as if he must take up the task of ushering in this entity back into the world. It is one of Campbell's great triumphs that this nebulous entity, as well as Ben's apparent yielding to it, is never described as anything but awesome and cosmic: fear has no place in this scenario. Campbell himself, in the acknowledgements to the novel, places it in the category of "visionary horror fiction," and indeed much of the novel is reminiscent of Algernon Blackwood's portrayal of the throbbing vitality of Nature, a portrayal as devoid of horror (in the sense of fear for the harm that might be caused to human beings) as Campbell's.

And yet, at the end Ben has a change of heart and seeks to combat the entity and thrust it back into the dark again. I find this transformation entirely unmotivated. It is true that Ben's self-immolation in the depths of the forest bring to mind the impromptu fairy tale he told as a boy—of the people who live "at the edge of the coldest place in the world" and whose responsibility it is to tend to the fires that will keep the ice from overrunning the world—but the thrust of Campbell's entire narrative has been leading up to the conclusion that the release of the ice-entity is in no way a horrific but simply an awesome event:

> The world and the stars had been less than a dream, nothing more than a momentary lapse in its consciousness, and the metamorphosis which was reaching for the world was infinitesimal by its standards, simply a stirring in its sleep, a transient dream of the awful perfection which would overtake infinity when the presence beyond the darkness was fully awake.

And yet, Ben, by choosing his family over the entity ("The only light he wanted to see now, too late, was the light in Ellen's and the children's eyes"), is also choosing the safe and bourgeois comforts of family life over the awesome and supremely impersonal force of Nature, even though Campbell has been suggesting all along that the former is utterly insignificant in relation to the latter.

What I am getting at in all this is that weird fiction should be *weird*. It should not try to copy the mannerisms of mainstream fiction by having laborious portrayals of "real" people, especially if these portrayals are developed at the expense of developing the actual weird scenario. Lovecraft was correct when he stated, long ago, that phenomena and not human beings are the true "heroes" of weird fiction. There really are very few "believable" characters in Poe, Lovecraft, Machen, Blackwood, Dunsany, and Ligotti (T. E. D. Klein is, to my mind, the only writer who has managed to depict vivid, realistic human figures without disfiguring the focus of his weird conceptions); we do not read these writers for "believable" characters, but (as Lovecraft wrote) for "a certain atmosphere of breathless and unexplainable dread of outer, unknown forces . . . a malign and particular suspension or defeat of those fixed laws of Nature which are our only safeguard against the assaults of chaos and the daemons of unplumbed space." In this formulation, ordinary people have no place.

The Canon of Weird Fiction

It has occurred to me that one of the implicit goals of my critical work is to lay down a canon of weird writing. No one need be reminded of the problematical nature of such an enterprise, although one hopes there may be less scepticism of it in light of Harold Bloom's *The Western Canon* (1994), which argues more cogently for the necessity of canon-formation than I can do. In essence, Bloom's argument is as follows:

There must be canons (and, indeed, there will always be canons whether anyone wants them or not) because there is only a limited time for reading amidst the myriad other activities of life. Such canons need not be exclusive, although by their very nature canons establish certain criteria that some works will meet and others will not; and any single critic's or reader's canon need be nothing more than suggestive, not prescriptive.

What is criticism, after all, but an individual's exercise of critical judgment? The degree to which that judgment is informed, coherent, and sensitive will determine its validity. Those readers and critics who object to criticism that is "subjective" miss the boat entirely: in searching for "objective" standards of valuation, they are attempting to turn criticism into an exact science (which it is not and never can be) and to bypass this whole issue of critical judgment—probably because they possess so little of it themselves. The root word of "criticism" is, after all, the Greek verb *kritein*, which means "to judge, distinguish, discriminate." The whole notion of distinguishing the good from the bad, the brilliant from the mediocre, has fallen into disfavour in our democratic age: either one dismisses the whole enterprise as offensively "elitist" (as if there is something wrong with excellence), or else artistic works are now valued or scorned on the basis of whether they do or do not conform to certain political ideals—many of which are, indeed, quite admirable when applied to the actual functioning of civilised society, but which are either irrelevant or pernicious when made into a bed of Procrustes into which literature must fit or forever be banished as "unwholesome." Fortunately, our field is sufficiently removed from many real-world concerns that it may be some time before weird fiction is judged acceptable on the basis of whether its author is or is not of a certain gender, sexual orientation, or race, and whether his or her work does or does not promote equality and/or harmony among the genders and races.

One seemingly "objective" standard that has frequently been put forth as a yardstick of quality is *endurance*; but I do not think many are aware how problematical this is. There are all sorts of political, social, and cultural factors that lead to the survival or disappearance of certain works, and abstract quality does not always enter into the matter. Consider some of the anomalies in the transmission of Greek and Latin literature. The reason we have only seven plays each by Aeschylus and Sophocles (out of the dozens each of them wrote) is that these fourteen were commonly taught in schools in antiquity. Since the motives for preservation here are *pedagogical* and not (or not only) *qualitative*, the survival of these fourteen plays can only be considered an accident. Ovid maintained that the Latin poet Cornelius Gallus was the greatest lyric poet of Rome; until the recent discovery of a lengthy fragment, the sum total of Gallus' work that had come down to us was exactly one line. The bountiful survival of the work of the mediocre biographer and philosopher Plutarch rests upon similarly non-literary factors.

Our field is peculiarly subject to the disappearance of great writers through no (qualitative) fault of their own. Weird fiction is a cultivated taste, and its readership has always been small; this makes publishers—especially in our financially straitened age—reluctant to issue such work, given its small returns. Machen, Dunsany, and Blackwood had no difficulty in marketing their work to major publishers in their lifetimes; but their work has fallen haphazardly in and out of print after their deaths. These and other meritorious writers will now be repeatedly forced to suffer the indignity of periodic resurrection. Conversely, I cannot imagine that anyone regards *Dracula* to be a work of the highest intrinsic merit; and its popularity and endurance seem not at all commensurate with its quality. To say that Dracula is the "definitive" treatment of the vampire trope is to yield to the cheap hyperbole of the dust jacket blurb.

Returning to the notion of a canon, it should be clear that no one has sufficient leisure to read all the works of weird fiction that have been written in the past two hundred years, even if anyone were so foolish as to undertake such a task. Some principle of selectivity must be had; and I can state unequivocally that my principle—hence my canon—is based upon the actual literary merits, as best I can assess them, of the works and authors I have read. There might conceivably be other criteria by which a canon is formed, but I am not interested in them. I am not, for example, interested in what weird fiction can tell us about our society because I am not interested in society. This may or may not be a deficiency on my part.

The overriding question is whether literary merit coincides with popular appeal. The question is relevant to the weird tale because of the widespread conception that weird fiction is, pure and simple, a "popular" literary mode and that there are no other criteria of value in this realm other than popularity or the insights that a given work or group of works may provide into "popular culture," whatever that is. I do not know how such a conception could have gained currency except through a very myopic view of the history of the field. Certainly, after the initial popularity of the Gothic novels of the late eighteenth century (most of which, by any aesthetic standard, are uniformly mediocre or worse and scarcely deserve the oceans of academic criticism of which they have been the beneficiaries), it could never be said that serious weird fiction—including the work of Poe, Le Fanu, Bierce, Machen, Dunsany, Blackwood, Lovecraft, Aickman, and so many others—was "popular" in any meaningful sense. The matter of popularity vs. literary merit really boils down to certain basic if uncomfortable truths about society: in particular, the truth that, for a variety of complex reasons, the "mass reading public" is incapable of assessing a literary work on its purely literary merits.

The brute fact of the matter is that public education in the English-speaking world—especially in America—does not inculcate literary values or render its charges capable of distinguishing literature from hackwork. Many untutored readers cannot make a distinction between what happens to tickle their fancy and what actually makes for a substantial work of literature. Since such readers are by far in the majority, and since the advent of democratic capitalism has given them purchasing power undreamed of in prior ages, it is natural that many otherwise talented writers would seek to cater to their tastes in order to make a living. This tendency became evident as early as the advent of the dime novels at the turn of the century—whose readership was almost exclusively among the ill-educated—and advancing through the pulp magazines to the paperbacks of today. Lovecraft was keenly aware of the situation and of its sociological causes:

> Bourgeois capitalism gave artistic excellence and sincerity a death-blow by enthroning cheap amusement-value at the expense of that intrinsic excellence which only cultivated, non-acquisitive persons of assumed position can enjoy. The determinant market for written ... and other heretofore aesthetic material ceased to be a small circle of truly educated persons, but became a substantially larger ... circle of mixed origin numerically dominated by crude, half-educated clods whose systematically perverted ideals ... prevented them from ever achieving the tastes and perspectives of the gentlefolk whose dress and speech and external manners they so assiduously mimicked This herd of acquisitive boors brought up from the shop and the

counting-house a complete set of artificial attitudes, oversimplifications, and mawkish sentimentalities which no sincere art or literature could gratify—and they so outnumbered the remaining educated gentlefolk that most of the purveying agencies became at once reoriented to them. Literature and art lost most of their market; and writing, painting, drama, etc. became engulfed more and more in the domain of *amusement enterprises*. (Letter to C. L. Moore, [7 February 1937])

If anyone has doubts about Lovecraft's assessment, one glance at any week's bestseller lists should relieve them. Critics who equate popular appeal with literary merit had best occupy their time writing studies of Danielle Steel and Sidney Sheldon.

The fatuous notion that "the popular writers of today become the classics of tomorrow" can be dispensed with very easily. In the first place, it is questionable how "popular" even such writers as Shakespeare and Dickens were in their time. There was no such thing as a "mass audience" prior to the twentieth century because it was only then that a numerical majority of individuals had both the literacy and the purchasing power to affect the sale of artistic work. Secondly, there have been a staggering number of very "popular" writers who are now totally and deservedly forgotten (how many readers today know or care about Dinah Maria Craik or Charlotte Mary Yonge or Marie Corelli, three of the most widely published writers of the nineteenth century?). Even such relatively recent bestselling writers as Harold Robbins and Irving Wallace have already achieved a merciful oblivion.

Who are, then, the canonical writers in our field? Leaving aside the Gothics, the list must begin with Poe and Le Fanu. We then come to the very fertile period of the later nineteenth and early twentieth centuries. In *The Weird Tale*, which somewhat fortuitously became a study of the leading writers of this period, I chose to discuss Arthur Machen, Lord Dunsany, Algernon Blackwood, M. R. James, Ambrose Bierce, and H. P. Lovecraft. I did not arrive at this list at the outset. I had been asked by Darrell Schweitzer to write essays on the first two writers for two critical anthologies he was editing; having done so, it occurred to me that I might write about the other two "modern masters" discussed by Lovecraft in the final chapter of "Supernatural Horror in Literature." I then added Bierce (largely because I rather like him and because I think Lovecraft underestimated him, although I later put forth the rationale that he represents a phase of weird fiction—psychological suspense—not found extensively in the other writers) and Lovecraft himself, whom I saw as in some sense culminating the weird fiction tradition in the period 1880–1940. (I do not, as a matter of fact, think that Lovecraft is uniformly "better" than the other five writers; each of them—even James, whom I do not value highly—has virtues he lacks.) But in the end I felt that this list of six writers really did represent a good canon of weird writing for the period in question. I cannot think of any other writers of the time who can rival them; admirable as the work of Hodgson, Chambers, Crawford, Benson, Howard, Clark Ashton Smith, and some others is, they must take a second rank to this "big six."

Turning to the second half of the century (the subject of my foll0w-up book, *The Modern Weird Tale*), my vaunting of Shirley Jackson, Ramsey Campbell, T. E. D. Klein, Thomas Ligotti, Peter Straub, and Dennis Etchison—and my devaluation of Stephen King, Clive Barker, and Anne Rice—should come as no surprise to anyone aware of my critical approach. I repeat that there are ways in which these latter writers could be raised in one's estimation, but I do not think it could be done on the basis of pure literary merit. And I repeat that that is the only basis which interests me.

Of course, the above names represent only the authors that I regard in the very front rank of weird fiction. There are any number of good writers of the second and third rank, and they are always worth reading. And our field has long been known for those solitary gems that otherwise non-weird writers have contributed over the years, whether it be Leonard Cline's *The Dark Chamber* (1927), Herbert S. Gorman's *The Place Called Dagon* (1927), or Iain Banks's *The Wasp Factory* (1980).

I do not know where the weird tale is going or where it is going to go. All the writers whom I rank at the top of the field (even Campbell, who has been publishing for more than thirty years) are either in the middle or even the beginning of their careers. With several promising new writers—of whom Kathe Koja and Norman Partridge can be cited—gradually emerging, a guarded optimism for continued literary contributions to the field may not be entirely unwarranted, in spite of limited markets, limited recognition, and either gleeful or lugubrious disquisitions on the death of horror. The days of horror's bestsellerdom may be over, and this would on the whole be a good thing. The field seems to have prospered most when its authors have worked in relative obscurity, writing for the sake of self-expression rather than for the sake of gain. I do not expect a renaissance of the Machen-Dunsany-Blackwood-Lovecraft type, but Ramsey Campbell, T. E. D. Klein, and Thomas Ligotti are hardly unworthy successors.

The Supernatural in Greek and Latin Literature

For the past half-century—ever since the publication of E. R. Dodds's *The Greeks and the Irrational* (1951)—we have come to understand that the supreme rationalism displayed by a small number of Greek philosophers, historians, poets, playwrights, and artists concealed the plain fact that the Greek populace at large was overwhelmingly superstitious, and that the Greek religion, far from being a harmless personification of natural forces, contained dark elements that hovered like ominous clouds over the Greek temperament. That the Greeks felt the presence of invisible or supernatural forces all about them; that they conceived their multitudinous gods as constantly and intimately involved in human affairs, usually to pursue vengeance against perceived slights or offenses; that they were guided in their daily actions by omens and portents, and implicitly believed in the power of oracles, prophetic dreams, and possession by gods and demons—all these are now a commonplace of scholarship. It is, accordingly, no surprise that the Greeks rudimentarily evolved many of the *topoi* that were later developed in tales of the supernatural: witches and monsters; ghosts and haunted houses; shamans, prophets, and other intermediaries between the natural and the supernatural worlds.

And yet, to discuss the "supernatural" in Greek literature is not to presuppose that the Greeks had actually evolved a notion of the "natural," or that they consciously utilized the "supernatural" for purely aesthetic ends. Indeed, it is plain that many of the entities and events that we might now consider supernatural were regarded as anomalous but natural by the Greeks, especially if they were brought about by the gods; these entities and events will, by and large, not be treated here. Moreover, the actual presentation of the supernatural in Greek literature rarely took the form of a clearly segregated work in prose, poetry, or drama, but was generally a feature—frequently an insignificant feature—of a larger literary work whose true focus lay elsewhere. Accounts of "supernatural" phenomena as related by historians, mythographers, or philosophers are by their nature non-literary, but often provide interesting sidelights into Greek popular folklore and can often illuminate the literary treatments to be studied here.

The Homeric poems (orally transmitted from as early a period as 1200 B.C.E. and probably codified around 750 B.C.E.) and the poems of Hesiod (c. 700 B.C.E.) contain the earliest instances of supernaturalism in Greek literature; and their focus is chiefly on bizarre monsters. Books 9–12 of the *Odyssey* relate Odysseus' adventures with all manner of fantastic entities. Perhaps the most gripping episode is the encounter with Polyphemus, the Cyclops (9.105f.). Homer is careful to note that Polyphemus is "not like a man" (9.190–91), suggesting that he lies somewhere between man and god. Hesiod (*Theogony* 139–46) declares that the race of Cyclopes (he names three of them—Brontes, Steropes, and Arges—but not Polyphemus) was borne by Earth (Gaia). It is Hesiod who explicitly states that the Cyclopes have only one eye (the word Cyclopes actually means "round-eyed"); Homer makes no mention of it, perhaps because this feature of the Cyclopes' anatomy would have been understood by his audience.

The Cyclopes are only one of several types of giants in Greek mythology. The Titans are mentioned only glancingly by Homer (*Iliad* 14.279), but are discussed by Hesiod (*Theogony* 207f.), who explicitly states that they are gods (*Theogony* 630). The Laistrygones encountered by Odysseus and his men are said to be "giants" (*Odyssey* 10.120), and in one instance they see "a woman / as big as a mountain peak, and the sight of her filled them with horror" (10.112–13; tr. Richmond Lattimore). Hesiod (*Theogony* 295f.) tells of various other monsters: Echidna, half nymph and half snake; the hound Cerberus (whom Hesiod declares to be fifty-headed, although later writers—e.g., Apollodorus 2.5.12—speak of him as three-headed); the Chimaera, part lion, part dragon, part goat; and Typhoeus (*Theogony* 820f.), evidently a manlike creature from whose shoulders grew a hundred snake-heads. It is interesting to note that these various creatures are, on the whole, merely enlargements of the human form or are composites of known animals. Hesiod suggests that these creatures were products of the dawn of time, before the advent of civilization. The sophisticated Alexandrian poet Apollonius of Rhodes (295–215 B.C.E.), in his *Argonautica*, speaks of the bronze giant Talos (4.1638f.), a descendant of a brazen race that sprang from ash-trees.

One of the most celebrated monsters in Greek literature is Medusa. Hesiod (*Theogony* 274f.) states that she is one of three Gorgons (the other two being Sthenno and Euryale), and the only mortal one; she has snaky locks and is capable of turning human beings to stone with her glance. No extent literary work treats Medusa in any great detail, and we must resort to the *Library* of the mythographer Apollodorus (fl. 140 B.C.E.) for the account of Perseus, who was commanded to fetch Medusa's head (2.4.1–3). He did so by cutting off the head by looking at a reflection of her in a bronze shield. Other Gorgons pursue him, but Perseus, wearing a cap that makes him invisible, escapes them. He then goes to Ethiopia, where he finds Andromeda (daughter of King Cepheus) prey to a sea monster (*thalassion ketos*); Perseus slays him and rescues Andromeda.

The Harpies ("snatchers") are only glancingly mentioned by Homer (*Odyssey* 20.77) and Hesiod (*Theogony* 267f.), who describes them as birdlike. Their most extensive treatment in extant Greek literature occurs in the *Argonautica* (2.187f.), which tells the story of Phineus, a prophet who offended Zeus and was rendered blind and subject to the Harpies, who snatch his food away from him; he appeals to the Argonauts, who chase the Harpies away. Apollonius suggests—but does not state explicitly—that they are birdlike creatures. Homer has no physical description of the Sirens, although he states that they are "enchanters / of all mankind" (*Odyssey* 12.39-40), but Apollonius (*Argonautica* 4.898-99) describes them has half-woman and half-bird.

The most celebrated witches, sorceresses, or enchantresses in Greek literature are Circe and Medea. In a lengthy passage (*Odyssey* 10.135-574) describes how Odysseus and his men came to her isle and saw men "whom the goddess had given evil drugs and enchanted" (10.213), turning them into lions and wolves. Like the hybrid creatures in H. G. Wells's *The Island of Dr. Moreau*, they retain some human characteristics ("the minds within them stayed as they had been / before": 10.240-41). When Circe turns Odysseus' own men into pigs, Hermes gives him "good medicine" (10.287)—the mysterious plant called "moly" (10.305)—to protect himself against Circe's magic. Circe then uses a wand to change Odysseus' men back to their original forms.

Medea (whose name means "the cunning one") has been treated in several great works, notably Euripides' play *Medea* (431 B.C.E.). Here Medea is depicted as alternately crafty and helpless. She has come from Colchis with Jason to Corinth following her assistance in helping him obtain the golden fleece, but she now feels alone and betrayed when Jason takes to his bed the daughter (never named) of Creon, king of Corinth. She appeals to Hecate, "my mistress, / Whom most I honor and have chosen as partner" (395-96; tr. Rex Warner), and prepares a dress and golden diadem that have been laced with poisons (*pharmakoi* 789). A Messenger reports the spectacularly grisly death of both Creon and his daughter (1121-1230) when the latter puts on the dress and diadem: the diadem "lets forth a fearful stream of all-devouring fire," and the flesh drops away from her bones. When Creon comes to assist her, he is unable to let go and also perishes. Books 3 and 4 of Apollonius' *Argonautica* also tells the story of Medea, although concentrating on the spells Medea uses to allow Jason to capture the golden fleece. Like Euripides, Apollonius states that Medea "practices witchcraft under the tutelage of the goddess Hecate" (3.478), using charms to allow Jason to protect himself while sowing the serpents' teeth and battling the warriors that spring up thereafter.

An instance of an unwitting sorceress is Deianira, Herakles' wife, who in Sophocles' play *Trachiniae* (c. 425 B.C.E.), who out of jealousy gives Herakles a robe that has been poisoned by the blood of Nessus, a centaur who had attacked her; Herakles killed him with arrows tipped with poison from the bile of the Lernaean Hydra, and now his blood is tainted with that poison. Deianira spreads the blood on the robe, because the dying Nessus had told her that it will act as a charm so that Herakles will never look at another woman. The charm works, but not in the way she assumes: Herakles puts on the robe and finds himself in torment—the robe has "eaten away / my inmost flesh" (1053–54).

Homer's celebrated account of Odysseus' visit to the realm of the dead (*Odyssey* 11) has a number of curious features. In the first place, the location of the realm is not under the earth, as in later Greek literature, but in a remote region apparently far to the west, near the land of the Cimmerians. Homer does not name the region aside from referring to it as "the house of Hades" (11.69), and later writers contract this to merely "in [the house] of Hades" (*en Haidou*). In Homer, Odysseus is commanded by Circe to seek out the shade of the prophet Teiresias for instructions on how to reach his homeland. Doing so, he also encounters other shades, including that of his own mother, whom Odysseus tries to embrace but who "fluttered out of my hands like a shadow / or a dream" (11.207–8). The suggestion is that the shades resemble the forms they had in life but are virtually immaterial. Homer also includes (11.576f.) a tableau of hapless figures suffering torture—Tityos, Tantalos, and Sisyphus—although there is no suggestion that their sufferings are a punishment for wrongs committed in life. The other living individual who descended to the underworld was Orpheus, in his fruitless attempt to rescue his wife Eurydice; but this story receives no notable treatment in extant Greek literature.

The Greeks wrote copiously of ghosts and haunted houses. Many of these accounts occur in works by historians, with little suggestion that they are any more anomalous than the tales of battles or political intrigues they discuss elsewhere. The first appearance of a ghost in Greek literature is that of the slain soldier Patroclus (*Iliad* 23.65f.), who berates his friend Achilles for not burying his corpse, thereby preventing him from crossing "the river" (Styx) and mingling with the other shades in the underworld. Achilles expresses wonder at Patroclus' appearance, and, like Odysseus, attempts to embrace him but fails. Plutarch (46–120 C.E.) mentions ghosts with particular frequency: in *Brutus*, Brutus confronts his "evil spirit," who says to him: "You shall see me at Philippi" (36.3–4); in *Cimon*, the ghost of a murderer is seen haunting the public bath where he was killed (1.2–7); in *Dion*, Plutarch asserts that the fact that a ghost appeared to Dion predicting his death should be accepted as evidence that supernatural phenomena are real and not merely the rambling of children and silly women (2.1–4). Pausanias tells of a particularly active ghost: one of Odysseus' sailors, after being killed by the townspeople of Temesa (in Italy) for raping a local woman, returns from the dead and kills people repeatedly until he is somehow driven away by a famous boxer (6.6.6–9).

Greek tragedy features some notable ghosts, although in most cases they appear to serve as means to advance the plot. In Aeschylus' *Persae* (472 B.C.E.), the Persian queen Atossa summons the ghost of Darius, who, like many of Homer's shades, is unaware of what has happened on earth since his death. In Aeschylus' *Eumenides* (458 B.C.E.) the ghost of Clytemnestra upbraids Orestes for murdering her and urges the Furies to plague him. The prologue of Euripides' *Hecuba* (c. 425 B.C.E.) is spoken by Polydorus, the son of Hecuba and Priam of Troy, who now "hovers as a wraith over my mother's head" (29).

Later Greek literature alternates between credulity in ghostly phenomena—see the odd work by Philostratus, the *Heroikos* (c. 230 C.E.), which speaks of the ghosts of the men of Troy haunting their old battlefields—and scornful scepticism, as in several works by Lucian of Samosata (115–180? C.E.). Much of Lucian's work is satiric or parodic, and his use of the supernatural is almost always for parodic purposes. *The Dead Come to Life* (*Anabiouetes*) depicts the ancient philosophers coming back to life; *The Downward Journey* (*Kataplous*) is a dialogue set in the underworld between Charon, Clotho, Atropos (two of the three Fates), and others. This work was probably inspired by Menippus (3rd century B.C.E.), a Cynic philosopher whose work exists only in fragments, and who devised the "Menippean satire," a form that mingled prose and verse. Menippus himself figures in *Icaromenippus*, in which he flies to the citadel of Zeus on wings patterned after Daedalus', and *Menippus, or The Descent into Hades* (*Menippus e Nekyomanteia*), in which he goes down to Hades and talks with Teiresias.

Lucian's most significant work of the supernatural is the *Lover of Lies* (*Philopseudes*), in which various interlocutors tell incredible stories—about a ghost of a dead wife who tells her husband where to find a lost slipper; a house haunted by an evil "phantom" (*phasma*), and whose bones are later found buried under the floor of a room; and, in a remarkable anticipation of the "sorcerer's apprentice" idea, a magician who can make inanimate objects move about and the grotesque results that ensue when an inexperienced pupil attempts the same thing—but the principal narrator, Tychiades, remains skeptical to the end. A *True Story* (*Alethon Diegematon*) has sometimes been seen as a forerunner of science fiction in its depiction of a galley that leaps into the sky, is swallowed by a 150-mile-long whale, and performs other miracles. The tale is, as with much of Lucian, a satire on the poets, historians, and philosophers "who have written much that smacks of miracles and fables" (1.2).

A work attributed to Lucian but probably not by him is *Lucius, or The Ass* (*Loukios, e Onos*), which apparently draws upon the same Greek work (now lost) that Apuleius used for his *Metamorphoses* (*Golden Ass*). The same events as in Apuleius are recounted, although in a far more condensed fashion: the narrator, Lucius of Patras, visits a friend, Hipparchus, whose wife is a witch. Lucius and a servant girl, Palaistra, sees the woman rub an ointment on herself and turn into a bird. Lucius wishes to do the same, but Palaistra uses the wrong ointment and he becomes an ass. After numerous humiliating adventures he eventually manages to find the roses that, when eaten, turn him back into a human being.

Phlegon of Tralles, a freedman of Hadrian (fl. c. 130 C.E.) wrote an eccentric work called *Peri thaumasion* (*On Wonderful Events*), in which he recounts the tale of Philinnion, a young woman who returned from the dead six months after her funeral because of her love for Machates, spending several nights with him before dying again. See William F. Hansen, *Phlegon of Tralles' Book of Marvels* (1996).

The literature of Rome is perhaps not as rich in the depiction of supernatural entities or events as that of Greece, but several imperishable works were nonetheless produced. Latin literature long remained dependent upon Greek models and sources, and many Latin works of the supernatural do little more than retell (usually in an inferior manner) episodes or scenarios found in celebrated Greek predecessors. The tragedies of the younger Seneca (4? B.C.E.–65 C.E.) are a prime example. *Hercules Oetaeus* retells Sophocles' story (in *Trachiniae*) of Deianira giving Hercules the poisoned shirt of Nessus; *Medea* retells Sophocles' immortal play, although here (perhaps because Seneca did not wish to incur invidious comparisons with his illustrious antecedent) the description of the deaths of Creon and his daughter from Medea's poisoned dress and diadem is highly truncated. The prologue of *Agamemnon* is spoken by the ghost of Thyestes; the prologue of *Thyestes* is a dialogue between the ghost of Tantalus and a Fury. In *Hercules*, Hercules brings back Theseus from the underworld, who then tells of Hercules' venture into the house of Dis, as he overpowers Cerberus and brings him back to the surface. This story was probably told numerous times in Greek tragedy and epic, but no example of it survives. A curious play in the Senecan tragic corpus, although obviously not by him, is the *Octavia*, a *fabula praetexta* (historical drama) set in the time of Nero. The ghost of Agrippina—Nero's mother, whom he has killed—predicts his death in a particularly grim manner. As is well known, Seneca's blood-and-thunder tragedies exercised considerable influence upon Elizabethan tragedy; see, e.g., A. J. Boyle, *Tragic Seneca: An Essay in the Theatrical Tradition* (1997).

The bizarre monsters that are so bountiful in Greek myth are relatively absent in Latin literature. The only supernatural creature that makes a frequent occurrence is the werewolf. The celebrated werewolf episode (61–62) in the *Satyricon* of Petronius (d. 65 C.E.) is told by Niceros, a former slave who recounts the story at Trimalchio's dinner. He and a friend are walking along the roadside among the gravestones that were commonly found there. All of a sudden the friend takes off his clothes, urinates on them, and thereby turns into a wolf. The clothes have turned to stone. The wolf is subsequently injured in the neck, and later the man himself is found—with a neck injury. This tale, told with Petronius' inimitable deadpan humor, might have been one of many such tales in his work, since the existing fragments of the *Satyricon* probably comprise less than a fifth of the total work. There are brief citations of werewolves in one of the *Elegies* (4.5) of Propertius (50? B.C.E.–16? C.E.) and in one of the *Eclogues* (8.97–99) of Virgil (70–19 B.C.E.).

Metempsychosis of this sort is the central feature in the *Metamorphoses* of Ovid (43 B.C.E.–17 C.E.). Although most of his accounts deal with transformations brought about by the gods, some are of a different sort; and in other cases, the final transformation is only a contrived expedient that allows Ovid to tell several gripping tales of the supernatural, in poetry that is fluid, elegant, but at times glib. We have a half-parodic retelling of the account of Perseus' slaying of the sea-monster and the rescue of Andromeda (4.663–764), a lengthy account of the witcheries of Medea (7.1–424), a rendering of the transformation of the maiden Scylla into a birdlike monster (8.1–151), and perhaps the most poignant surviving account (although many others must once have existed) of the failed attempt of Orpheus to rescue his dead wife Eurydice from the underworld (10.1–85). The most extended treatment of metempsychosis occurs in the *Metamorphoses* (or *Golden Ass*) of Apuleius (fl. c. 155 C.E.).

Latin accounts of the supernatural generally focus on witches, ghosts, and haunted houses, usually in conjunction. In Latin, ghosts are variously referred to as *larvae, lemures, manes,* or *umbrae* (literally, "shadows"). The Romans in fact held a festival, the Lemuralia, in May to appease the ghosts of the dead. One of the earliest accounts of ghosts, although manifestly parodic, is in the *Mostellaria* of Plautus (250?–184 B.C.E.), probably based upon a Greek play, *Phasma* (262 B.C.E.) by Philemon. The title approximately translates to "ghost story" (from *mostellum*, a diminutive of *monstrum*, "monster" [or, in this case, "ghost"]), and tells of a young wastrel, Philolaches, who, as a means of disguising his prodigality during the absence of his father, Theopropides, tries to convince his father that his house is haunted by the ghost of a man whom the previous owner had murdered and buried in the house. The ploy falls apart fairly quickly. The curious thing is that this scenario is closely duplicated in the celebrated letter (7.27) of Pliny the Younger (61?–113 C.E.) to Licinius Sura, in which Pliny debates the veracity of ghostly legendry. He tells of a house in Athens that is thought to be dangerous to its occupants because the ghost of an old man in fetters is frequently seen. A skeptical philosopher, Athenodorus, investigates and, led by the ghost, finds the remains of bones wrapped in chains buried in the courtyard. The pseudo-Virgilian poem *Culex* (probably dating to the early 1st century C.E.) is an amusing account of the horrors of the underworld as told by the ghost of a gnat.

The witch (variously termed *malefica*, *maga*, or *saga*) is a common feature in Latin literature, and her powers seem well-nigh infinite. A character in Apuleius describes them: "[she] hath power to bring down the sky, to bear up the earth, to turn the waters into hills and the hills into running waters, to call up the terrestrial spirits into the air, and to pull the gods out of the heavens, to extinguish the planets, and to lighten the very darkness of hell" (*Metamorphoses* 1.8; tr. William Adlington). Apuleius later speaks oddly of how witches bite off portions of the faces of dead people and use them in sorcery (2.21). Horace's *Epode* 5 is an imperishable account of the witch Canidia, who with three other witches plans to kill a boy and, from his remains, make a love-philter to torment a lover who had scorned her. But the boy curses the witches, vowing to return as a ghost "and claw your faces with my curved and spectral nails" (5.94; tr. Charles E. Passage). *Epode* 17 is another poem about Canidia, in which the poet pleads with her to cease her incantations; Canidia scornfully replies that she will instead hurl even more spells at Horace.

Two epic poets of the Silver Age treat of witches and ghosts. The *Bellum Civile* (sometimes called the *Pharsalia*) of Lucan (39–65 C.E.), a poem about the Civil War between Caesar and Pompey, is notable for the entire absence of the conventional gods of the Graeco-Roman pantheon; but Lucan is not above incorporating the supernatural in other ways. In a lengthy passage (6.419–830) Pompey's son, Sextus Pompeius, consults the witch Erictho, who lives in deserted tombs, goes out only during stormy nights, and eats the flesh of the living and the dead. Sextus wishes to know the best place to fight Caesar's forces; Erictho wants the battle to be at Pharsalus, since she knows that there will be many corpses on which she can feast. When Sextus asks her the outcome of the battle, she says she must resurrect a recent unburied corpse and make him speak. She uses a "lunar poison" (*virus lunare* 669) to reanimate the corpse, then utters a spell. The corpse speaks, but utters an ambiguous message that nonetheless predicts the defeat and death of Pompey's army.

In the *Thebaid* of Statius (45?–96? C.E.), an account of the battles between the descendants of Oedipus, the shade of Oedipus' father, Laius, is summoned by Mercury (2.1–33) and appears to Oedipus' son Eteocles disguised as the prophet Tiresias; he warns him against his brother Polynices' plot against him, then reveals his true form, shedding "phantom blood" (*vanum cruorem* 2.126) over him. The entire passage is full of a powerful atmosphere of weirdness and eldritch landscape descriptions. A later passage (4.406–645) tells of Tiresias going into a haunted wood, making sacrifices to Hecate, and summoning shades from Hades. He asks the shade of Laius to foretell the outcome of the war, but the latter gives a puzzling prediction. Both Lucan and Statius wrote in the florid, hyperbolic style typical of the Silver Age, but at times this only enhances the spectral atmosphere of the passages.

The supernatural figures powerfully in the greatest of Latin epics, Virgil's *Aeneid*, the account of how the Trojan warrior Aeneas left Troy to found Rome. In the description of the fall of Troy that occupies Book 2, Virgil tells of how Aeneas, finding Helen cowering in a corner and blaming her for the city's destruction, is about to kill her in rage, but his mother, the goddess Venus, appears to him and says that the events have been brought about by the gods; she reveals a spectacular tableau of Neptune, Juno, Apollo, and Jupiter all taking part in the razing of Troy (2.589–633). In a later passage (2.772f.), Aeneas encounters the ghost of his dead wife Creusa; indeed, the appearance of the ghost is Aeneas' first indication that his wife has died. Most of Book 6 is occupied by the celebrated account of Aeneas' visit to the underworld. Landing at Cumae (on the southern Italian coast, near modern-day Naples), he asks the Sibyl to be allowed to visit the shade of his father Anchises in the underworld, since he knows that there is an entrance to the underworld near Avernus (a lake near Cumae). The Sibyl makes the pungent comment: *facilis descensus Averno* (6.126; "the descent to Avernus is easy"), but the return is a bit more difficult. The Sibyl instructs Aeneas to pluck a golden bough (*aureus ramus* 6.137) from a wood sacred to Proserpina, queen of the underworld. He does so, and, after making sacrifices at the entrance of a dark and evil-smelling cave, he and the Sibyl begin their descent. They initially encounter horrific allegorical monsters (Grief, Revenge, Fear, etc.), then the phantoms of Greek monsters (centaurs, Scyllas, the Chimaera). They cross the river Styx in Charon's boat, and the Sibyl gives a drugged honeycake to Cerberus to lull him to sleep. Then occurs Aeneas' poignant encounter with the shade of Dido, the Carthaginian queen who had committed suicide when Aeneas abandoned her to found Rome. The Greek and Trojan heroes appear, some bearing the injuries they had suffered in life. They come to a fork in the road, one leading to Dis or Tartarus, the other to Elysium. Taking the latter, they encounter the shade of Anchises, who utters his imperishable prophecy of the future greatness of Rome.

Not perhaps to be classified as strictly supernatural, but nonetheless memorable, are such things as Poem 63 of Catullus (84?–54? B.C.E.), a spectacularly bizarre description (written in a strange meter found almost nowhere else in extant ancient literature) of the madness and castration of Attis, who is in love with the Phrygian goddess Cybele, and *Satire* 15 of Juvenal (60?–140? C.E.), a grisly depiction of cannibalism in Egypt.

The Criticism of Weird Fiction

The analysis of the theoretical foundations of the supernatural tale coincided almost exactly with the emergence of the supernatural as a distinctive literary mode. Only nine years after Horace Walpole published *The Castle of Otranto* (1764), John and Anna Laetitia Aikin wrote the trenchant essay, "On the Pleasure Derived from Objects of Terror" (1773), addressing the still vexed issue of why readers enjoy the apparently unpleasant experience of being frightened. Ann Radcliffe, in the posthumously published essay "On the Supernatural in Poetry" (*New Monthly Magazine*, 1826), made the critical distinction between terror, which "expands the soul, and awakens the faculties to a high degree of life," and horror, which "contracts, freezes, and nearly annihilates them." Sir Walter Scott, in a number of papers—such as his introduction to a new edition of Walpole's *The Castle of Otranto* (Ballantyne, 1811), his reviews of Maturin's *Fatal Revenge* (*Quarterly Review*, May 1810) and Mary Shelley's *Frankenstein* (*Blackwood's Edinburgh Magazine*, March 1818), and the essay "On the Supernatural in Fictitious Composition" (*Foreign Quarterly Review*, 1827)—broached numerous subjects pertaining to the supernatural in literature.

The latter half of the nineteenth century saw little work, either of a theoretical or of an historical nature, on the supernatural tale. As is well known, Poe was not recognised as a leading literary figure until he was championed by Baudelaire and other French writers; and Poe has remained a controversial figure to this day. Few critics today, however, would deny his centrality as a pioneer in the supernatural tale as well as in the short story in general. The study of the supernatural at this time was perhaps hindered by the fact that few authors could be termed "supernatural writers" *tout court*, and accordingly there seemed little justification for segregating this work from the general run of literature. Even the study of Gothic fiction did not prosper in the later 19th century, largely because it had fallen into disrepute as the product of tyros and hacks seeking to capitaliae on a naïve reading public.

Things began to change in the early 20th century. A landmark work was Edith Birkhead's *The Tale of Terror* (Constable, 1921), a still valuable treatise on the Gothic novel that led the way to several other such studies. The first account of contemporary supernatural fiction was Dorothy Scarborough's *The*

Supernatural in Modern English Fiction (Putnam, 1917), but this study tends to be overly schematic and obsessed with the mere cataloguing of supernatural themes and tropes. Nevertheless, Scarborough did draw attention to the fact that supernatural fiction was being bountifully written in her day; indeed, Philip Van Doren Stern later identified the late nineteenth and early twentieth centuries as the "Golden Age" of the supernatural tale, a judgment with which it is difficult to dispute.

It was at this time that H. P. Lovecraft wrote his pioneering study, "Supernatural Horror in Literature" (first published in the *Recluse*, 1927, revised in the *Fantasy Fan*, 1933–35, and published in nearly definitive form in *The Outsider and Others* [Arkham House, 1939]). Lovecraft maintained that the "weird tale" must embody a defiance or subversion of natural law—must, in other words, depict phenomena defying (current) conceptions of entity as determined by science. As such, such non-supernatural modes as the mystery story, the *conte cruel*, the psychological horror tale, and even tales of the "mundanely gruesome" are, in theory, rigidly excluded; in practice, however, Lovecraft did make exceptions for some of Poe's and Bierce's non-supernatural tales, along with a few others. Lovecraft's treatise is largely an historical account. His study of the early Gothic novels is routine (and heavily indebted to Birkhead); but he recognized the central importance of Poe in transferring the sense of weirdness to human psychology, discussed Hawthorne, Bierce, and others brilliantly in short compass, and, most prophetic of all, identified the four "modern masters" of the early twentieth-century supernatural tale as Arthur Machen, Lord Dunsany, Algernon Blackwood, and M. R. James—a judgment confirmed by subsequent scholarship.

But Lovecraft's monograph is only one of a number of studies of the theory and practice of supernatural fiction made by leading practitioners down to the present day. M. R. James wrote several pertinent essays, notably "Some Remarks on Ghost Stories" (*Bookman* [London], December 1929); other works such as Lafcadio Hearn's "The Value of the Supernatural in Fiction" (in *Interpretations of Literature* [Dodd, Mead, 1915]), Walter de la Mare's lengthy introduction to his son Colin de la Mare's anthology *They Walk Again* (Dutton, 1931), Oliver Onions's "Credo" in *Collected Ghost Stories* (Nicholson & Watson, 1935), and Edith Wharton's preface to *Ghosts* (Appleton Century, 1937) all bespeak a desire by supernatural writers to probe the sources and aims of their work. Oddly enough, such leading figures as Machen, Dunsany, and Blackwood wrote little on the subject; but suggestive hints of their attitudes can be found in their respective autobiographies. In recent times two writers stand out for mention, Ramsey Campbell and T. E. D. Klein. Campbell's bountiful essays and reviews—now collected in *Ramsey Campbell, Proba-*

bly, ed. S. T. Joshi (PS Publishing, 2002)—show a keen analytical mind consistently defending the literary status of the supernatural tale. Klein has written a long essay, "Dr. Van Helsing's Handy Guide to Ghost Stories" (*Twilight Zone*, August-November 1981), and the handbook, *Raising Goosebumps for Fun and Profit* (Footsteps Press, 1988), which, although at times flippant, exhibit a thorough familiarity with the history of the field. Less astute is Stephen King's *Danse Macabre* (Everest House, 1981), a rather slipshod account of the horror literature that King appreciated in his youth. *Clive Barker's Shadows in Eden*, ed. Stephen Jones (Underwood-Miller, 1991), is a wide-ranging collection of Barker's somewhat cocksure opinions on the field and his defense of his brand of over-the-top horror as represented by his *Books of Blood*.

Theoretical and historical studies of supernatural fiction have increased in quantity and perspicacity in the last half-century. The Swiss scholar Peter Penzoldt, in *The Supernatural in Fiction* (Peter Nevill, 1952; Humanities Press, 1965), relied heavily on Lovecraft's theoretical presuppositions, and, although revealing an amusing squeamishness in the face of the explicit horrors of Machen, Crawford, and others, produced fine analyses of Lovecraft, Blackwood (with whom he was acquainted), and others. In the highly influential *Introduction à la littérature fantastique* (Editions du Seuil, 1970; Eng. tr. by Richard Howard as *The Fantastic* [Case Western Reserve Univ. Press, 1973), Tzvetan Todorov, utilising a structural approach, maintains that the "fantastic" (*fantastique*) occurs only when the reader "hesitates" between adopting a natural or supernatural explanation for the phenomena in a given literary work. If the phenomena are resolved naturally (e.g., as in Ann Radcliffe), then the work is deemed "uncanny" (*l'étrange*); if the events are resolved supernaturally (e.g., as in M. G. Lewis), then the work is deemed "marvelous" (*merveilleux*). This perspective appears to privilege such "ambiguous" works as Henry James's *The Turn of the Screw*, relegating the great majority of supernatural tales to the apparently inferior category of the marvelous. Terry Heller, in *The Delights of Terror: An Aesthetics of the Tale of Terror* (Univ. of Illinois Press, 1987), relies on Todorov's categories, as well as Wolfgang Iser's theories of the implied reader, in probing the different aesthetic responses elicited in the reader by the different types of terror tales.

Several works probe the supernatural tale from a philosophical perspective. Rosemary Jackson's provocative *Fantasy: The Literature of Subversion* (Methuen, 1981), in spite of a confusing use of terminology (by "fantasy" she apparently means the genre of supernatural horror), maintains that horror tales subvert our "norms" of the possible—although the "norms" are interpreted culturally rather than metaphysically. S. T. Joshi, in *The Weird Tale* (Univ. of Texas Press, 1990), asserts that the best supernatural writers effect a refashioning of the universe in accordance with their philosophical predispositions; he also maintains that the weird tale did not exist as a concrete genre in the period under discussion (roughly 1880–1940), but that it was a literary mode to which writers of many different types could resort for specific philosophical or aesthetic purposes. In a loose follow-up, *The Modern Weird Tale* (McFarland, 2001), Joshi treats post–World War II work, claiming that the weird tale had now (to its detriment) become a formulaic genre; he vaunts the literary merits of Shirley Jackson, Ramsey Campbell, T. E. D. Klein, and Thomas Ligotti over such best-selling figures as Stephen King, Clive Barker, and Anne Rice. In *The Philosophy of Horror* (Routledge, 1990), Noël Carroll asserts that horror literature is characterized by monsters that represent "disturbances of the natural order." Like Todorov's, this definition would have the effect of relegating a substantial proportion of supernatural literature to some other genre (Carroll believes that tales of supernatural events, without any concomitant "monster," are merely tales of *dread,* while stories portraying abnormal psychologies are tales of *terror*). Of tangential interest is Victoria Nelson's *The Secret Life of Puppets* (Harvard Univ. Press, 2001), a study of how supernatural fiction, film, and art have replaced religion as a vehicle for our culture's need for a non-rational view of the universe.

In the 1930s the "fandom" movement emerged, and has continued unabated to this day. Although this movement has sometimes degenerated into uncritical adulation, it has nonetheless resulted in the production of a substantial body of biographical, bibliographical, and critical work, mostly by young enthusiasts and independent scholars. The *Fantasy Fan* (1933–35) did not generate much actual criticism, but was a focus of fan interest in the pulp writers, especially those who wrote for *Weird Tales* and the early science fiction pulps. *Fantasy Commentator* (1943–52), edited by A. Langley Searles, was much superior and published articles that are still valuable today. Searles revived his magazine in 1978 and is still issuing it. *Nyctalops* (1970–83, 1991) and *Whispers* (1973–97) also published sound work, although both magazines gradually became dominated by short fiction and poetry. Necronomicon Press's *Lovecraft Studies* (1979f.) and *Studies in Weird Fiction* (1986f.) produced work of a more scholarly tenor, much of it valuable. Both journals are indexed in the MLA Bibliography, bringing academic recognition to the field. Necronomicon Press also published *Necrofile* (1991–99), which became the leading journal for substantive reviews of contemporary supernatural fiction. *Locus* and *Science Fiction Chronicle,* although chiefly devoted to science fiction, contain much news relevant to supernatural horror. Darrell Schweitzer has assembled several volumes of essays by leading critics in the field, among them

Discovering Classic Horror Fiction I (Starmont House, 1992) and *Discovering Modern Horror Fiction I* and *II* (Starmont House, 1985, 1988).

The field has never lacked for bibliographical chronicling, much of it done by non-academicians. Donald H. Tuck's *Encyclopedia of Science Fiction and Fantasy through 1968* (Advent, 1974–83; 3 vols.) remains valuable, although much outdated and sprinkled with errors. E. F. Bleiler's *Guide to Supernatural Fiction* (Kent State University Press, 1983)—the ultimate revision of his pioneering *Checklist of Fantastic Literature* (Shasta, 1948)—is invaluable in supplying plot synopses of thousands of supernatural novels and tales; but both his criteria for inclusion and his critical judgments are subject to debate. The pinnacle of such bibliographical work is Mike Ashley's *The Supernatural Index* (Greenwood Press, 1995), an immense index of anthologies of supernatural fiction. Ashley is now at work on a similar compilation for single-author collections. Ashley assisted Frank H. Parnell in the invaluable *Monthly Terrors* (Greenwood Press, 1985), an index to hundreds of magazines in the field, including *Weird Tales*; Ashley and Marshall Tymn have compiled *Science Fiction, Fantasy, and Weird Fiction Magazines* (Greenwood Press, 1985), a critical account of these magazines. Hal W. Hall has done outstanding work in charting criticism of supernatural fiction, in such works as *Science Fiction and Fantasy Reference Index, 1878–1985* (Gale Research Co., 1987; 2 vols.) and its supplements.

Critical reference works include *Horror Literature*, ed. Marshall Tymn (Bowker, 1981), and *Horror Literature*, ed. Neil Barron (Garland, 1990); both their titles and their methodology are identical, presenting chapters by various hands on selected periods and topics in supernatural literature, with annotated bibliographies of major works. Barron's compilation—now revised as *Fantasy and Horror* (Scarecrow Press, 1999)—has been criticized for giving excessive coverage to transient contemporary works rather than to the landmark works and authors of the past who have stood the test of time. Frank N. Magill's *Survey of Modern Fantasy Literature* (Salem Press, 1983; 5 vols.) features essays on many works of supernatural fiction by various hands. *The Penguin Encyclopedia of Horror and the Supernatural*, ed. Jack Sullivan (Viking Penguin, 1986), is a meticulously assembled work with abundant contributions by leading scholars. E. F. Bleiler's *Supernatural Fiction Writers* (Scribner, 1985; 2 vols.; rev. ed. by Richard Bleiler [Scribner, 2002; 2 vols.]) presents a discussion by various hands of more than 150 writers, although several of them are only of tangential relevance to supernatural literature; more pertinent is *Gothic Writers*, ed. Douglass H. Thomson, Jack G. Voller, and Frederick S. Frank (Greenwood Press, 2002). David Pringle's *Horror, Ghost, and Gothic Writers* (St. James

Press, 1998) presents comprehensive bibliographies and critical summaries of many leading writers.

General surveys of the field have, on the whole, been mediocre or worse, especially as regards contemporary work. Glen St. John Barclay, in *Anatomy of Horror* (St. Martin's Press, 1978), apparently believes that most writers of supernatural fiction are only fit for the insane asylum. Walter Kendrick's poorly researched *The Thrill of Fear* (Grove Weidenfeld, 1991) finds merit only in the luridness of modern supernatural literature. Not much better, although more academically rigorous, is David Punter's *The Literature of Terror* (Longman, 1980), a ploddingly chronological treatment based on "Marxist and sociological" principles. The revised edition (Longman, 1996; 2 vols.) shows astounding ignorance of contemporary work (there is no mention of Shirley Jackson, Clive Barker, T. E. D. Klein, Dennis Etchison, and many other leading figures), and a poor understanding of Lovecraft, Campbell, and others. The best historical study may be Les Daniels's *Living in Fear: A History of Horror in the Mass Media* (Scribner, 1975), although of course it is now much outdated. Some studies of selected historical periods—such as Julia Briggs's *Night Visitors: The Rise and Fall of the English Ghost Story* (Faber & Faber, 1977) and Jack Sullivan's *Elegant Nightmares: The English Ghost Story from Le Fanu to Blackwood* (Ohio Univ. Press, 1978)—are somewhat better. The early Gothic novels, in spite of their admitted literary inferiority to late work, continue to receive disproportionate coverage, perhaps because an accepted canon of later supernatural work has not yet been determined.

Studies of individual authors remain sketchy. Some writers, such as Poe, Lovecraft, and Stoker, have been exhaustively and minutely covered, while others—such as Machen, Dunsany, Blackwood, and even Bierce—have failed to receive coverage commensurate with their literary merit. Certain cult authors such as Robert E. Howard, Clark Ashton Smith, and M. R. James are discussed widely in the fan press, but only some of this material is of value. In short, it would appear that, while many valuable studies in both the theory and practice of supernatural fiction have been written, much work remains to be done.

The Theory and Practice of Satirical Criticism

Over the years I have dabbled in what I have chosen to call "satirical criticism." I am by no means the inventor of this rarely practiced literary genre, but I like to believe that there are reasons—having nothing to do with the mere expession of bile and vitriol—why it may yield some benefits for readers, critics, and even the authors and works that are the objects of this opprobrium.

Satirical criticism involves the fusion of literary criticism—even in the humble guise of book reviewing—with satire. It is, of course, easy to poke fun at bad writing, but doing so in a way that justifies the term "satirical criticism" requires something other than insult or abuse; and the underlying principle—or, perhaps, the hoped-for objective—is to illuminate the deficiencies of a literary work in a particularly pungent manner so that its failings can be exposed to all concerned.

It would be difficult to specify the creator of satirical criticism, but in this country one of its pioneers was Edgar Allan Poe, whose various reviews are laced with vicious attacks on his literary enemies. Ambrose Bierce, perhaps the greatest satirist in American literature, was also a noted exemplar. Bierce did not write many formal book reviews, or literary criticism in general, but his journalism—which dwarfs his collected fiction and poetry many times over—is replete with towering condemnations of politicians, clergymen, and other worthies. Bierce is frequently regarded as an indiscriminate hater, misanthrope, pessimist, or what have you, but he did not consider himself such. When a contemporary writer, John Bonner, took him to task for what seemed to him mere billingsgate, Bierce replied keenly:

> John Bonner, does it really seem to you that contempt for the bad is incompatible with respect for the good?—that hatred of rogues and fools does not imply love of bright and honest folk? Can you really not understand that what is unworthy in life or letters can be known only by comparison with what is known to be worthy? He who bitterly hates the wrong is he who intensely loves the right; indifference to the one is indifference to the other. Those who like everything love nothing; a heart of indiscriminate hospitality becomes a boozing ken of tramps and thieves. Where the sentimentalist's

love leaves off the cynic's may begin. You have lived and written to little purpose if you have yet to learn why the good do not make the bad behave themselves.[1]

H. L. Mencken practiced satirical criticism with flair and panache, in the hundreds of review columns he wrote for the *Smart Set* (1908–23), *American Mercury* (1924–33), and elsewhere. From his earliest days as a reviewer, he evolved a fairly consistent and rigorous standard of what passed for good writing, and he was unremitting in his condemnation of what failed to measure up to that standard. Simultaneously, he recognized that a satirical flourish to his book reviews would not only make them entertaining to readers, but underscore the follies and absurdities of the work being reviewed. Consider a passage from his riotous review of a best-selling sentimental novel by one Marjorie Benton Cooke, *Bambi* (1914—*not the basis of the celebrated 1942 film*):

> A sweet, sweet story. A string of gum-drops. A sugar-teat beyond compare. Of such great probabilities, of such searching reports of human motive and act, the best-seller is all compact. . . . But do not laugh too much, dear friend, however hard your heart, however tough your hide. The mission of such things as *Bambi* is, after all, no mean one. Remember the fat woman—how it will make her forget that she is fat. Remember the tired business man—how it will lift him out of his wallow and fill him with a noble enthusiasm for virtue and its rewards. Remember the flapper—how it will thrill her to the very soles of her feet and people her dreams with visions of gallant knights and lighten that doom which makes her actual beau a baseball fan and corrupts him with a loathing for literature and gives him large, hairy hands and a *flair* for burlesque shows and freckles on his neck.[2]

As for me, generally speaking I unleash my satirical criticism in instances when I encounter authors or works that are, from an abstract literary perspective, so far beneath contempt that satire is the only recourse; at the same time, I continue to use the most rigorous tools of the literary critic in my analysis. As Juvenal of old said, *Difficile est saturam non scribere* ("It is difficult not to write satire" [*Satires* 1.30]). I began working in this mode in the reviews I wrote for *Necrofile* (1991–99), the predecessor to the present esteemed jour-

---

1. Ambrose Bierce, "Prattle" (*San Francisco Examiner*, 3 November 1895); in *A Sole Survivor: Bits of Autobiography*, ed. S. T. Joshi and David E. Schultz (Knoxville: University of Tennessee Press, 1998), 215–16.

2. H. L. Mencken, "Mush for the Multitude" (*Smart Set*, December 1914); in *H. L. Mencken on American Literature*, ed. S. T. Joshi (Athens: Ohio University Press, 2002), 183.

nal; that was when Ellen Datlow, in one of the introductions to *The Year's Best Fantasy and Horror*, referred to me as "the *nastiest* reviewer in the field" (her emphasis). I took that comment as a compliment.

Some tender-hearted individuals—even among my supporters—appear to believe that the *tone* of my "satirical criticism" is to be deprecated. They complain that I come off sounding "arch" or "pretentious" or "holier than thou." *People, the adoption of that tone was quite deliberate!* The essential purpose of satire is to provoke, to annoy, to irritate, to offend, even to outrage; and the fact that I appear to done exactly that in blogs, articles, and reviews suggests that I have succeeded in my goal. But I do maintain that I have a more serious purpose in mind than merely dialing up a few zingers to hurl at the objects of my derision. Chiefly, I regard my satirical criticism as a kind of public service, whereby I fervently seek to save readers from wasting their hard-earned money on the rubbish that I eviscerate. What could be nobler than that? Okay, that comment itself was somewhat satirical, but not entirely so—and it underscores a truly serious point, especially as it applies to our humble field.

The plain fact of the matter is that criticism of weird fiction is still at a very primitive stage, and the number of critics who could be said to have the critical judgment, educational background, and (perhaps most importantly) the courage to direct an unflinching gaze toward the contributions in our field, both past and present, is woefully small. Some critics who may otherwise be capable of the job seem to feel that the very attempt to sort good writing from bad is somehow not a legitimate function of criticism, whereas I see it as its central mission. To a degree—but only to a degree—the decision as to what is "good" or "bad" is subjective; but one finds, both in this field and others, a general consensus among informed critics as to who the leading figures are, even if judgments on individual writers vary, and perhaps vary widely. As Lovecraft once said, critics of poetry may differ as to the relative merits of Pope and Shelley; but all sound critics of poetry will agree that Pope and Shelley are true poets whereas, say, Edgar A. Guest is not. Evaluative judgments are not meant to be prescriptive but suggestive: they are designed to provoke discussion as to what actually constitutes good writing, in the hope that other critics—as well as general readers—will be compelled to confront this fundamental issue head-on.

Ever since I entered this field in the late 1970s, I was struck by the amount of mutual backpatting going on among fans and writers of all sorts. In part this tendency was inspired by the perceived need to stay on good terms with leading authors, editors, and publishers in the hope of cultivating their favor and thereby advancing one's career; but in large part, I believed, it was simply a result of a lack of sound critical taste. This was, indeed, a chief motivating factor in my co-founding of *Necrofile*. I in particular, not feeling any obligation to toady up to the bigwigs in the field, wrote blistering reviews of books I genuinely felt to be markedly inferior, especially if they were by popular writers whom others did not venture to criticize. I continue to write censorious reviews and articles today, even though they occasionally alienate certain writers to whom I would like to extend invitations to contribute to my anthologies. But I also write reviews (and articles) on authors and works I judge to be meritorious, including Ramsey Campbell, Thomas Ligotti, T. E. D. Klein, Caitlín R. Kiernan, Jonathan Thomas, Michael Aronovitz, Steve Rasnic Tem, Jason V Brock, and a host of others. Generally speaking, I do not write satirical reviews of novice or insignificant writers, under the age-old principle that it is unwise to hit a fly with a sledgehammer—or, in modern parlance, to "punch downward."

There has now developed, over the past several years, an even more distressing tendency for certain writers and their followers to band together in tightly knit cliques; these individuals are so terribly insecure that they cannot endure the slightest criticism, however well intentioned or constructive. Or is it that they are actually convinced that they have already attained the pinnacle of literary achievement, and therefore that criticism of any sort is a kind of *lèse-majesté*? I have no idea. But whatever the cause, the development of these cliques is unfortunate on many levels. It results in extreme touchiness, resentment, groupthink, and all manner of other bad things that inhibit honest and straightforward criticism. I trust I may be pardoned for at times baiting these timorous folk. Given how quick they are to express blubbering outrage and self-righteous indignation, they easily fall into the trap I set for them.

It remains an unfortunate fact that there are few venues for the expression of honest criticism of weird fiction—fewer than there were several decades ago. We have reached a stage where, in the old adage, "everyone's a critic," if by that we mean that we are to take seriously the readers' comments found on Amazon.com, many of which (both the positive and the negative ones) are manufactured for the express purpose of puffing up or tearing down a given author or work, irrespective of the merits or demerits of that author or work. In other contexts, it is regarded as somehow "bad form" to speak harshly of a work, even if there is nothing at all personal in the review.

This will never do. Not all books are good; indeed, relatively few of them are. And everyone is *not* a critic: relatively few of us are properly trained in the principles of literary criticism or endowed with the all-important quality of *critical judgment* (i.e., the quality that allows us to distinguish the good from the bad, the original from the hackneyed, the scintillating from the mundane), such that we can pass an even approximately valid judgment on the work in question. The need to separate the wheat from the chaff is even more important now—when we are deluged with publications of a wildly varying nature from big presses, small presses, and authors who cannot achieve print except by self-publishing—than it was decades ago, when certain individuals called *editors* exercised a modicum of gatekeeping. So if satirical criticism can drive some particularly boneheaded author to give up writing and become a more useful member of society, where is the harm in that?

Women and the Ghost Story

There is a certain artificiality in segregating literary or other artistic work by gender. Studies have repeatedly shown that readers are unable to tell the difference between work written by men and work written by women if the authors' names are concealed; and many attempts to identify characteristically "male" or "female" traits in writing have a tendency to descend to conventional stereotypes. That said, there is some virtue in focusing on the many distinguished women writers who have contributed to the development of the literature of horror and the supernatural, for they have been at the forefront of the field since its inception as a genre—perhaps more so than in any other literary genre.

The Gothic novels that appeared in their hundreds in the half-century following the publication of Horace Walpole's *The Castle of Otranto* (1764) could be said to have constituted the first instance of the emergence of "popular" fiction in English literature, and three writers took center stage in the movement: Ann Radcliffe, Matthew Gregory ("Monk") Lewis, and Charles Robert Maturin. But whereas Lewis (*The Monk*, 1796) and Maturin (*Melmoth the Wanderer*, 1820) came to be known for a single noteworthy work of Gothic fiction, Radcliffe wrote six novels, all of which were immense bestsellers, chief among them *The Mysteries of Udolpho* (1794), which in many ways came to define the Gothic novel. Its vivid setting in the Appenine Mountains of Italy, its classic portrayal of the "woman-in-peril" motif, and its mingling of historical fiction and terror were all copied by countless imitators, and "Mother Radcliffe" was arguably the most popular writer in the English-speaking world during the years 1790-1825. She wrote no short fiction, however, so she goes unrepresented in this volume. Moreover, her focus on the "explained supernatural"—the suggestion of the supernatural, later to be explained away as the result of trickery or misconstrual—was later rightly criticised by Sir Walter Scott as something of a disappointment and a copout, and subsequent ventures into "weird fiction" focused more clearly and unequivocally on the "reality" of the supernatural occurrence.

One of the more curious episodes in Gothic fiction was the now celebrated contest in 1816 that led to the writing of Mary Shelley's pioneering short novel *Frankenstein* (1818)—a work that not only fostered the development of weird fiction but also laid the groundwork for the later emergence of science fiction. Perhaps it is not surprising that for many decades thereafter it was believed that Mary's more famous husband, the poet Percy Bysshe Shelley, had helped her to write the book (even though his own early ventures into Gothic fiction, *Zastrossi* [1810] and *St. Irvyne* [1811], are almost laughably bad) or actually wrote it himself. Such speculations typify the denigration of female accomplishment that has dominated human history: it was no doubt offensive to many believers in male superiority that a woman barely twenty years old could write such a profound and compelling work while such of her more illustrious male counterparts, such as the poet Shelley and Lord Byron, produced next to nothing in the contest. (A fourth participant, Dr. John William Polidori, did write the notable novelette "The Vampyre" [1819].) Mary Shelley went on to write several other novels as well as a brace of weird stories, of which "Transformation" (1830) is something of a pendant to *Frankenstein* in some of its themes and motifs.

In the post-Gothic period, the one titanic literary figure to emerge was Edgar Allan Poe (1809–1849), who refined the outmoded Gothic tropes and rendered them imperishably potent in the compact mode of the short story. But, especially in England, the Victorian age saw the emergence of an array of women writers who focused on the "ghost story" to convey their fascination with the supernatural. There are, indeed, some faint supernatural episodes even in such novels as Charlotte Brontë's *Jane Eyre* (1847) and Emily Brontë's *Wuthering Heights* (1848); and a close friend of the Brontës, Elizabeth Gaskell, made frequent departures from her writing of novels of English domestic life to pen the occasional weird tale. And she was by no means alone: Mary Elizabeth Braddon, Amelia B. Edwards, Margaret Oliphant, and Mrs. J. H. Riddell followed in her wake, joining such male figures as Edward Bulwer-Lytton, J. Sheridan Le Fanu, Charles Dickens, Rudyard Kipling, and W. W. Jacobs in filling Victorian periodicals with tales of terror. Even the eminent Anglo-American novelist Henry James—who wrote an early and appreciative essay on Braddon— could not resist the tendency toward the weird, and his recurring work in the weird tale came to full flower in the short novel *The Turn of the Screw* (1898).

In America, the influence of Poe in the later nineteenth century was even more pronounced. His younger contemporary Fitz-James O'Brien led the way, although his early death in the Civil War no doubt deprived us of a number of weird tales along the lines of "What Was It?" and "The Diamond Lens." Another figure who fought in the Civil War, Ambrose Bierce (1842–1914?), became Poe's most notable disciple, adhering closely to his mentor's strictures on the "unity of effect" by writing stories whose austere compactness and focus on the psychological effects of terror rendered them almost unbearably intense. Bierce was an unabashed misygonist, but that did not stop him from promoting the work of his younger contemporary Gertrude Atherton, whose powerful weird stories are only a small portion of her prodigious work as novelist, short story writer, and chronicler of the history and topography of her native California.

Bierce and Atherton represent what might be called the "West Coast School" of supernatural writing in America during the period 1880–1940, a period that many have called the Golden Age of weird fiction. The East Coast School, dominated by Henry James and his colleague and disciple Edith Wharton, also generated fine work, but work that was perhaps more closely allied to the conventional "ghost story." In New England, Sarah Orne Jewett, Charlotte Perkins Gilman, and Mary E. Wilkins Freeman all took occasional respite from their focus on gritty realism to write weird tales whose power resides precisely in their evocation of the hard, unforgiving landscape of their native land and the dour, grizzled denizens it produces. Gilman's "The Yellow Wall Paper" (1892) seems to be a textbook case of the kind of psychological horror that can uniquely affect women—it was inspired by her own bout with post-partum depression—but a closer reading of the story suggests a supernatural undercurrent (the psychic possession of the hapless woman confined to the attic bedroom by a previous denizen of the place) that many critics have failed to detect.

Nearly all the Victorian writers mentioned above indulged in the supernatural only as a kind of hobby—a respite from their more recognized work in mainstream fiction. Even Le Fanu, who (aside from Poe) perhaps came closest to being a "professional" weird writer, confined the weird to his short stories and novellas; most of his novels, even the celebrated *Uncle Silas* (1864), do not involve the supernatural and rarely venture even into psychological or Gothic horror. Perhaps it was not possible to make a career out of weird writing at this juncture: E. Nesbit, who wrote two early collections of weird tales, achieved far greater success in writing children's books (some of which do involve elements of fantasy, if not the supernatural) than in weird fiction designed for adults.

But with the turn of the twentieth century there emerged, somewhat fortuitously, a cadre of towering figures who transformed weird fiction into a genre that could attain the highest aesthetic levels. It is no doubt an historical accident that all these writers—Arthur Machen, Lord Dunsany, Algernon Blackwood, M. R. James, and H. P. Lovecraft—are men; and even a good many of the second-tier figures who helped to make this era such a rich period of weird fiction—William Hope Hodgson, Walter de la Mare, L. P. Hartley, Robert Hichens—are also male. But, as before, mainstream writers dabbled in the weird to no little extent: even putting aside the obscure American novelist and translator Edna W. Underwood, whose eccentric volume *A Book of Dear Dead Women* (1911) is only now gaining some attention, we can point to the highly regarded Southern writer Ellen Glasgow and to such British figures as Marjorie Bowen, May Sinclair, and, preeminently, Virginia Woolf as examples of the ineluctable attraction of the weird upon temperaments of a very different sort.

It should also be noted that, during the long history of *Weird Tales* (1923–54) and its fellow pulp magazines, women were a not insignificant presence: Francis Stevens (pseudonym of Gertrude Barrows Bennett), Everil Worrell, Leah Bodine Drake, Mary Elizabeth Counselman, and many other women made frequent appearances in the pulps and attracted a devoted following. During the 1950s and 1960s, weird fiction suffered something of an eclipse, as mystery fiction and science fiction came to the fore; but the mainstream writer Shirley Jackson elevated the weird to the highest literary status in such works as "The Lottery" (1948) and *The Haunting of Hill House* (1959).

The sudden and unexpected emergence of supernatural fiction as a best-selling phenomenon—begun with the publication of Ira Levin's *Rosemary's Baby* (1967), fostered by William Peter Blatty's *The Exorcist* (1971), and culminating in the many novels of Stephen King—might be said to be a largely male phenomenon, as such other writers as Peter Straub, Clive Barker, and Dean R. Koontz contributed to the immense popularity of the weird as a literary and media phenomenon; but no one would have expected Anne Rice, a predominantly mainstream writer whose *Interview with the Vampire* (1976) was initially published with little fanfare, to become the queen of the weird as she has become in the past few decades. Many other women writers who do not always attain bestseller status but whose work is second to none in quality—Caitlín R. Kiernan, Nancy Kilpatrick, Nancy A. Collins, Lois H. Gresh, Elizabeth Hand, Gemma Files, Kathe Koja, Kelly Link—have made the present era an inexhaustibly rich one for the expression of weird motifs and conceptions.

Is there any specifically "female" approach to the weird? It would be demeaning and stereotypical to say that women writers have focused more on the human emotions elicited by a weird scenario rather than the weird phenomenon itself, or even that women writers can portray women characters more emphatically and realistically than male writers can. All we can say is that women have contributed to the development of weird fiction in ways that perhaps can only be paralleled by the female dominance of the detective story with such writers as Agatha Christie, Margery Allingham, Ngaio Marsh, P. D. James, Ruth Rendell, Sue Grafton, and countless others. Let us be content to read the weird work of women—and men—and enjoy the pleasant shivers they can send up our spines.

The Haunted House

The earliest tales of haunted houses date to Greco-Roman antiquity. One of the most celebrated is found in Pliny the Younger's letter to Licinius Sura, in which he speaks of a "large and spacious mansion [in Athens] with the bad reputation of being dangerous to its occupants"(7.27; trans. Betty Radice). It is significant that the source of this place's bad reputation proves to be the ghost of a murdered man buried in the courtyard: the union of ghosts with haunted houses becomes a staple of later Gothic literature, chiefly as the most direct means of suggesting a moral or aesthetic *motive* behind a "haunted" house: a house must be haunted by something, and a ghost is the most convenient sign that the house's very purpose of providing tranquility and safety to its occupants has been perverted by hidden crime or injustice.

In the outpouring of Gothic novels beginning in the later 18th century, the haunted castle was by far the preferred setting. Such a structure could, as it were, house a variety of symbolic meanings: its many rooms, hidden passageways, and deserted wings suggest the rambling contents of the subconscious mind; its decaying antiquity points to appalling acts lost in the dimness of the forgotten past. It may be true that, in such works as Walpole's *The Castle of Otranto* (1764) and Radcliffe's *The Mysteries of Udolpho* (1794), to say nothing of their legions of inferior imitators, the castle's function as a locus of terror is either contrived or implausible; but what this points to is that the castle itself—as Eino Railo in *The Haunted Castle* (Routledge/Dutton, 1927) was one of the first to point out—becomes not merely a neutral stage setting but an active, perhaps the most significant, character in the work. In later Gothic writing, such as Brontë's *Wuthering Heights* (1847) or Le Fanu's *Uncle Silas* (1864), the house becomes "haunted" only by the arrival of a redoubtable figure (Healthcliff and Uncle Silas, respectively) who use it as the springboard for their demonic activities. As for Hawthorne's *The House of the Seven Gables* (1851), the home of the Pyncheons is haunted not so much by a ghost (although the figure of the wronged Matthew Maule hovers constantly, if metaphorically, in the background) but by the ineluctable weight of sadness that has crushed and impoverished an entire family. Bulwer-Lytton's "The Haunted and the Haunters; or, The House and the Brain" (1859) retains its rank as perhaps the prototypical haunted house tale.

Poe's "Metzengerstein" (1832) is, in short compass, a remarkably faithful duplication of the "haunted castle" topos, although there is good reason to believe the tale a sly parody of already stale Gothic conventions. But in "The Fall of the House of Usher" (1839) Poe transformed the haunted house by fusing its being so intimately with that of the human beings who occupy it that its fate is sealed with their own; the word "house" in the title becomes a pun, referring simultaneously to its own physical collapse and the demise of the familial line. Poe was, manifestly, seeking to transform the Gothic mode into something psychologically viable in the modern age. His house of Usher is set in a never-never-land not clearly identifiable as either in Europe or the United States; by transferring the source of horror away from hoary antiquity (which in America was in short supply) to the tortured complexities of the human mind, he allowed horror to manifest itself at all times and anywhere. His posthumous disciple Ambrose Bierce managed to situate horror in a land even more recently settled by people of his race, the American West. In such tales as "The Middle Toe of the Right Foot" (1890) and "The Spook House" (1889), Bierce evoked all the terror and melancholy inherent in the ill-made shacks of the California mining towns, booming at one moment and deserted the next. On the other side of the country, the haunted house served as a powerful adjunct to the intimate, domestic horror of Mary E. Wilkins Freeman's "The Shadows on the Wall" and other tales in *The Wind in the Rose-bush* (1903), as it did in a more complexly psychological manner in Henry James's *The Turn of the Screw* (1898).

Bram Stoker's *Dracula* (1897) harks back to the Gothic novels by resurrecting the trope of the haunted castle; but by transferring that castle to eastern Europe rather than the Mediterranean, he leaves himself open to the charge of ethnocentrism. And yet, the opening scenes in Castle Dracula are far more compelling than the long-winded episodes in England. The intimate connection between the ghost and the haunted house was renewed by M. R. James and other British writers of ghost stories. For James, the ghost was the preeminent horrific entity, and its manifestation was nearly always for the purposes of supernatural revenge. And yet, in "Count Magnus" (1904), the hapless Mr. Wraxall can only be accused of excessive curiosity when he suffers a hideous fate after probing the secrets of Count Magnus's mausoleum. James's masterful "Number 13" (1904) finds horror in a modern hotel room, something H. P. Lovecraft approximately duplicated in "Cool Air" (1928), set in a decrepit New York brownstone. E. F. Benson's "Negotium Perambulans ..." (1923) masterfully embeds a loathsome entity in an ancient church, something Stoker managed far less successfully in *The Lair of the White Worm* (1911).

The two leading British supernaturalists of the early twentieth century, Arthur Machen and Algernon Blackwood, rarely utilized the haunted house. For Blackwood, both terror and wonder resided far more potently in the untenanted wilderness; although his first book was entitled *The Empty House* (1906), its finest story, "A Haunted Island," is set in the wilds of Canada. Perhaps only *Jimbo* (1909) is worth considering here, a poignant tale in which a boy is caught in a house of his imagination, trapped by his own fears. Machen wrote almost no haunted-house stories, although in some sense the whole of London was for him the locus of horror and fascination, as *The Three Impostors* (1895) reveals. William Hope Hodgson masterfully combined local and cosmic horror in *The House on the Borderland* (1908).

H. P. Lovecraft, although influenced by Machen and Blackwood as well as by Poe and Bierce, nonetheless looked forward, recognizing that many of the Gothic props had become stale through overuse and reliance upon outmoded aesthetic and philosophical conceptions. In "The Shunned House" (1928) the occupant, a psychic vampire, is dispatched by being doused with sulphuric acid. *The Case of Charles Dexter Ward* (written 1927, published 1943) is somewhat more traditional, although the entities that Dr. Willett encounters in Joseph Curwen's hidden cellar are far from orthodox. As for Leonard Cline's *The Dark Chamber* (1927), the haunted house proves to be nothing less than an immense library in which the protagonist has recorded all the minutiae of his life—a transparent symbol for the labyrinthine caverns of his disturbed mentality.

The modern prototype of the haunted house is Shirley Jackson's *The Haunting of Hill House* (1959), although that novel is somewhat hampered by a puzzling surfeit of unsystematized supernatural effects. The house that the four psychic investigators come to explore is one whose function lies in rending the fabric of emotional ties that binds human beings to each other; it is for that reason that, as the novel's memorable opening paragraph states, "whatever walked there, walked alone." Jackson expands this conception in *The Sundial* (1958), in which a neurotic family believes that their house alone will survive an imminent and otherwise universal cataclysm. Robert Bloch magisterially simulates the supernatural in the Bates Motel in *Psycho* (1959), "haunted" only by the vile crimes that take place in it.

In the supernatural fiction of the past three decades, the haunted house topos has not been used with any great frequency, perhaps because the increasing urbanization of the Anglo-American population renders it implausible. Recency of construction of most modern dwellings, a population rapidly shifting locales as time and circumstance warrant, and the absence of generations dwelling either consecutively or simultaneously in the same residence make it difficult to envision a particular structure, whether residential or public, as the victim of a specific spectral manifestation. Perhaps this is why a few writers have chosen to seek horror in the rural milieu, as Thomas Tryon did in *The Other* (1971) and T. E. D. Klein did in "The Events at Poroth Farm" (1971). For the writers of urban horror, a house becomes "haunted" not by reason of past events but as a result of an almost random supernatural victimization, as in the house of Regan MacNeil in William Peter Blatty's *The Exorcist* (1971), where the climactic scene occurs in Regan's otherwise ordinary and modern bedroom. Stephen King similarly transforms the seemingly bland Overlook Hotel in *The Shining* (1977) into something far more sinister, as David J. Schow does with a seedy tenement in *The Shaft* (1990). But the transcendent haunted house novel of our time must be Ramsey Campbell's *The House on Nazareth Hill* (1996), which fuses domestic conflict and centuries-old supernaturalism into a potent mix.

II. The Classics

The Life and Career of Ambrose Bierce

Ambrose Bierce was a private man. For all the millions of words he wrote in more than forty years as a journalist, and the hundreds of thousands of words he penned as a prolific correspondent, he made few direct statements about many of his most deeply held beliefs, and he was not given to chatting about his daily activities. To this degree, and to this alone, Ambrose Bierce matches the popular caricature of him—the misanthropic recluse spewing venom at the world.

And yet, it was Bierce himself who wrote his "memoirs" (as he termed them in a letter of 1908), by which he presumably meant the eleven essays he published in the first volume of his *Collected Works* under the general title "Bits of Autobiography." Most of these pieces had appeared in the newspapers and magazines for which Bierce wrote, the earliest (and best) of them, "What I Saw of Shiloh," as early as 1881. But if Bierce meant "Bits of Autobiography" to constitute his memoirs, are we to believe that nothing significant occurred in his life after 1875? For although the last item, "A Sole Survivor," is clearly the rumination of an old man who has seen his friends die one by one, the chronological sequence of "Bits of Autobiography" ends with his English visit of 1872–75.

Fortunately, there is in the remarkable richness of Bierce's corpus a wealth of autobiographical material—interpreting that phrase in a wider sense than merely a chronicle of the bare events of his life, to cover his piquant and challenging views of society and politics and his dicta on the principles of literature—that allows us to augment those "Bits of Autobiography" and present a few further glimpses into the long life and career of the saturnine journalist and master of the short story.

It is not surprising that Bierce offers yield little information about his upbringing. Born in 1842 to a poor and religiously (perhaps even fanatically) devout family of farmers in Meigs County, Ohio, he must have spent the years of his youth, the youngest of ten Bierce children (each with a first name beginning with the letter A), attempting to earn a hard living from the earth. Although he proclaimed himself a lifelong atheist, Bierce must have absorbed some elements of his parents' extreme Christian views, for he exhibited a lifelong puritanical intolerance for unchastity (especially in women) and judged friend and foe alike by an unwavering and rigid moral standard that took no account of differing customs or changing times.

It was mere circumstance that allowed Bierce to expand his physical and mental horizons beyond the narrow confines of his youthful environment. He first stayed briefly with his uncle Lucius Verus Bierce, a well-known politician and lawyer who took Bierce in at his residence in Akron, Ohio, in 1859, more than a decade after Bierce's own family had moved to Indiana. Later that year Bierce enrolled for a year at the Kentucky Military Institute, but of his tenure there nothing is known. Then, while Bierce was idling at home in Indiana in the spring of 1861, the Civil War broke out.

Bierce's immediate enlistment in the Ninth Indiana Volunteers appears to bespeak more a wish to be where "something was going on" (as he put it late in his life, when he was preparing to go to Mexico) than any devotion to one side or the other of the conflict. It is true that Bierce had served in 1857 as a printer's devil on an abolitionist newspaper, the *Northern Indianan*, but, again, little is known of that experience. Throughout his life Bierce would express a rueful wistfulness over the horrific struggle and his role in it. When, in 1903, he returned to West Virginia, the scene of his earliest fighting in the war, he told correspondent that the grave of a Confederate soldier had recently been found and remarked: "I'm going over to beg his pardon."[1]

If nothing else, Bierce's participation in some of the bloodiest battles of the Civil War—Shiloh, Chickamauga, Franklin—allowed him in later years to set down some of the most memorable accounts we have of those conflicts; and although several were written more than forty years after the events, they harmonize in every significant particular with the known facts. Bierce's memories of the war are found not only in his formal essays; many shorter and more informal recollections scattered throughout his journalistic work, reprinted here for the first time, substantially augment our knowledge of Bierce's involvement in the war.

Eight of the eleven "Bits of Autobiography" concern Bierce's experiences during and immediately following the war; did he, perhaps, believe that the most exciting period of his life was lived by 1865? In a sense it was: physically he would never be the same (the gunshot wound in the head, received in 1864, was nearly fatal, and for the rest of his life he was susceptible to searing headaches as a result of his injury), while his psychological state as a veteran who had somehow survived when so many of his companions had perished can only be conjectured. Although Bierce left the army for good in 1866, for the whole of his life he considered himself more soldier than civilian, and it is no surprise that his first collection of tales focuses on that distinction in its very title.

But for the immediate future there was work to be considered. A stint as an aide to the Treasury Department in Alabama during Reconstruction proving markedly unsatisfactory, Bierce joined his old friend and erstwhile commander, General William B. Hazen, in a trip to the uncharted wilderness of the West on an exploratory mission. He abandoned the party at San Francisco in early 1867; although he did not know it then, he would, for the next thirty years, be intimately identified with the Bay Area. What led Bierce to become a writer is unclear; certainly, his earliest pieces—a few poems and an essay on female suffrage for the *Californian*—are stiff and undistinguished. But he got a needed break when, after writing a number of unsigned items for the *San Francisco News Letter and California Advertiser*, he was hired as its regular columnist late in 1868. Bierce's career as an editorialist had begun.

The paragraphs of random commentary Bierce wrote for the *News Letter* are a testament more to his energy than to his emotional maturity; for the 2500-word columns that appeared weekly almost without a break for more than three years are, in actual substance, very much the callow reflections of a young man eager to prove to the world—or, at least, to the local community—his wit, his outrageousness, and his defiance of convention. In the rough-and-tumble world of post-'49er San Francisco, where several other newspapers competed with the *News Letter*, including the *Chronicle*, the *Bulletin*, the *Call*, and the *Alta California*, Bierce's provocative opinions on religion, women, and politics found a receptive audience; and, as early as the summer of 1869, they also found recognition in the pages of so august a journal as the *Nation*, which felt that the western firebrand was worth introducing to its refined readership.

It was in the *News Letter* that Bierce articulated a defense of the unrelenting satire that would consume much of the rest of his career. From the beginning he was faced with the naive criticism that satire of his sort—the tart, at times biting satire of Juvenal, Swift, and Voltaire, which did not refrain from naming names, which disdained the tickle of a feather and stung with the rapier's slash—was somehow inherently improper, beyond the bounds of civilized discourse, and the product of personal spite. It may be true that some of Bierce's earlier and cruder work is mere vilification, although even this has its amusing qualities; but the overwhelming bulk of his work features satire that is both pungent and thought-provoking, marked by a carefully considered intellectual stance even at its most vicious. Few perceived that the objects of Bierce's scorn were condemned in such a way as clearly to suggest his approval of their opposite.

Given Bierce's notoriety, it is perhaps not surprising that he courted and won the well-bred society lady Mary Ellen ("Mollie") Day for his wife, marrying her on Christmas Day of 1871. Bierce's silence about his wife, and about the course of their long and often troubled marriage, is telling; even in private correspondence she is rarely mentioned, although we have several affecting letters by Bierce to his three children as well as to the wife of his nephew Carlton, whom he seemed to regard with as much tenderness as his own off-spring. As with his relations with his parents, Bierce's attitude toward Mollie can only be inferred with caution from his creative work—from his celebrated definition of "Marriage" in *The Devil's Dictionary* ("The state or condition of a community consisting of a master, a mistress and two slaves, making in all, two") to the numerous paragraphs in the *News Letter* and elsewhere on the miseries of married couples, the loathsomeness of babies, and the alarmingly frequent suicides, homicides, and infanticides within the family circle.

By the spring of 1872, when Bierce apparently found himself discontent-ed with the narrow literary horizon of San Francisco, he boldly resettled in England. Although the dozen letters he wrote to the *Alta California* in the fall and winter of 1872 read in part like the notes of a wide-eyed tourist, it is like-ly that he felt the move to be permanent—dependent, of course, upon his suc-cess as a writer. His stay lasted only a little more than three years, but it proved remarkably fertile. He wrote hundreds of columns for the semiweekly magazine *Figaro*, dozens of stories and sketches for Tom Hood's comic paper *Fun* (and also *Tom Hood's Comic Annual*), as well as work (not yet traced) for at least two other periodicals. He and Mollie also found time to begin their fam-ily: a son, Day, was born in December 1872, while another, Leigh, arrived in April 1874. It was at this time that Bierce's first books appeared, albeit pseu-donymously: *The Fiend's Delight* (1873), *Nuggets and Dust* (1873), and *Cobwebs from an Empty Skull* (1874), consisting of various scraps derived from his earli-er California work and from his *Fun* contributions. In later years Bierce wished upon these little books an oblivion he felt they deserved; but if noth-ing else they exhibited his sardonic wit in a form more permanent than news-papers or magazines. It is not to be denied that in some ways these books shared the celebrity enjoyed in England at that time by California writers, among them Bierce's longtime friend Joaquin Miller (whose *Songs of the Sierras* was the sensation of 1871) and Mark Twain, who was sojourning in England concurrently with Bierce and whom Bierce met on a few occasions.

Perhaps the most peculiar of Bierce's experiences in England was his work in 1874 on two issues of a paper entitled the *Lantern*. Bierce wrote every word of the paper, unaware that it was secretly funded by the exiled Empress of France as a vehicle for attacking her bitter enemy, Henri Rochefort. Bierce later found out about the charade, writing up the event in "Working for an Empress"; and after the paper folded he resumed his work for *Figaro* and *Fun*.

Bierce himself clearly enjoyed dallying with the English literati of Grub

Street and hopping from London to Bath to Leamington, with an occasional jaunt into France; but when, in the spring of 1875, Mollie became pregnant with their third child (Helen, born in October) and returned to San Francisco, Bierce regretfully followed to tend to his family. For the next two years there is silence, although we know that Bierce worked for the United States Mint in San Francisco, where he had been briefly employed in 1867.

The next stage of his career was shaped by Frank Pixley, who in the spring of 1877 founded a weekly paper named the *Argonaut* and invited Bierce to write for it. Bierce resumed the writing of a column of miscellaneous comment. In the *News Letter* Bierce had taken over a column called "The Town Crier," a title he retained in Figaro"; now he revived the name he had used previously for only a single column in the short-lived *Lantern*—"Prattle." For the next twenty years—in three different papers—the Prattler would be the terror of San Francisco: no politician, cleric, writer, actor, or private individual could know whether he or she would be skewered with Bierce's pen. The *Argonaut* columns reveal both considerable expansion of Bierce's horizons—his London stay had shown him that the world, not just California, was a bountiful haven of fools and scoundrels—and a marked advance in style. Bierce quickly became a master of the most condensed literary forms—fables, epigrams, definitions, poetic couplets and quatrains—but he occasionally ventured into more expansive ruminations on the world around him and on his own three and a half decades of life. His earliest memories of the Civil War and of his English stay appear in the *Argonaut*.

In the summer of 1879 Bierce's contributions to the *Argonaut* ended abruptly. For the next year and a half we find him mired in the frustrating proposition known as the Black Hills Placer Mining Company. Gold had been discovered in the Dakota Territory, and Bierce's old colleague General Sherburne B. Eaton (who had supervised his work as a Treasury aide in 1865 and who was the company's New York attorney) urged Bierce to come out and share in the wealth expected from the venture. In the summer of 1880 Bierce was sent there by Eaton and John McGinnis, Jr., the company's vice president, to be the General Agent overseeing the progress of the mining. Romantic as this may sound, one should not picture Bierce sitting by a trickling stream panning for gold; this was big business. It was, unfortunately, a very badly run business, as Eaton and McGinnis provided almost no support to Bierce against the machinations of the company's president, General Alexander Shaler, the duplicitous treasurer, Marcus Walker, and various other individuals who appeared to resent Bierce's authority—indeed, his very presence—perhaps because of his inexperience in the business and what may have been his cantankerous attitude. Although we have little evidence of the nature of the enterprise besides that contained in Bierce's letters to Eaton and McGinnis, it appears the company was very poorly operated—with sometimes too many people in charge, at other times none at all. Bierce lasted as long as he could in the face of poor (or nonexistent) pay, hostility from workers whose salaries were far in arrears, lawsuits from all sides, and the ever-present physical danger of robbery or death at the hands of brigands. Bierce left the job in late 1880, and some years later the company itself collapsed; but for years thereafter Bierce was vexed by a lawsuit that emerged from the boondoggle.

Upon his return to San Francisco, Bierce found that Frank Pixley would not rehire him. But shortly thereafter, in March 1881, another weekly paper, the *Wasp*, offered Bierce his usual page of "Prattle." For the next five and a half years Bierce worked tirelessly on the *Wasp*, contributing his usual commentary on the follies of the world, along with poems, humorous sketches, and—in small numbers—actual short stories. Bierce's first real story, "The Haunted Valley," had appeared in the *Overland Monthly* in 1871. The many brief comic pieces he wrote for *Fun* in England, few longer than a thousand words, qualify as stories only for lack of anything else to call them. During his *Argonaut* stint he wrote only one story, "The Famous Gilson Bequest," but for the *Wasp* he produced such tales of horror and the Civil War as "A Holy Terror," "George Thurston," and "An Imperfect Conflagration." How Bierce became attracted to the horror tale is not entirely clear; certainly he must have read Poe, and he retained Poe's devotion to the short story and the short poem for the whole of his life. Perhaps the morbid humor he displayed in both his journalism and his comic sketches required little alteration for transition into tales of supernatural or psychological horror. Whatever the case, Bierce was began to achieve recognition in another arena: his journalism may have attracted the notice of contemporary San Franciscans, but his tales garnered readers who knew nothing of the local personalities lambasted every week by the Prattler.

Politics—both local and national—came increasingly under Bierce's scrutiny during his *Wasp* years. His political convictions clearly developed over the course of his life, and it is impossible to pin him down to any specific party line. In the end he came to believe that hypocrisy and "rascality" owed allegiance to no party, and that his stance—"pox on both your houses"—was the one that best accorded with political reality. To say that Bierce's political satire—or his satire as a whole—was merely the product of an inflexible "misanthropy" is short-sighted and superficial. There is no reason to disbelieve his declaration: "I like many things in this world and a few persons."[2] But there is much reason to believe that his witnessing of the increasing corruption of American politics had much to do with his increasing censoriousnesss. The assassination of President Garfield in 1881 seemed to confirm all Bierce's fears.

By the fall of 1886 Bierce again found himself out of a job; perhaps the *Wasp*'s purchase in 1885 by Colonel J. P. Jackson, not a man after Bierce's heart, rendered continued work untenable. For years he had struggled with increasingly severe asthma, and he moved continually from one rural or mountain locale (Auburn, Angwin, Los Gatos) to another; not coincidentally, he found in these moves a convenient opportunity to escape from his wife and the burdens of childrearing. It was while living in Oakland in the spring of 1887 that Bierce's life took its most dramatic turn; for it was then that the twenty-three-year-old William Randolph Hearst knocked at his door and asked him to become the chief editorial writer for the *San Francisco Examiner*.

Hearst readily dropped out of Harvard when his father gave him a chance to run the paper, and he immediately hired the best-known local journalists of the day. It is a testament to Bierce's local fame that his "Prattle" column was for several years the only signed contribution on the editorial page of the *Examiner*, which at that time was rather more subdued than its flamboyant incarnation of the late 1890s. Bierce plunged into his work with renewed vigor, producing weekly columns of unprecedented length (sometimes longer than 3000 words) and wondrously scintillating wit, but also writing many short stories: in his first four years at the *Examiner*, he published such tales as "One of the Missing," "A Son of the Gods," "A Tough Tussle," "Chickamauga," "A Horseman in the Sky," "The Coup de Grâce," "The Suitable Surroundings," "A Watcher by the Dead," "An Occurrence at Owl Creek Bridge," "The Realm of the Unreal," as well as the little-known "The Fall of the Republic," a long political satire later rewritten as "Ashes of the Beacon." Bierce's continuing outspokenness embroiled him in many controversies, but he gave as well as he got—usually better. It is noteworthy, however, that two personal dilemmas—his separation from Mollie in 1888 over his discovery of what he took to be love letters to her from a Danish admirer, and the death the next year of his sixteen-year-old son Day in a sordid duel over a girl—find virtually no mention in either his published work or his surviving correspondence.

The 1890s were, at least on paper, a decade of triumph for Bierce. His *Tales of Soldiers and Civilians* was published by a local publisher (the edition is dated 1891, but it probably appeared in early 1892) after being rejected by major houses in New York; it was reprinted in 1892 in England as *In the Midst of Life*, and although Bierce then used that title in subsequent editions, several remarks in letters lead one to believe that he preferred his original title. In 1892 his translation (with G. A. Danziger) of Richard Voss's *The Monk and the*

Hangman's Daughter appeared in book form, as did his first collection of verse (culled from his newspaper columns), *Black Beetles in Amber*. The volume emerged under the imprint of the Western Authors Publishing Association, a firm he and Danziger had established; for the next decade he would wrangle with Danzig over the profits of the book and the rights to the *Monk*. In 1893 his collection of horror tales, *Can Such Things Be?*, was published; in 1898 an augmented edition of *In the Midst of Life* appeared from Putnam's, and the next year that publisher issued his *Fantastic Fables*.

Beyond these literary successes (tempered by the fact that three of the publishing houses folded a year or two after the books they published appeared), Bierce found himself at the nation's political center. In early 1896 Hearst sent Bierce to Washington to lobby against the efforts of Collis P. Huntington, one of the most notorious of the "railroad barons," to pass a funding bill that would give Huntington nearly a century to repay a debt to the government for the building and maintenance of the Southern and Central Pacific Railroad. Bierce, for once agreeing with Hearst on a point of policy, believed Huntington to be a mere thief who had already pocketed too much of the government's money, and he entered the fray with gusto. His sixty or so articles on the matter, from February to May, were written for both the *San Francisco Examiner* and the *New York Journal*, which Hearst had recently acquired; most of the pieces were apparently sent to the newspaper offices by telegraph. There is little doubt that Bierce's articles were instrumental in swaying both the public and members of Congress (many of whom had initially been inclined to vote for the Huntington bill) to defeat the measure. These pieces alone are sufficient to establish Bierce as a forerunner of the Muckraker movement of the following generation.

Bierce claimed to suffer health problems upon the completion of his work in Washington, but his contributions to the *Examiner* continued unabated. By November he had returned to San Francisco. The next year, 1897, Bierce tendered his resignation from the Hearst staff, on this occasion because he objected to the severe editing and rewriting of his contributions in the New York paper. (It was probably not the first occasion for such an act, and it definitely was not the last.) Hearst, having many other concerns and probably not wishing to exercise rigid supervision of his staff, managed to lure Bierce back to work, but the editorial tampering continued.

In 1898 that Bierce commenced a long series of articles on the Spanish-American war and its ramifications in the Philippines and on American relations with China. Here he was manifestly not in Hearst's corner, seeing the war as merely a naked grab for power.[3] These articles, if perhaps less superficially dramatic than his broadsides against Huntington, reveal a seasoned understanding of political reality that was exceptionally rare for their period, and leagues beyond the impish abuse of local politicians that characterized Bierce's earliest work. They may stand as his most distinguished newspaper writing.

In December 1899 Bierce's work for the *Examiner* again lapsed briefly; but this time it was not because he went on strike. Bierce had finally decided for health reasons to uproot himself from his adopted home town, the town that had stood in mingled terror and admiration of him for thirty years. He settled in Washington, D.C., where his contributions were wired to both the *New York Journal* (which became, in early 1902, the *New York American*) and the *Examiner*. His literary output declined both in quantity and in substance: the columns became skimpier ("Prattle" gave way to "The Passing Show," which in turn gave way to "The Views of One" and other brief pieces), and relatively few works of fiction appeared, with the notable exception of the revised "Ashes of the Beacon," which took up an entire page of the *American* and *Examiner* in February 1905. Another personal tragedy—the death of his son Leigh of pneumonia in March 1901—is mentioned tersely in a few letters.

In 1905 Hearst finally put forward to Bierce a proposal that seemed promising: Bierce would eventually cease his newspaper work and write exclusively for the newly purchased magazine, *Cosmopolitan*. At first he jumped at the task, writing an array of stories as well as several additional satires of the "Ashes of the Beacon" type. But Bierce's regular column, "The Passing Show," proved to be unsatisfying, as he found himself unable to discuss contemporary affairs pertinently in a column that would be published a month or two after the items were written. A shift to a less topical column, "Small Contributions," proved no more satisfactory; and the title unwittingly reflected both the size and nature of his work for the magazine. The only book publication of note during this period was *The Devil's Dictionary*, which Doubleday issued in 1906; Bierce did not care for the lackluster title *The Cynic's Word Book*, used to avoid offending readers' religious sensibilities.[4] It was also at this time that Bierce attempted valiantly to secure the publication of his young pupil George Sterling's remarkable poem of fantasy and imagination, "A Wine of Wizardry"; after being rejected by many standard magazines, it appeared in *Cosmopolitan* itself, accompanied by an essay on it by Bierce. Perhaps Bierce felt indebted to Sterling for the his financing of Bierce's second collection of verse, *Shapes of Clay* (1903). Whatever the case, the Hearst papers used the occasion to create a kind of literary tempest in a teapot, with many of Bierce's enemies upbraiding him for advocating a poem so out of tune with the placid decorum of the verse of the day.

By the spring of 1909 Bierce had had all he could stomach of *Cosmopoli-*

tan, and his resignation signaled the definitive end of his work for Hearst. For more than twenty years Bierce had given the best years of his literary life to the Hearst publications, and in his rumination on those years, "A Thumbnail Sketch," which curiously does not appear among the "Bits of Autobiography," Bierce concluded that the relation had been of mutual benefit. Certainly, his contributions of 1887–99 represent the pinnacle of his journalistic work, and a case could be made that they constitute the most remarkable American journalism of the century.

It was tragically short-sighted of Bierce not to reprint much of this material in the twelve volumes of his *Collected Works,* which his friend, the publisher Walter Neale, issued between 1909 and 1912. Bierce's low view of journalism in general clearly skewed his assessment of his own work; and of course his journalism has now gained added historical value as the commentary of a keen mind on the political and social events of the period. But no reader of this body of work—which makes up the bulk of the latter two-thirds of this book—can come away unimpressed with the verbal witchery, the glittering wit, the merciless satire, the towering rhetorical fire, and, most important, the depth of thought and keenness of perception of Bierce's editorial columns. One must compare them with the average run of work written in the newspapers at this time to gain a true sense of its superiority. Even if Bierce on occasion embodies his own definition of "Positive" ("Mistaken at the top of one's voice"), there can be little doubt that most of his views are well-considered, sincerely held, and expressed with dazzling wit and acerbity.

For the last eight or nine years of Bierce's life we are largely reliant on his correspondence, which either was more voluminous during this time or merely happens to survive more copiously than for earlier periods. Bierce continued to play his hand close to the vest, treating in a sentence or a phrase matters we would like to see dealt with in paragraphs or pages; but it is all we have. The assembling, editing, and proofreading of the *Collected Works* was occupying much of his time, but Bierce found occasion to return triumphantly, and a little ruefully, to San Francisco in 1910 and 1912; he had overcome his resolve not to visit the city after its destruction by the earthquake and fire of 1906, of which he heard much from friends like Sterling.

By 1913 Bierce was tiring of his idle life in Washington. He was writing little save letters, and, although now past seventy, felt the need to involve himself in something. The Mexican Civil War offered an opportunity. Many of his letters of the latter half of 1913 speak of his inclination to see what was going on there, and then to continue to South America. Was this merely an elaborate deception? Did Bierce in fact not go to Mexico (beyond a brief foray in November 1913)? The puzzle of Bierce's disappearance—attested by the provocative "1842–1914?" that follows his name in library catalogues—has certainly augmented his reputation as a mystery man of American letters, and in all likelihood the truth will never be known. His biographer, Roy Morris, Jr., has argued that Bierce did not in fact go to Mexico; but the existence of a letter written from Chihuahua on December 26, 1913, of which Morris was evidently unaware, makes such a view unlikely. What exactly happened to Bierce may never be known for certain, but the evidence suggests that he perished in very early 1914, possibly mistaken for a spy.

Bierce's frequent strictures on the uselessness, even the perniciousness, of literary biography extended to autobiography, but they did not prevent him from writing of his own life from time to time. Perhaps he did not have the energy or inclination to write of the entirety of his life; perhaps he felt that much of his life was not worth writing about. Perhaps, too, he did not have the patience to wade through the oceans of his journalism over forty years to abstract items that might flesh out the high points of his literary and personal existence beyond those harrowing days as a raw soldier and the intoxicating few years as a man of letters in London. But at least that journalism has been left for future hands to sift, and we hope that the following volume presents at least some bits of autobiography of which Bierce might have approved.

It is true that some of this material is not "autobiographical" in the narrowest sense; but surely a writer's opinions on the world around him—and, especially, the evolution of those opinions from youth to maturity—are as much a part of his life as the bare physical events he experienced. It is indisputable that the "life" of many a writer is largely made up of writing; but for such persons the life of the mind can certainly rival that of the body in compelling interest. We make no apologies, therefore, for presenting what amounts to an anthology of Bierce's journalistic work in addition to his consciously autobiographical writing; for this work provides as transparent an index to Bierce's literary and philosophical development as anyone could wish. Perhaps, too, it will help to expand the general understanding of Bierce beyond that of a skilled writer of short stories; for those stories, brilliant as they are, are dwarfed at least in quantity by the editorial commentary Bierce expounded over nearly half a century of newspaper work. Such diligent and untiring work, which brought him his share of fame, notoriety, and obloquy, should not be forgotten.

The Ghost Story, 1870–1920

The term "ghost story" has been widely employed to denote an entire range of literary works that suggest the existence of supernatural entities, whether they be actual ghosts or other creatures such as vampires, werewolves, witches, or revenants (the dead revived to a semblance of life); the term has even been used, over the objections of some theorists, to denote works embodying supernatural scenarios of a broader kind, such as haunted houses, fantastic voyages, or speculative tales of the future. In recent years the terms "supernatural fiction" or "weird fiction" have been proposed as more representative of the wide range of conceptions exhibited by such literature, but whatever genre designation one uses, the works to be studied here have in common the suggestion of at least a single departure from mimetic realism, whether that suggestion is ultimately explained away naturalistically or is made for symbolic, metaphorical, or allegorical purposes.

In the United States, the shadow of Edgar Allan Poe (1809–1849) loomed large in this domain for a century after his death. Although relatively few of Poe's works could be considered ghost stories or even supernatural tales in the strictest sense, he effected a radical revolution of the conventions of Gothic literature that had already become stale in the two generations after their initiation in Horace Walpole's *The Castle of Otranto* (1764). The Gothic novels of that period were almost entirely a British phenomenon, and the lone American representative of any consequence, Charles Brockden Brown, did not attain widespread recognition. American writers were faced with a curious historical dilemma in translating British Gothic fiction to their shores: since most of that fiction was set in the mediaeval age (in order to render the exhibition of supernatural phenomena more plausible by a patina of remoteness and primitive superstition), how does one write Gothic fiction in a land that had no mediaeval period? Poe solved the problem by transferring the locus of terror to the baffling workings of the human mind ("The Tell-Tale Heart"; "Ligeia") or by setting his tales in a nebulous never-never-land ("The Fall of the House of Usher") or by transferring his characters to remote settings (*The Narrative of Arthur Gordon Pym*). But what Poe established for a century and a half by his meticulous example was the radical superiority of the short story as a conveyer of fear, so that the novel of the supernatural became a rare exception.

Poe—and to a lesser degree his younger contemporary Fitz-James O'Brien, whose promising career as a supernaturalist ("What Was It?"; "The Diamond Lens") was cut short by his death in the Civil War—did not garner disciples immediately. It took a generation or two for successors to emerge, but when they did so they not merely developed his intense investigation of aberrant psychology but, curiously, adapted the ghost story to the purposes of regionalism. Accordingly two distinct schools, one on the West Coast and the other on the East Coast, emerged as inheritors of Poe's legacy.

The West Coast School

The most distinguished of the West Coast school was Ambrose Bierce (1842–1914?). His taste for the supernatural developed early in his career, if the satirical squib "The Discomfited Demon," a dialogue between a devil and a ghoul included in *The Fiend's Delight* (1873), is any indication. But the bulk of Bierce's tales of psychological and supernatural horror were produced when he became William Randolph Hearst's chief editorial writer for the *San Francisco Examiner* in 1887. During the next six years he generated one of the most impressive bodies of short fiction in all American literature, most of it collected in two landmark volumes, *Tales of Soldiers and Civilians* (dated 1891, but actually issued in February 1892) and *Can Such Things Be?* (1893). The former volume, of course, also contained his gripping tales of the Civil War, many of which can themselves be considered works of psychological horror by the grim, at times bitterly cynical investigation of their characters' emotional traumas as they face the horrors of war. But the latter volume—especially as Bierce revised it for the third volume of his *Collected Works* (1909–12)—is exclusively devoted to stories of the supernatural, ranging from the spectacular supernatural-revenge tale "The Middle Toe of the Right Foot" (*Examiner*, 17 August 1890) to the ambiguous "The Death of Halpin Frayser" (*Wave*, 19 December 1891), perhaps the pinnacle of his supernatural output in its appalling suggestions of mother-son incest and the death of that son by the "lich" (soulless revenant) that his mother has become. A later tale, "The Moonlit Road" (*Cosmopolitan*, January 1907), displays a trilogy of narratives—by Joel Hetman Jr.; his father, Joel Herman Sr. (now going by the name Caspar Grattan); and his mother, the late Julia Hetman, "through the medium Bayrolles." Each of these figures is missing a vital piece of information that could have averted tragedy; instead, the misunderstandings cause Julia's death at the hands of her own hustiand.

It is difficult to deny that Bierce's tales of the Civil War and of psychological horror are considerably superior to his supernatural tales. The latter are almost always ghost stories, such as the lacklustre and unimaginative "Beyond the Wall" (*Cosmopolitan*, December 1907), and in many cases the climax of the tale is merely the confirmation that something supernatural has actually occurred. The satire that is at the very heart of Bierce's work finds its most piquant expression in those non-supernatural tales, whether of soldiers or civilians, that display human beings psychologically crushed by the weight of fear—whether it be the fear of death as embodied by a corpse ("A Tough Tussle," *Examiner*, 30 September 1888; "A Watcher by the Dead," *Examiner*, 29 December 1889), or the fear of being thought a coward in battle ("George Thurston," *Wasp*, 29 September 1883; "Killed at Resaca," *Examiner*, 5 June 1887).

Bierce's achievement, in such tales as "The Middle Toe of the Right Foot" and "The Boarded Window" (*Examiner*, 12 April 1891), was to convey the latent horror to be found in the deserted mining camps and boomtowns of the West, where spectacular wealth, decadence, and lawlessness could be followed by the sudden departure of its generally crude and ill-educated denizens for greener pastures. This was the dark side of the settlement of the West whose more wholesome facets had been presented by Bierce's early colleague Bret Harte. These ghost towns could then serve as potently as the focus of supernaturalism as the hoariest castle of old Europe.

Almost by accident Bierce produced a few pioneering tales that looked forward to future developments of the form. "Moxon's Master" (*Examiner*, 16 April 1899), although possibly derived in some degree from Poe's "Maelzel's Chess-Player" (1836), effectively exhibits a robot gradually developing quasi-human emotions and can be thought of as a work of proto-science fiction. Even more significant is "The Damned Thing" (*Town Topics*, 7 December 1893), although it may owe something to Fitz-James O'Brien's "What Was It?" In this account of an invisible monster, Bierce probes the notion of "colors that we cannot see" (i.e., infrared and ultraviolet rays); as his protagonist proclaims melodramatically at the end: "And, God help me! the Damned Thing is of such a color!" The influence of this tale on such later stories of invisible monsters as Algernon Blackwood's "The Wendigo" and H. P. Lovecraft's "The Colour out of Space" and "The Dunwich Horror" is patent.

Bierce gradually gathered around him a band of like-minded colleagues and disciples who both vaunted his own work and strove to capture something of his psychological insight and sense of place. Perhaps the most distinguished of these is W. C. Morrow (1854–1923), son of slave-owning parents in Selma, Alabama, who came to California in 1879. For the next twenty years he wrote voluminously for the *Argonaut* and other San Francisco papers, publishing dozens of short stories as well as the acclaimed novel *Blood-Money* (1882), a scathing exposé of the ruthlessness of the railroad industry in the state. The piquantly titled *The Ape, the Idiot, and Other People* (1897) contains only fourteen stories, and not necessarily his best ones. The great majority are tales of psychological suspense, but his most famous story, "The Monster-Maker" (*Argonaut*, 15 October 1887), is a gripping account of a crazed surgeon who, when a despairing man wishes to be euthanised, uses the body for an experiment in creating a headless but animate entity. It may perhaps be misleading to refer to Morrow as merely a disciple of Bierce, for the chronology of his tales suggests that he himself may have influenced Bierce or that they mutually influenced each other. Another colleague, Emma Frances Dawson (1851–1926), included some ghost stories in *The Itinerant House and Other Stories* (1897).

The East Coast School

The East Coast school of supernatural writing might itself be said to have split into two branches, one centreing around the New England regionalists and the other coalescing around the imposing figure of Henry James. A quartet of women writers—Mary Eleanor Wilkins Freeman (1852–1930), Sarah Orne Jewett (1849–1909), Charlotte Perkins Gilman (1860–1935), and Olivia Howard Dunbar (1873–1953)— emphatically drew upon the craggy landscape and history of New England as a means of simulating the hoary mediaevalism that in Europe facilitated the introduction of the supernatural. Freeman's volume of ghost stories *The Wind in the Rose-Bush* (1903) does not necessarily represent her at her best; the tales, all written for *Everybody's Magazine* in the year prior to their book publication, focus almost claustrophobically upon the pinched lives of New Englanders trapped by archaic notions of decorum and propriety, leading to cruelty, neglect, and outright savagery that entail inevitable supernatural vengeance. The title story of this collection, for example, features the ghost of a neglected child, while "The Southwest Chamber" features a malevolent old woman whose hatred survives her death.

If Freeman's supernatural tales are set in an increasingly urbanised milieu, Jewett's tales draw poignantly upon the wild and unforgiving landscape of the untenanted Maine woods to evoke fear. Although she produced no single volume of ghost stories, Jewett throughout her career employed the supernatural as a means of adding depth to her portrayal of character and landscape. Her most celebrated work, *The Country of the Pointed Firs* (1896), contains only one incidental supernatural episode, but several short stories tread the borderline between psychological and supernatural horror. Perhaps her most successful tale in this regard is "In Dark New England Days" (*Century Magazine*, October 1890; in *Strangers and Wayfarers*, 1890), in which two sisters, Betsey and Hannah Knowles, after a long, hard life, lose a fortune in silver coins and curse the right hand of the man they suspect of the crime, Enoch Holt; subsequently three members of the Holt family, including Enoch, lose their right hands. Ambiguity is maintained to the end as to the perpetrator of the crime and whether the supernatural has genuinely come into play, but the story is an unforgettable depiction of the cheerless poverty of an ageing New England family. "The Foreigner" (*Atlantic Monthly*, August 1900) is a powerful portrayal of a French-born woman who marries a New England sea captain but is never accepted by the community; on her deathbed she and her one friend see the ghost of her mother, who comes to bear her spirit away.

Charlotte Perkins Gilman wrote relatively little fiction in the midst of a busy career as magazine editor and crusader for women's rights, but she did produce several ghostly tales. "The Giant Wistaria" (*New England Magazine*, June 1891), is a seemingly lighthearted but ultimately grim story of a ghost of a woman who had had a child out of wedlock—and who, it is suggested, was murdered along with her baby by her own shame-stricken family. Gilman's signature piece, however, is "The Yellow Wall Paper" (*New England Magazine*, January 1892), which has become emblematic as a feminist tract; its central scenario is reflected in the title of Sandra Gilbert and Susan Gubar's pioneering study of literary feminism, *The Madwoman in the Attic* (1979). And yet it has not been widely observed that this tale of a woman who, suffering from postpartum depression, is all but imprisoned in the attic of an old house in New England to which her husband has taken her for a "rest cure," is in fact a tale of the supernatural, and not merely one of progressive madness. The tale provides numerous clues that the attic was not a place where, as the protagonist initially believes, children were housed but where a madwoman, or perhaps even a succession of madwomen, has been confined, and that the protagonist is insidiously possessed by the spirit of one of these until at the end she identifies herself with one of the previous occupants. This supernatural interpretation need not in any way contradict the feminist message of the text, where the infantilisation of women and the condescension of male physicians in regard to women's ailments are emphasised; in many ways the reinterpretation of "The Yellow Wall Paper" as an authentic ghost story enhances the feminist message by hinting at generations of psychological abuse of women.

Another feminist, Olivia Howard Dunbar, wrote a handful of ghost stories that similarly underscored her sociopolitical concerns. "The Shell of

Sense" (*Harper's*, December 1908) is a remarkable ghost story narrated in the first person by the ghost of a woman whose husband has married her sister, and whose fluctuating emotions—love, jealousy, resentment, pity—are effectively captured by Dunbar's elegant prose. Perhaps Dunbar's greatest weird tale is "The Long Chamber" (*Harper's*, September 1914), in which a woman who had subordinated her life to that of her husband sees a ghost who inspires her to achieve independence and emotional fulfilment. Dunbar's ghost stories are marked by exquisitely orchestrated prose, delicate character portrayal, and skill at employing the supernatural as a symbol for profound thematic concerns.

From the cramped quarters of the New England regionalists to the social expanse of Henry James's Europe and America would seem a significant shift, but James too could invoke the claustrophobia of ghosts and haunted houses almost in spite of the flaccid orotundity of his prose. Of *The Turn of the Screw* (1898) it is difficult to speak in small compass, and many scholars have accepted Edmund Wilson's thesis that the tale is by design irresolvable: there is an insufficiency of clues as to whether the events depicted—a governess tending to a man's two small children believes herself haunted by the ghosts of Peter Quint, the man's former valet, and Miss Jessel, the governess's predecessor—are supernatural or psychological in origin. The supernatural interpretation appears to dominate at the start, but as the narrative proceeds the reader's increasing suspicions about the reliability of the governess's account throw the matter into doubt—a doubt that is maintained to the end. Some scholars of the genre, most notably Tzvetan Todorov in *The Fantastic* (1970), have found this tale so compelling as to vaunt it as the prototypical fantastic narrative, although this kind of ambiguous weird tale is in fact quite rare: the great majority of horror tales resolve fairly clearly into the supernatural or the psychological mode. James of course wrote an abundance of other weird tales—collected by Leon Edel in *The Ghostly Tales of Henry James* (1949)—but his most innovative venture might have been his final work, the unfinished novel *The Sense of the Past*, depicting a man who falls into the past and fears that he will remain there.

James's fellow expatriate F. Marion Crawford (1854–1909) was considerably less subtle in his horror tales, and it is of some significance that, although immensely prolific and popular, he himself never bothered to collect his scattered tales of the supernatural; they were assembled only posthumously in *Wandering Ghosts* (1911). It certainly cannot be said that Crawford showed any inclination to follow James in the meticulous dissection of the shifting psychological states of his characters; nevertheless, his most celebrated weird tale, the much-reprinted "The Upper Berth" (1886), is a triumph of cumulative horror. This account of a cold, wet, oozy entity that haunts the upper berth of a passenger ship is made the more effective by its narration by a bluff, no-nonsense protagonist named Brisbane. Of "The Dead Smile" (*Ainslee's*, August 1899) it is impossible to speak without a smile: this venture into unrestrained, "oh my god" horror is nonetheless effective in its very excess of lurid prose and its suggestions of incest.

More in line with James's style and methodology was the work of his friend Edith Wharton (1862–1937), the final representative of the conventional ghost story. Wharton collected her earlier supernatural tales in *Tales of Men and Ghosts* (1910) and more definitively in her last volume, *Ghosts* (1937), which includes an illuminating essay on the ghost story. And yet, even her most artfully crafted weird tale, "Afterward" (*Century Magazine*, January 1910), is nothing more than a skilful portrayal of supernatural revenge. Another, more distant colleague, of James's, the Californian Gertrude Atherton (1857–1948), could be said to have effected a union between the East Coast and West Coast schools of ghostly writing. Her principal collection of supernatural tales, *The Bell in the Fog* (1905), is dedicated to James, and its title story (*Smart Set*, August 1903) features a lonely writer, clearly based on James, who believes that a little girl he encounters near his ancestral estate in England is the revenant of a girl whose portrait hangs in his home.

What is surprising is the degree to which, during this period, the most unlikely writers made forays into the weird, either for the space of a single story or perhaps an entire volume. The architect Ralph Adams Cram produced a slim body of ghost stories, *Black Spirits and White* (1895), including the masterful tale of a haunted locale, "The Dead Valley." Julian Hawthorne, although labouring under the shadow of his celebrated father, Nathaniel (himself a highly skilled manipulator of supernatural imagery in novel and tale alike), regularly included at least one token ghost story in nearly every one of his story collections of the last two decades of the nineteenth century, although his greatest contribution was the ten-volume *Lock and Key Library* (1909), a still-valuable anthology of mystery and supernatural tales from world literature. Perhaps most surprisingly of all, William Dean Howells, the reigning dean of American letters, filled two entire volumes, *Questionable Shapes* (1903) and *Between the Dark and the Daylight* (1907), with a series of somewhat attenuated supernatural tales. At the turn of the twentieth century several popular magazines, such as *Collier's*, *Saturday Evening Post*, and *Ainslee's*, opened their pages to the weird, and leading short-story writers of the period did not fail to supply them. Although O. Henry skirted the supernatural in several tales, only one, the much-reprinted "The Furnished Room" (1904), can be considered an authentic ghost story.

Looking Forward

A scattered array of novelists and short-story writers around the turn of the twentieth century produced, almost by accident, a body of work that carried the supernatural tale into new directions, directly influencing the generations that followed them. These writers either abandoned or so radically modified the conventional ghost and haunted house that they became pioneers in spite of themselves. Indeed, by the end of the nineteenth century the standard literary ghost had in some quarters become an object of derision and mockery. The advance of scientific knowledge rendered increasingly unlikely the reality of ghostly manifestations, and such writers as John Kendrick Bangs and Frank R. Stockton had no compunction in poking fun at the form. Bangs's much-reprinted "The Water Ghost of Harrowby Hall" (in *The Water Ghost and Others*, 1894) is prototypical: a female ghost who creates a nuisance by dousing the phlegmatic owner of a decrepit old house with water is finally dispatched by being led out into the bitter cold of a Christmas Eve and being frozen. In Stockton's best-known supernatural tale, "The Transferred Ghost" (*Century Magazine*, May 1882), a ghost is assigned to haunt a house even though the ghost's body is still living.

A highly surprising contributor to the new trend in supernatural writing was Robert W. Chambers (1865–1933)—surprising because, although he wrote some scintillating weird tales early in his career, he later prostituted himself with an unending succession of shopgirl romances that ensured his material comfort but spelled his aesthetic undoing and ultimate oblivion in the Gehenna of outdated bestsellerdom. And yet, *The King in Yellow* (1895), his second volume, drawing a bit affectedly upon his early experiences as an art student in Paris, is nonetheless remarkable in the nightmarish intensity of some of its tales. "The Repairer of Reputations" depicts a New York of the 1920s that has arisen white and austere from the horrors of Victorian architecture and in which euthanasia chambers are available to assist those who wish to slough off the burden of a tiresome existence. "The Yellow Sign" potently describes an artist pursued by a hideous hearse driver who himself seems to be not merely dead but rotting. Later works by Chambers mingle humour and horror in increasingly ineffective ways, the nadir being reached in *Police!!!* (1915), whose interesting conceptions—mammoths in the glaciers of Canada, a group of "cave-ladies" in the Everglades, a school of minnows the size of railroad cars—are spoiled by flippancy and a meretricious love interest.

Chambers's *In Search of the Unknown* (1904), however, introduces the notion of hybridity that a number of other writers also developed. Its opening chapters—originally published as a story, "The Harbor-Master" (*Ainslee's*, August 1899)—terrifyingly depicts a creature that appears to be half-human and

half-fish, with the suggestion that an entire colony of such entities dwells under the sea. The popular Irvin S. Cobb (1876–1944), chiefly known as a hu-
mourist, utilised this same conception in "Fishhead" (*All-Story Cavalier*, 11
January 1913), about a rustic mixed-blood fisherman who has an anomalous
affinity to the enormous catfish that populate the Kentucky lake near which
he dwells. Gouverneur Morris (1876–1953) also enjoyed tremendous popularity as a short-story writer, and in "Back There in the Grass" (*Collier's*, 16
December 1911) he continues the theme of hybridity in presenting a colony
of foot-high half-human, half-snake entities on a Polynesian island. The early
work of Edward Lucas White (1866–1934) can also be cited in this context,
for many of the horror tales in *The Song of the Sirens* (1919) and *Lukundoo*
(1927) were written in the first decade of the twentieth century but not published until their book appearance. "The Snout" (written in 1909) concerns a
band of thieves who come upon a half-man, half-pig in the rich mansion they
seek to rob.

There is considerable evidence to suggest that this theme of hybridity was
a response both to concerns regarding the biological integrity of the human
species in light of Darwinian evolution and to fears of miscegenation in the
wake of the immense influx of immigrants in the period 1890–1920. Another
horror story by Cobb, "The Unbroken Chain" (*Cosmopolitan*, September
1923), is openly racist in its premise. A Frenchman whose ancestry can be
traced back to an African slave experiences an access of "hereditary memory"
when he cries out in an obscure African language as he is run over by a train—
an echo of his ancestor's death by a rhinoceros. Robert W. Chambers's later
novel *The Slayer of Souls* (1920) clumsily mingles supernaturalism with the "yellow peril" topos, depicting a band of Asians, descended from the "devil-
worshipping" Yezidis of central Asia, threatening to overthrow the U.S. government.

Cobb's "Fishhead" was published in one of the numerous magazines of
Frank A. Munsey's publishing empire. Munsey, whose first magazine, the
Golden Argosy, began issuance in 1882, was very accommodating to stories of
fantasy, terror, and proto-science fiction (notably the work of Edgar Rice
Burroughs, whose stories of Tarzan began appearing in 1912), but these forerunners of the pulp magazines tended to cater to the poorly educated by purveying contrived, shoddily written tales generated by a cadre of hack writers
who could write stories of any given genre almost at will. They—along with
such other early magazines as the *Black Cat* (1895–1923) and the *Popular
Magazine* (1903–27), issued by Street & Smith—may have had a role in the
eventual banishing of weird material from the standard "slick" magazines, a

tendency radically augmented by the full-fledged emergence of the pulps in the 1920s.

The horror fiction of this period, diverse as it is, is united by its demonstration that the use of the supernatural, whether it be a ghost, a haunted house, or some less classifiable phenomenon, need not result in mere shudder-coining. The supernatural was shown to enhance the portrayal of character, the probing of aberrant psychology, and the depiction of landscape in all its historic and cultural richness. That some of the leading writers of the period chose this venue to express their literary concerns confirms the viability of the ghost story as art form no less worthy of critical attention than its congeners in mimetic realism.

Arthur Machen and Weird Fiction

Born in Caerleon-on-Usk in southern Wales, Arthur [Llewellyn Jones] (1863–1947) was from youth fascinated with the Roman ruins nearby (Caerleon was the site of the Roman legionary fortress of Isca Silurum). Although failing his examination for the Royal College of Surgeons in 1880, he decided to head to London in any event. Just before leaving Wales, he printed 100 copies of his poem *Eleusinia* (Joseph Jones, 1881; rpt. Necronomicon Press, 1988), but later became ashamed of it and destroyed as many copies as he could obtain; only two copies are known to exist. The poem is, in fact, a creditable performance in highlighting the mystical aspects of the Eleusinian mysteries of ancient Greece; it is the first expression of the attitude (it cannot be dignified by the term philosophy) by which Machen governed his entire life and work.

Machen was forced to work at odd jobs—tutor, cataloguer, editor, translator—chiefly in Grub Street; indeed, over the course of his life he wrote an immense number of essays, articles, and reviews for many British newspapers and magazines, the great majority of which remain uncollected. Among Machen's productions during this difficult time of great poverty—he dwelt in a garret apartment on Clarendon Road, London, and subsisted largely on green tea and tobacco—were a translation of the *Heptameron* of Marguerite de Navarre (Privately printed, 1886) that long remained standard, as well as such eccentric works as *The Anatomy of Tobacco* (Redway, 1884), an owlish parody of scholarship in its analysis of different types of tobacco, and the engaging but insubstantial picaresque novel *The Chronicle of Clemendy* (Privately printed, 1888).

The death of his father in 1887 ensured Machen economic independence for the next fourteen years, and it is during this period that he produced much of the work for which he would be best known—work that also played a significant role in making the Yellow Nineties so distinctive. Aside from translating the entirety of Casanova's *Memoirs* (Privately printed, 1894; 12 vols.), Machen produced *The Great God Pan and The Inmost Light* (John Lane/Roberts Brothers, 1894), *The Three Impostors* (John Lane/Roberts Brothers, 1895), and the stories in *The House of Souls* (Richards, 1906). These volumes represent the core of Machen's weird work.

In "The Great God Pan," Dr. Raymond, a practitioner of "transcendental medicine," performs an experiment on a servant girl, Mary, that involves surgery on her brain so that she "see[s] the Great God Pan." She becomes a hopeless idiot. Raymond's friend, Mr. Clarke, later collects several documents that relate various disturbing episodes. In the first of them, a teenager named Helen V., living in a small town in Wales, drives a little boy, Trevor W., mad when he sees her playing with a "strange naked man" in the woods. Later the boy suffers another fit when he sees the sculptured head of a faun or satyr. Helen later befriends a girl named Rachel M., and it is suggested that she once took her into the woods, where Rachel suffered some nameless trauma.

In the next document, a man in London named Charles Herbert tells his friend Villiers of his disastrous marriage to a woman named Helen Vaughan, who "corrupted my soul." Villiers's friend Austin tells him that three years earlier Charles and Helen had been involved in a scandal in which a man had been found in front of their house, dead of fright. Villiers is a friend of Clarke, and when Villiers shows Clarke a portrait of Helen Vaughan, he initially mistakes it for the servant girl Mary. Later it is discovered that several prominent men—the artist Arthur Meyrink, the prominent socialites Lord Argentine and Lord Swanleigh, among others—have committed suicide; their only apparent connection is their common acquaintance with a mysterious woman named Mrs. Beaumont. Villiers ascertains that Mrs. Beaumont is none other than Helen Vaughan. The manuscript of a Dr. Robert Matheson is then presented: he has witnessed the extraordinary suicide of a woman—clearly Helen Vaughan—after bizarre transformations involving a descent into the depths of the life principle.

The story caused a scandal upon its first appearance, for it was regarded as virtually pornographic in its suggestiveness, although Machen presents the sexual innuendoes so obliquely that they are scarcely recognizable: Mary had been impregnated by Pan and given birth to Helen, Helen had then mated with a satyrlike creature in the woods, and had then lured other men to their dooms by her evil seductiveness. The tale is hampered by an implausible reliance on coincidence and by a mystery framework that becomes mundane once the secret is out. Nevertheless, the story made Machen's reputation and has proved highly influential: two prominent works that rely heavily upon it are H. P. Lovecraft's "The Dunwich Horror" (1929) and Peter Straub's *Ghost Story* (1979).

In *The Three Impostors; or, The Transmutations*, Mr. Dyson and Charles Phillipps marvel at the wonders to be found in the heart of London. One day Dyson runs into a man, Mr. Wilkins, pursuing a "young man with spectacles." By way of explanation, Wilkins tells Dyson the "Novel of the Dark Valley," a wild account of his adventures in a mining camp in the American West as the secretary of an evil man named Smith—the young man he is now pursuing. A woman calling herself Miss Lally then encounters Phillips, saying that she is desperately looking for her brother. Supplying her background, she tells him the "Novel of the Black Seal," a gripping masterpiece of terror about the theories of Professor Gregg, a celebrated ethnologist, regarding the existence of a pre- or sub-human race of devilish creatures dwelling in caves in Wales and perhaps elsewhere, and who seek to overthrow the human race for dominance of the earth. Dyson then meets a man named Mr. Burton, who tells him the "Novel of the Iron Maid" (first published in *St. James's Gazette*, 13 September 1890), about a Mr. Mathias in London who collects torture devices; Mathias inadvertently gets caught in an iron maiden and dies. Dyson then runs into a woman named Miss Leicester, who tells the "Novel of the White Powder," a potent tale of her brother, Francis, who takes a tonic to revive his energies but learns too late that a careless apothecary had allowed the tonic to deteriorate into the *Vinum Sabbati* (the wine of the [witches'] sabbath), with the result that he degenerates into a mass of protoplasmic slime. Dyson then stumbles upon a diary entitled the "History of the Young Man with Spectacles," in which Joseph Walters tells of falling under the influence of a scholar named Dr. Lipsius, who persuades Walters to help him steal a coin of immense value, a gold Tiberius, from a Mr. Headley. It dawns upon Dyson and Phillipps that the various characters they have met are all seeking to hunt down the young man with spectacles; at the conclusion Dyson and Phillipps find that the "three impostors" have done exactly that.

Machen's avowed model for this book were two popular works by Robert Louis Stevenson, *New Arabian Nights* (1882) and *The Dynamiter* (1885). Machen has followed both Stevenson's episodic structure and his rather arch and jaunty style. The implication of the story is that the "novels" (from the French *nouvelle*, tale) told by the "three impostors" are all fabrications designed to trick Dyson and Phillipps into revealing whatever they know about the young man they are pursuing. These "novels" are virtually self-standing stories, and the two best ones, "Novel of the Black Seal" and "Novel of the White Powder," have frequently appeared as separate narratives. Because of its prior magazine publication, "Novel of the Iron Maid" is omitted from some editions, including the Knopf (1923) edition, for which Machen wrote a new preface.

An Anglo-Catholic, Machen came to believe that the advance of science posed a dangerous threat to romance, sentiment, religion, and perhaps all human existence, and he sought to battle it as best he could; but his grasp of science and philosophy was weak at best, and his arguments are easily refuted.

They are embodied most exhaustively in a treatise on aesthetics, *Hieroglyphics: A Note upon Ecstasy in Literature* (Richards, 1902). Here Machen condemns what he takes to be the literature of mundane realism (his chief whipping-boys are Jane Austen and W. M. Thackeray), which he believes lacks the "ecstasy" that raises them above mere transcripts of reality. This treatise cannot properly be taken as a justification of supernatural literature; Machen's chief praise goes to such works of romance as *Don Quixote* or the works of Dickens, to which he remained perennially devoted. But the work can be seen as an indirect justification for the type of story Machen was evolving.

The short novel *A Fragment of Life* (written 1899–1904; first published in *Horlick's Magazine*, February–May 1904; rpt. in *The House of Souls*) may be Machen's most finished tale, although it is only on the borderline of the weird. Here what appears to be a tedious chronicle of the life of a bourgeois married couple, Edward and Mary Darnell, takes a remarkable turn when Edward begins imperceptibly to feel the mystical call of his Welsh heritage, and in the end he and Mary return to a fuller life in Wales. This transformation is handled with exquisite delicacy and subtlety, and there is only the barest hint that some supernatural phenomenon has been at work on Edward's temperament.

Somewhat similar is Machen's greatest novel, *The Hill of Dreams* (Richards, 1907), written in 1895–97. This heart-rending account of Lucian Taylor, a Welshman who comes to London to seek his fortune as a writer, appears transparently autobiographical, but it is so not so much in terms of the surface events as in Lucian's complex emotions as he strives to express the inexpressible. This work too is only marginally weird; only its remarkable fourth chapter—in which Lucian, so spiritually attuned to the Roman ruins at Isca Silurum that he imaginatively transports himself back to Roman times—can be said to hint of the supernatural.

The Hill of Dreams was an excruciating work for Machen to write (as he relates in the preface to the Knopf [1923] edition), because he was striving to shed the imitativeness, in both style and manner, that had dogged some of his earlier work—in particular, the episodic novel *The Three Impostors*, obviously an imitation of Robert Louis Stevenson. This work contains some of the most powerful supernatural tales Machen would ever write, notably "Novel of the Black Seal" and "Novel of the White Powder." The former is a component of a loosely defined group of tales in which Machen wrote of the "Little People"—the fairies and changelings who, according to Welsh legend, dwelt in obscure corners of the countryside. Machen transformed this benign folklore into an horrific topos, notably in "The White People" (*Horlick's Magazine*, January 1904; *The House of Souls*), perhaps his greatest weird tale; "The Red Hand" (*Chapman's Magazine*, December 1895; *The House of Souls*), a masterwork of suggestiveness that hints of the existence of "Little People" in the very midst of London; "The Shining Pyramid" (*Unknown World*, 15 May and 15 June 1895; in *The Shining Pyramid* [Secker, 1925]), a rather tepid rehash of "The Red Hand"; and some later works. In the essay "Folklore and Legends of the North" (*Literature*, 24 September 1898), Machen expressed the belief that modern advances in anthropology justified his conception: "Of recent years abundant proof has been given that a short, non-Aryan race once dwelt beneath ground, in hillocks, throughout Europe, their raths have been explored, and the weird old tales of green hills all lighted up at night have received confirmation. Much in the old legends may be explained by a reference to this primitive race. The stories of changelings, and captive women, become clear on the supposition that the 'fairies' occasionally raided the houses of the invaders."

In 1897 Machen wrote a series of prose poems later collected in *Ornaments in Jade* (Knopf, 1924), but none were published at the time. These delicate works defy description or summarization, but they represent some of the most ethereal examples of Machen's work. Such a tale as "The Idealist," in which a man leads the prosy life of a clerk by day but escapes into his own world of the imagination by night, perhaps express Machen's religio-mystical temperament more satisfactorily than many of his more ambitious works.

By 1901 Machen's inheritance had run out, and he was forced to seek employment. He worked for most of the decade as a bit player in Frank Benson's Repertory Company and also wrote voluminously for such papers as the *Academy* (1907–12), the *London Evening News* (1910–21), *T.P.'s Weekly* (1908–28), the *Lyons Mail* (1919–23), and the *Observer* (1926–37). Little of this work is of enduring value, and Machen made efforts to collect only some of it, in such volumes as *Dog and Duck* (Cape, 1924), *Dreads and Drolls* (Secker, 1926), and *Notes and Queries* (Spurr & Swift, 1926). In 1907 he wrote the novel *The Secret Glory* (Secker, 1922), partly a satire on the British school system and partly another expression of mysticism. Machen inexplicably did not allow the last two chapters he had initially written to be published, even though the novel makes little sense without them. They were finally issued as *The Secret Glory: Chapters Five and Six* (Tartarus Press, 1991). In some senses similar to *A Fragment of Life* in recording Ambrose Meyrick's glorious return to his Welsh homeland, this novel has virtually no weird elements.

World War I brought a different, and perhaps unwelcome, kind of fame to Machen. Early in the war he wrote a story called "The Bowmen" (*London Evening News*, 29 September 1914), telling of how hard-pressed British troops at an unnamed battle were miraculously saved by the ghosts of British archers from the Hundred Years' War; perhaps because it appeared in a newspaper, the story was taken for a real occurrence and quickly led to the legend of the "Angels of Mons," where angels came to the rescue of British and French troops at Mons. Eyewitnesses testified to seeing the ghosts or angels, and Machen's repeated assertions that he had made the whole story up went for naught. A publisher capitalized on Machen's notoriety by issuing *The Angels of Mons: The Bowmen and Other Legends of the War* (Simpkin, Marshall, Hamilton, Kent, 1915). A more substantial work written during the war was the short novel *The Terror* (serialized in the *Evening News*, 16–31 October 1916; Duckworth, 1917), a chilling account of animals revolving from human control. Machen blunderingly tried to justify the horrors of war with his religious beliefs in *War and the Christian Faith* (Skeffington, 1918).

By the 1920s Machen had attained considerable fame both in England and the United States (largely from the reprints of his early work by Knopf, beginning in 1922), but his own creative fires were waning. Although he produced three superlative autobiographies, *Far Off Things* (Secker, 1922), *Things Near and Far* (Secker, 1923), and *The London Adventure* (Secker, 1924), and a long-winded account of the mysterious disappearance of an 18th-century woman, *The Canning Wonder* (Chatto & Windus, 1925), Machen did little fictional work. By the end of the decade he had again lapsed into severe poverty, but efforts by friends and colleagues (including T. S. Eliot) secured a Civil List pension for him in 1931, allowing him modest financial security for the rest of his life. Two years earlier Machen had left the London that had fascinated him for half a century and returned to Wales.

In his later years he wrote only the slim weird novel *The Green Round* (Ernest Benn, 1933; Arkham House, 1968), an insubstantial narrative of a man who goes to a quiet resort in Wales but is plagued by a strange, stunted being whom he can see but others cannot, and the collections *The Cosy Room* (Rich & Cowan, 1936) and *The Children of the Pool* (Hutchinson, 1936). The former gathers his later stories; the latter contains previously unpublished work. Perhaps the only notable tale is "The Bright Boy," an account of a perverted old man who retains the appearance of a young boy. An uncollected story, "The Dover Road" (in *Missing from Their Homes* [Hutchinson, 1936]), about a mysterious disappearance, has some fine moments of mystery and suspense.

Machen's horror fiction, although highly uneven, has been immensely influential. Championed in the United States by, among others, Alfred A. Knopf, Carl Van Vechten, and Vincent Starrett—who assembled two volumes of miscellany, *The Shining Pyramid* (Covici-McGee, 1923) and *The Glorious Mystery* (Covici-McGee, 1924)—Machen exercised a significant influence on H. P. Lovecraft and his associates, as well as upon such later writers as Peter Straub,

T. E. D. Klein, and Tim Lebbon. In many ways his own life—or, rather, the telling of it—was his greatest creation, and he stands as the prototypical example of the impoverished, unrecognized author working in obscurity to produce eccentric and esoteric works for the delectation of the few.

The Weird Work of Robert Hichens

The neglect that has engulfed the weird work of Robert Hichens (1864–1950) is as inexplicable as it is undeserved. Had Dorothy L. Sayers not reprinted "How Love Came to Professor Guildea" in her first *Omnibus of Crime* (1928) and thereby ensured its status as a much-reprinted classic, it is likely that Hichens would now be virtually forgotten as a weird writer, just as his prolific and best-selling mainstream work has all but fallen into oblivion. And yet, Hichens is far more than merely a "one-story" writer: if "Professor Guildea" does indeed remain his finest weird tale, there are numerous others that deserve to be ranked just below it. His collection, *Tongues of Conscience* (1900), can stand next to any single volume by Algernon Blackwood, Lord Dunsany, Arthur Machen, or H. P. Lovecraft as a compendium of powerful, finely crafted horror fiction.

Much of what we know about the life of Robert Smythe Hichens comes from his autobiography, *Yesterday* (1947). From this book we learn that Hichens was born on November 14, 1864, at Speldhurst, Kent, the son of a clergyman. His grandfather had founded a stockbroking firm, Hichens & Harrison, and upon his death he left his son, Hichens's father, a fortune. Hichens attended a private school, Hurstleigh, just outside Tunbridge Wells, and also took riding and music lessons. When he was fifteen, his father abandoned his parish and moved to the city of Clifton in Gloucestershire. The move was disturbing to young Robert in several ways, chiefly in the sudden absence of the dogs and horses to whom he had become devoted at Speldhurst. Hichens admits that he was "exceedingly fond of dogs,"[1] and from this bare mention we can gain an inkling of the uncanny understanding of animal mentality that Hichens reveals in some of his best weird fiction.

Entering Clifton College, Hichens sought to pursue a career in music and become an organist. He was later removed from Clifton College and instructed by George Riseley, organist at Bristol Cathedral. At this time Hichens wrote a full-length adventure novel, *The Coastguard's Secret*, published in 1886.

---

1. Robert Hichens, *Yesterday: The Autobiography of Robert Hichens* (London: Cassell, 1947). Further citations will occur parenthetically in the text.

But literature was not his major interest; still determined to become a musician, he entered the Royal College of Music in London. Although he wrote lyrics to numerous popular songs of the day, Hichens ultimately came to realise that he did not quite have the talent to become a professional musician. Accordingly, his father sent him to the London School of journalism—which, at that time, was really nothing more than an informal gathering of several young men under the tutelage of a professional journalist, David Anderson. Hichens wrote not merely journalism but also short stories for the school's paper, *Mistress and Maid,* and shortly thereafter he sold several tales to the *Pall Mall Magazine.* That magazine's editor, Frederic Hamilton, devised the idea for one of Hichens's earliest weird tales, "A Tribute of Souls." The story was published with a joint byline in 1897.

In 1893, Hichens had nearly died of peritonitis. His doctor urged him to take a sea voyage, and Hichens decided to go to Egypt. In the course of this voyage Hichens met E. F. Benson and Lord Alfred Douglas; the latter introduced him to Oscar Wilde. The result of this acquaintance was the anonymously published novel, *The Green Carnation* (1894), an enormous bestseller that catapulted Hichens to fame once his authorship was revealed. *The Green Carnation* is a tart sendup of the decadent aestheticism of Wilde and Douglas, both of whom appear in thinly disguised roles. From this time forward, Hichens found a ready market for his fiction, whether it was weird, adventure, romantic, or mainstream.

But Hichens himself, if he could not become a musician, was at least determined to be a music critic. He was offered such a position for a London newspaper, the *World,* taking over the responsibilities from George Bernard Shaw. Some years later, however, he refused an offer to join the staff of the *Daily Telegraph* (at a salary of £2000) in order to concentrate on fiction writing. His wide travels continued—to Morocco (where he wrote the powerful weird tale "The Charmer of Snakes"), Algeria (where his stay with Trappist monks no doubt inspired the haunting "The Face of the Monk"), Rome, Sicily, and elsewhere. Early in his autobiography he looks down "the vista of years, during which I have occupied several delightful country, houses in England and Switzerland, some nice London flats, two villas on Lago di Como, Sicily, a bungalow by the Nile, a house on the desert edge near Heliopolis, tents in the Sahara Desert, in the wilds of Morocco, among the mountains and valleys of Palestine, etc., etc." (29). These wide travels lend an unmistakable sense of topographical realism to his tales.

By the first decade of the twentieth century, Hichens was a best-selling author and in comfortable circumstances. He speaks casually of his acquaintance with the celebrated authors of his day—F. Marion Crawford, Edith

Wharton, Frank Harris, Thomas Hardy, Somerset Maugham, Joseph Conrad, Edgar Wallace—as well as of the composer Edward Elgar. He and H. D. Traill wrote a play, *The Medicine Man*, for Henry Irving and Ellen Terry, but it was a failure. *The Garden of Allah* (1904), set in Algeria, was probably his greatest commercial triumph.

Hichens never married. Several of his tales betray a fascination with "the eternal feminine," and he acknowledges his bafflement at the actions and motives of women when he remarks (of his own mother): "Who knows what goes on secretly in the mind of a woman?" (20). Around the age of twenty, Hichens had fallen passionately in love with a woman violinist at Clifton College; but her parents did not approve the marriage, and Hichens appears never to have had another serious romance for the rest of his long life.

When World War I broke out, Hichens was residing at his seaside cottage in Tankerton, but shortly thereafter he moved to London, serving for three years in the Special Constabulary. His life as a popular author was abruptly interrupted in the early 1930s when he lost a fortune in financial speculation. As a result, he wrote the crime novel, *The Paradine Case* (1933), one of his most successful books. Although he notes selling the film rights to MGM and expressing interest in the fact that his favourite film star, Greta Garbo, was to be featured in the film, he nowhere mentions in his autobiography the fact that Alfred Hitchcock was to be its director.

Hichens spent most of World War 11 in Switzerland. Although almost seventy-five, he attempted to volunteer for war work of some kind, but was not summoned for duty. He died in Zurich on July 20, 1950.

The oblivion that has overtaken all of Hichens's weird work except "How Love Came to Professor Guildea" is in some sense understandable, for not only are the best of his tales long—some would say overly long—novelettes difficult to accommodate in anthologies, but many of them return obsessively to a single idea: the transference or survival of the soul after the death of the body. It is difficult to know how seriously Hichens took this idea: did he believe in it himself, or was he merely using it as a literary device? The number of tales in which this idea recurs, even with significant variations, points to actual belief, as does the following passage from *Yesterday*, where Hichens reports his early interest in spiritualism:

At that time I was interested in "spiritualism," as it was called . . . and I attended several séances, and knew various people who claimed to have occult powers. I have never been convinced that the souls of those we call dead are able to communicate with the living, and have expressed my lack of conviction in at least one book and been taken to task for it. But on the

other hand, some have called me credulous. For I believe that certain people, specially endowed, are able at times to foretell the future correctly, and
to foresee what is coming to those whom they call their "clients," or for
friends who consult them. And I have no doubt at all that apparitions of the
dead have been many times seen haunting the places in which they have
formerly lived and loved and perhaps—though not always—suffered. I have
myself lived for a time in a house which was haunted by its former owner, a
famous Englishman. I never saw the apparition of him, but an intimate
friend of mine did on at least four occasions. And it was, I believe, seen in
daylight by a famous actress when she was staying with me. (77)

The concluding part of this passage appears to suggest the inspiration for
Hichens's first weird tale, "The Return of the Soul," published in the *Pall
Mail Magazine* in 1895 (as "A Reincarnation") and reprinted in *The Folly of
Eustace* (1896). The soul-transference theme is also evident in this tale as well
as Hichens's two weird novels, *Flames: A London Phantasy* (1897) and the
powerful *The Dweller on the Threshold* (1911). Hichens was never content to
write merely a spook story: he never wished merely to send a shudder up a
reader's spine. The title of his collection *Tongues of Conscience*—containing
"Sea Change," "The Cry of the Child," "How Love Came to Professor
Guildea," and "The Lady and the Beggar"—is apt, for it suggests that it is the
protagonists' guilt or unease over some past action that brings down the
supernatural manifestation upon them. A painter unwittingly lures a young
boy to perish at sea; a scholar causes the death of his own child by excessive
and single-minded study; a hard-hearted professor is plagued by a ghost that
loves him; a woman is haunted by a beggar whose pleas for charity she cruelly
ignored: these are the scenarios in which Hichens finds a wealth of human
torment and misery, and it is the slow, meticulous accumulation of details—
both supernatural and emotional—that allows each character in these tales to
gain the fully rounded humanity that brings them to life. And it is this same
attention to detail—as, for example, in "Professor Guildea," when the ghost is
first suspected by the bizarre actions of a parrot—that creates the uncanny
realism of the supernatural events Hichens etches so subtly and delicately.
Hichens requires the expansiveness of the novelette to convey the richness of
his weird scenarios, and some of them attain a cumulative power that creates
that rarest fusion in literary art—the fusion of horror and pathos.

The Dweller on the Threshold, Hichens's most sustained contribution to
weird fiction, is a remarkable short novel. Serialised in the *Century Magazine*
(November 1910–April 1911) and published as a book by The Century Co.
in March 1911, it is the most exhaustive treatment of a theme that appears to
have obsessed its author: psychic possession, or the transference of personality

from one body to another. Much of the weird work of Robert Hichens re-volves around this theme, but he treats it in such variegated ways that he can-not be accused of repetition. One of his earliest weird tales, "The Return of the Soul" (1895), focuses on this motif, as do, in their various ways, such tales as "The Charmer of Snakes" (1897) and "The Black Spaniel" (1905), both of which deal with the transference of a human soul into the body of an animal. Hichens's other weird novel, *Flames: A London Phantasy* (1897), also utilises this theme, but is marred by prolixity. That cannot be said for the compact and intense *Dweller on the Threshold*, which can well be seen as the capstone of Hichens's weird work, fully equal to the celebrated novella "How Love Came to Professor Guildea" (1900).

The secret of the success of this novel is its portrayal of character. We are here introduced to two clergymen, the Rev. Marcus Harding, the rector of a fashionable London parish, and his senior curate, the Rev. Henry Chichester. The latter was once "marred . . . by a definite weakness of character" but has now become anomalously "aggressive"; Harding, on the other hand, had once been a domineering figure but now fails to project "self-confidence." It is clear that some kind of personality exchange has occurred, as Evelyn Malling, a psychic investigator, detects at once. But how could this have occurred? Malling eventually learns that Harding had compelled Chichester to engage in occult "sittings," for the ostensible purpose of enhancing his subordinate's strength of will, but in reality for the sake of penetrating the veil beyond death and "to communicate with the spirit world." But the effect of these re-peated sittings was, in fact, to cause Harding's strength of will to be trans-ferred into the soul of Chichester.

The gradualness with which this whole scenario is conveyed to the reader is a masterstroke of subtlety and careful psychological delineation. At its cen-tre is a long and peculiar sermon delivered by Chichester, whose upshot clear-ly suggests that he wishes to take Harding's place, both in his religious office and in his very life. The sermon, focusing upon an apparent *doppelgänger* who looks through the window of a house and sees himself sitting by the fire, clearly shows that Chichester himself is the Dweller on the Threshold—although, curiously, that term is never used in the text of the novel.

A central role in this scenario is played by Harding's wife, Lady Sylvia Harding. While her highly unfeminist portrayal may be politically incorrect—she is depicted as a "woman who, intensely, almost exaggeratedly feminine, can live in any fullness only through another, and that other a man"—the characterisation is probably not inaccurate for a certain segment of society at this time, given how few opportunities women had for an independent exist-ence. Accordingly, Lady Sylvia, who initially is fervently desirous of securing advancement for her husband, gradually transfers her allegiance to Chichester, whom she sees as the stronger man and therefore more worthy of her devotion.

Robert Hichens has waited a century or more for his weird work to be resurrected. If that work comprises only a small proportion of his prodigally bountiful output, it may nonetheless grant him a more enduring celebrity than the bestsellers that entranced a prior generation. The best weird fiction is often written by those who do not specialise in it; the insight into character and situation that such writers derive from their more orthodox work lends their weird creations a depth and poignancy not often seen in work of this kind. That Hichens finds weirdness as much in the baffling intricacies of human personality as in the manifestations of ghosts and revenants is a testimonial to his perception of the irremediable strangeness of human life.

Clark Ashton Smith's Juvenilia

The Black Diamonds is a full-length novel of almost 90,000 words written by Clark Ashton Smith (1893–1961) around 1907, when he was fourteen. It is remarkable that so youthful a writer could have produced such an extended narrative, with numerous clever plot-twists culminating in a satisfying resolution; but it is only the most substantial of a number of surviving texts of its kind.

Smith attested that around 1905 he began producing a number of tales of Oriental adventure, based largely upon the *Arabian Nights.* Among the works found in his papers (now in the John Hay Library of Brown University) are stories—some of them fragmentary—with such titles as "The Brahmin's Wisdom," "The Curse of Runjat Singh," "The Emir's Captive," and several others, many of them written in a distinctive purple ink. Smith notes that he discovered William Beckford's *Vathek* in 1908, but *The Black Diamonds* does not appear to bear any influence from that work, hence its provisional dating to 1907.

The Black Diamonds is, to be sure, not a literary masterwork in its own right, but it is a rousingly entertaining narrative that keeps the reader's interest from beginning to end. Unlike Smith's later work, it is almost entirely non-supernatural; the only suggestion of supernaturalism occurs in the episode in which the Fire-Worshippers' "Lake of Fire" appears to exhibit miraculous curative properties. Even here, though, the leader of the Fire-Worshippers maintains that these properties "are within the realm of nature," although he fails to elaborate upon the claim. But *The Black Diamonds* does not require the supernatural to maintain interest: its bewilderingly convoluted plot is sufficient for the purpose.

Readers familiar with Smith's work will be curious to know how *The Black Diamonds* relates to the four early tales that he published in 1910–12: "The Malay Krise" (*Overland Monthly,* October 1910), "The Ghost of Mohammed Din" (*Overland Monthly,* November 1910), "The Mahout" (*Black Cat,* August 1911), and "The Raja and the Tiger" (*Black Cat,* February 1912). There does not appear to be much of a connexion, as these latter tales are manifestly written under the influence of Rudyard Kipling's Indian stories. (Smith had in fact conceived a volume entitled *Tales of India,* and stories from this uncompleted collection constituted early versions of three of the tales he published at this time.) The Kipling influence is entirely absent from *The Black Diamonds.*

Lovers of weird fiction may perhaps regret that Smith virtually gave up fiction-writing from about 1911 to 1929; but in this period, of course, he produced—largely under the guidance of George Sterling—some of the most remarkable poetry in all American literature, and much of this poetic work readily falls within the realm of the weird. While *The Black Diamonds* and the other tales of this period reveal surprising precocity and promise in prose narration, no one should regret Smith's decision to master the craft of poetry—and master it he did.

It is not untoward to ask the indulgence of readers and critics in evaluating *The Black Diamonds*. As the product of a fertile young imagination; as an experiment in extended narrative; as the single longest work of fiction Clark Ashton Smith would ever write—in all these ways and more it should earn our admiration; its implausible incidents, its stilted dialogue, and its wooden character portrayals can be easily forgiven. Not the least engaging of its features is its charming naïveté, and there are many scenes or turns of phrase that suggest the slow emergence of a boy into young manhood. The highest tribute that a reader can pay to *The Black Diamonds* is to regard it as its author himself very likely wished it to be regarded—as just an entertaining story.

The Sword of Zagan, at slightly over 39,000 words, is considerably shorter than *The Black Diamonds*, although it appears (from the greater maturity of its prose) to have been written sometime after the latter. And, it must be admitted, it is in many ways inferior to *The Black Diamonds*, a novel of extraordinarily convoluted plot, lively characters, and a delectable hint of the supernatural. By contrast, *The Sword of Zagan* is plainly an adventure story, resembling not so much the *Arabian Nights* as, perhaps, some of Kipling's tales set in India or the Middle East. An unusual amount of bloodletting occurs in the novel: the body-count is as high as in any of today's action films, and characters major and minor seem to die—or appear to die—with startling rapidity. And yet, one can sense a far greater technical assurance in the managing of prose, a paring down of incidents to those that have a direct bearing on the climax (aside from the awkwardly inserted "tales" in Chapter XVI), and a love-element that was apparently foreign to Smith's temperament while he was writing *The Black Diamonds*.

Several of the shorter tales also reveal noteworthy features—features that we can recognise from Smith's later prose work. "The Emir's Captive" is distinctive in that it manifestly takes the side of the Saracens in their battles against the British during the Crusades: let us recall that Smith could trace his ancestry directly back to English forbears through his British father. "The Haunted Gong," set in San Francisco's Chinatown, foreshadows many of Smith's later stories. As in such works as "The City of the Singing Flame" and "The Treader of the Dust," this real-world setting serves only as the springboard for imaginative voyages into far more exotic realms. "The Bronze Image" and "The Fulfilled Prophecy," set in India, again evoke Kipling—not merely the Kipling who wrote poignantly of both the British and the Indians in such works as *Kim,* but who probed the hidden realms of wonder and mystery lurking in the immense subcontinent in such tales as "At the End of the Passage" or "The Mark of the Beast." "The Haunted Chamber," though set in England, features an Indian character as a servant. It is also notable for being one of Smith's few tales utilising what might be called the pseudo-supernatural, in which the supernatural (in this case, a ghost) is suggested, only to have the phenomenon explained away naturalistically at the end.

The numerous fragments in this collection give a hint of the prodigious fertility of a young imagination so bursting with ideas that they could not all be captured in finished prose. It is particularly regrettable that Smith did not—or perhaps could not—finish such substantial fragments as "The Opal of Delhi" (first version) and "The Guardian of the Temple," for they would certainly have taken their place among the more meritorious of his early tales. And yet, it is very likely that these unfinished efforts were of significant formative value in teaching Smith the craft of fiction writing. As H. P. Lovecraft once said, the only practice for writing is writing; and it is only by trial and error that one can gain a concrete idea of what conceptions can be captured in prose or verse and what conceptions must, for lack of coherence or proper denouement, forever remain elusive.

Smith early on learned that some of his *Arabian Nights* conceptions could indeed best be encapsulated in verse. Kipling's verse may again have been a partial influence, but Edward FitzGerald's translation of the *Rubaiyat* is perhaps considerably more significant—and not only in regard to the a-a-b-a rhyme-scheme Smith adopted in some of his early poems. Interestingly, a fair proportion of this work is in a rather naively moralistic vein. Smith would quickly learn that the elementary morality found in "The River of Life" and "The Departed City" would not do in mature work: it is not that morality has no place in verse (or prose), but that it must be expressed with subtlety and indirection, and by means of image, metaphor, and symbol rather than by plain statement. Especially under the guidance of his mentor, George Sterling, Smith evolved the notion of "pure poetry" and exemplified it from his very first volume, *The Star-Treader and Other Poems* (1912), to his last.

Miscellaneous as Smith's juvenile tales and poems are, the mere fact that

Smith chose to bestow some of them upon a friend (Dr. W. C. Farmer) rather than merely destroy them suggests that he saw some value in them, even if that value was largely formative. As a means of providing a window into the early mind, heart, and imagination of Clark Ashton Smith, these works are of inestimable value; and not a few of them can claim an intrinsic value as well. How Smith's fantastic imagination metamorphosed from the exoticism of the East to the even more remote exoticism of interstellar space is something that scholars of his work must chart; for us it is sufficient to read and appreciate these delectable works in the spirit in which they were intended—as the initial offerings of a creative mind that would soon take the entire cosmos as its haven.

Algernon Blackwood and John Silence

John Silence–Physician Extraordinary (1908) is a landmark work—as much in the realm of weird fiction as in the career of its author, Algernon Blackwood (1869–1951). It was one of Blackwood's first successes—both artistic and commercial—and made much of the rest of his literary work possible. And that body of work may well establish him as the greatest weird writer in all literature.

It is unlikely that Algernon Henry Blackwood ever thought of becoming a literary man, for until he was close to forty he pursued almost every other career except that of writer. Born in Kent, England, and the son of a distinguished father—Sir Stevenson Arthur Blackwood, who ultimately became Secretary of the Post Office—Blackwood spent his youth absorbing the rigid Evangelical teachings of his parents, although secretly rebelling by surreptitiously reading the *Bhagavad Gita* and theosophy. Throughout his life Blackwood remained a religious mystic, but one who vigorously opposed the dogmas of conventional religion.

Much of Blackwood's adolescence and early manhood was spent in travel—and the whole of his literary work reveals the expansion of mental horizons he gained from his visits to four continents. After spending time at a series of private schools in England, he was sent for a year-long stay (1885–86) at the School of the Moravian Brotherhood in Konigsfeld, Germany. He spent the summer of 1887 in Switzerland, after which his father sent him to Canada for business. In 1888 Blackwood enrolled in Edinburgh University in Scotland but withdrew the next year.

Returning to Canada in 1890, Blackwood attempted to start a dairy farm, but it failed and he lost much of his investment. After an idyllic summer in the Canadian backwoods in 1892 (later the setting for some of his most powerful tales of supernatural horror, including "The Wendigo"), Blackwood came to New York, where he became a reporter for the *Evening Sun*. The brutal contrast between the pristine forests of Canada and the phantasmagoric civilisation of New York was, I believe, a crucial turning point for Blackwood. Consider his description of the metropolis in his piquant autobiography, *Episodes Before Thirty* (1923):

> The awful city, with its torrential, headlong life, held for me something of the monstrous. Everything about it was exaggerated. Its racing speed, its roofs amid the clouds with the canyon gulfs below, its gaudy avenues dripping gold that ran almost arm in arm with streets little better than sewers of human decay and misery, its frantic noise, both of voices and mechanism, its lavishly organized charity and boastful splendour, and its deep corruption in the grip of heartless and degraded Tammany—it was all this that painted the horror into my imagination as of something monstrous, non-human, almost unearthly.

It is scarcely to be wondered that Blackwood developed a kind of mystic pantheism that saw all good to be housed in the untenanted wilderness and all evil in the teeming labyrinths of modern urban life.

Blackwood returned to England in 1899, remaining involved in a variety of business ventures but still giving apparently little thought to writing. He had, indeed, written various articles on his early travels as well as a few stories (the first was "A Mysterious House" [1889]); but now he not only continued his travels—to France, to his old school in Germany, and to the Danube (the setting for his later masterpiece, "The Willows")—but also turned increasingly to literature. His essays and stories began appearing with some regularity in the magazines of the day; but it was only a chance meeting with a friend, Angus Hamilton, that led to Blackwood's submission of his first volume, *The Empty House and Other Ghost Stories*, to the publisher Eveleigh Nash. The book was published in 1906, and—although the significant collection *The Listener and Other Stories*, containing "The Willows," "The Old Man of Visions," "The Woman's Ghost Story," and other fine tales, appeared in 1907— it was only *John Silence* that made Blackwood a bestseller.

To trace the history of the "psychic detective" in literature would be a fascinating exercise. Here we can perhaps pinpoint two significant forerunners: Dr. Martin Hesselius, the German doctor who appears (though oftentimes fleetingly and tangentially) in the tales that make up Joseph Sheridan LeFanu's landmark volume, *In a Glass Darkly* (1872), most notably "Green Tea" and "Carmilla"; and, of course, Professor Van Helsing, the antagonist of Count Dracula in Bram Stoker's *Dracula* (1897). It is, indeed, significant that both Hesselius and Van Helsing make pretensions to medical knowledge; for Blackwood never uses the term "psychic detective" about John Silence, referring to him only as a "psychic doctor."

Of course, the influence of Sherlock Holmes (recall that by 1908 three collections of tales and three short novels by Sir Arthur Conan Doyle about the cerebral detective had appeared) is also evident in the figure of John Silence. In "A Psychical Invasion" he sits in his consulting room and listens to a woman telling the story of a haunted house; later he engages in pseudo-Holmesian ratiocinative detection, perceiving at a glance that a character has been taking drugs. In "The Nemesis of Fire" there is, as throughout the Holmesian saga, a tantalising reference to an unwritten John Silence case.

It might seem as if this element of scientific rationality would be fatal to the atmosphere of cosmic wonder that Blackwood is clearly attempting to create in these tales; and, indeed, this tension persists throughout the volume and also figures in the differing roles John Silence plays from one story to the next. The most orthodox instance is "A Psychical Invasion," where Silence is summoned to a house apparently haunted by some of its former tenants; he promptly "solves" the case. In "Ancient Sorceries" Silence acts merely as an interlocutor, listening to the account of a man's strange experiences in a small town in France and adding only a few concluding comments in a somewhat pedantic know-it-all detective fashion. "The Nemesis of Fire" introduces John Silence's assistant, a man named Hubbard, who acts as a Dr. Watson-like narrator while Silence energetically probes and solves another haunting. Hubbard returns as the narrator of "The Camp of the Dog." In "Secret Worship" Silence acts as a literal *deus ex Machina*, rescuing the hapless narrator at the last minute from spiritual and perhaps physical death. "A Victim of Higher Space"—a story not published in the 1908 volume, although written at about the same time (it was first collected in *Day and Night Stories*, 1917)—finds Silence back in his consulting room, although with a new assistant, Barker.

It might be startling at first to hear John Silence say, in "The Nemesis of Fire," that "I have yet to come across a problem that is not natural, and has not a natural explanation"; but what he means is that the seemingly supernatural can really be encompassed within the realm of a kind of higher rationality that takes both spiritual and physical phenomena into account. In a sense Blackwood is perhaps trying to have his cake and eat it, too—trying to retain the mystery of an awesome universe while at the same time remaining within the domain of human reason—and if the attempt is not always successful, then it has still resulted in the creation of some of the most powerful vignettes in weird fiction.

H. P. Lovecraft, who thought some of the tales immeasurably powerful, nevertheless criticised Blackwood for "credulousness regarding 'occultism' which causes him to employ now and then a professional mediumistic jargon of woefully weakening effect." It is true that when a "knowledge of occultism" is attributed to him, John Silence expostulates in mock horror, "Oh, please—that dreadful word!" But this may be a case of protesting too much. Silence clearly claims to be a clairvoyant, and in "The Nemesis of Fire" he and other characters hold a kind of séance as a way of bringing forth the supernatural entity.

Blackwood himself did indeed reveal a certain "credulousness" in the oc-cult. His early studies in Buddhism and Hinduism endowed him with a fixed belief in reincarnation. In his brief school days at Edinburgh he participated in a number of séances. Then in 1900 he joined the Hermetic Order of the Golden Dawn. His dissatisfaction with this occultist organisation led him into a splinter group, the Holy Order of the Golden Dawn, headed by A. E. Waite, and he remained a member until 1914. Indeed, the Blackwood schol-ar Mike Ashley believes that the character of John Silence himself is based upon a member of this group, although his identity is as yet uncertain. Blackwood himself acknowledges in his enigmatic dedication to "M. L. W." that John Silence is indeed derived from some real person.

There are other autobiographical connexions in the John Silence tales. The most obvious instance is "Secret Worship," whose opening pages trans-parently and movingly convey Blackwood's respect for the simple piety of the Moravian Brothers and irritation at their stern discipline. An early article, "About the Moravians" (*Methodist Magazine*, February 1891), anticipates many features of the story:

> To the visitor anxious to see a Moravian settlement to its best advantage, no place offers greater attractions than Königsfeld. Remote from the world, it is a perfect model for its earnest, active life and at the same time its perfect peacefulness. Here the round of life goes on undisturbed from year to year. . . . A long day of hard study is commenced at six o'clock with a reading out of the Bible, the same portion being read in all Moravian settlements all the world over at the same time. . . . Nothing was more conspicuous in this school . . . than the beautiful spirit of gentleness and merciful justice, tem-pered by true brotherly sympathy, with which the boys of as many temper-aments as nationalities were taught to live.

The extensive references to Egypt in "The Nemesis of Fire" are intriguing: although Blackwood did not visit Egypt in person until 1911, his fascination is already evident; and many of his later works (notably "Sand" in *Pan's Garden* and "A Descent into Egypt" in *Incredible Adventures*) are the direct results of his absorption of the mysteries of this ancient land. "The Camp of the Dog," although set in Scandinavia, clearly echoes Blackwood's camping trips in Canada.

The overriding dangers of a serial character are, of course, monotony and repetitiousness. Blackwood manages to avoid these pitfalls by ingenious varia-tions in narration. As already mentioned, Blackwood's assistant, Hubbard, narrates two stories in the first person ("The Nemesis of Fire" and "The Camp of the Dog"), playing a far more active role in the actual events of the tales than Dr. Watson ordinarily would. Three other stories—"A Psychical Invasion," "Secret Worship," and "A Victim of Higher Space"—are told in a fairly orthodox first person; indeed, the fact that "A Psychical Invasion"—presumably the first of the John Silence stories—does not feature Hubbard suggests that John Silence was not initially conceived as having an assistant and that Hubbard was added later precisely for the purpose of imparting diversity to the narratives. From this perspective the most effective story is "Ancient Sorceries," featuring an interesting mixture of pseudo-first-person narration (the monologues of Arthur Vezin) and third-person narration.

But none of these narrative devices would be effective if the tales themselves did not have the power and substance of theme to bear them. In the best of the John Silence stories, Blackwood has discovered a secret that many other weird writers have come upon but that few others have tapped as cannily: the aptness of the novelette form for conveying supernatural horror. This form allows for all the dramatic intensity that Poe sought in his quest for "unity of effect" while at the same time developing the textural richness of a novel in its expansive scope. Blackwood's tales are the more remarkable because not much "happens" in them; instead, it is the slow accumulation of telling details that fosters an insidious atmosphere of almost unendurable tension and foreboding. Blackwood was a master of narrative pacing, and all his best tales build to an apocalyptic climax that fully justifies their length.

John Silence–Physician Extraordinary was an immediate success, partially because of an aggressive advertising campaign on the part of Blackwood's publishers. As Mike Ashley notes in his definitive *Algernon Blackwood: A Bio-Bibliography* (1987): "A distinctive poster depicting a bearded John Silence gazing out of an open balcony window at the night sky bore the slogan 'JOHN SILENCE–the Most Mysterious Character of Modern Fiction.' The advertisement held the distinction of being the largest illustrated book poster to appear on hoardings in England at that time."

The result for Blackwood was especially felicitous. It allowed him to spend the next six years in a mountain village in Switzerland and write some of his most remarkable weird work: the story collections *The Lost Valley* (1910), *Pan's Garden* (1912), and *Incredible Adventures* (1914), the latter being perhaps the greatest weird collection of all time; the delightful children's stories *Jimbo: A Fantasy* (1909) and *The Education of Uncle Paul* (1909); and the novels *The Human Chord* (1910), *The Centaur* (1911), and *A Prisoner in Fairyland* (1913).

The rest of Blackwood's career, indeed, was a vain attempt to duplicate the potency of these imperishable works. Although such novels as *Julius LeVallon* (1916), *The Wave* (1916), *The Garden of Survival* (1918), and *The Bright Messenger* (1921) have their moments of power, and there are some worthy tales in such later collections as *Day and Night Stories* (1917), *The Wolves of God* (1921), *Tongues of Fire* (1924), and *Shocks* (1935), it seems as if Blackwood's creative energies were dissipating. In the late 1920s he returned to children's writing, producing a number of delightful stories and novels, including *Dudley and Gilderoy* (1929) and *The Fruit Stoners* (1934).

But Blackwood showed vigour to the end. In the mid-1930s he began a new career reading stories on BBC radio, and he even became a pioneering presence in the new medium of television, where his long, gaunt, skeletal face was the perfect embodiment of weirdness. Throughout World War II—even though his residence in London was destroyed in the Battle of Britain and he was almost killed—Blackwood continued his radio talks; this valiant work led ultimately to his becoming a Commander of the British Empire.

Algernon Blackwood has left a legacy of weird writing unsurpassed in both quality and quantity. The fact that his reputation now survives, if at all, on the basis of a few anthology chestnuts like "The Willows" and "The Wendigo" surely casts doubt on the facile belief that literary merit always prevails. In his long life he watched his best work slowly go out of print; one hopes that successive reprints of his novels and tales will help to elevate him once again to the place he deserves in the literature of the weird.

The Weird Work of M. P. Shiel

In the original version of "Supernatural Horror in Literature," H. P. Lovecraft wrote:

> Matthew Phipps Shiel, author of many weird, grotesque, and adventurous novels and tales, occasionally attains a high level of horrific magic. "Xélucha" is a noxiously hideous fragments [*sic*], but is excelled by Mr. Shiel's undoubted masterpiece, "The House of Sounds", floridly written in the "yellow nineties", and re-cast with more artistic restraint in the early twentieth century. This story, in final form, deserves a place among the foremost things of its kind. It tells of a creeping horror and menace trickling down the centuries on a sub-Arctic island off the coast of Norway; where, amidst the sweep of dæmon winds and the ceaseless din of hellish waves and cataracts, a vengeful dead man built a brazen tower of terror. It is vaguely like, yet infinitely unlike, Poe's "Fall of the House of Usher".[1]

It is evident that Lovecraft had not yet read Shiel's true masterpiece of weirdness, the novel *The Purple Cloud* (1901). Frank Belknap Long lent this book to Lovecraft in May 1927, referring to it as "the most unutterably terrible book ever written."[2] Lovecraft's own response, when he read the book shortly thereafter, was equally enthusiastic:

> "The Purple Cloud" was magnificent, despite a perceptible weakening or letting down of the tone in the latter half. . . . It deals with vague Black Powers & White Powers battling for the earth's supremacy—how the former were released by the visit of a man to the frightful lake & carven column at the North Pole, & how all the human race save him & one other were thereupon wiped out with prussic-acid vapour. But it is in the *details* that the power lies. Ugh! What pestilential death-ships & dead cities! This book is worth buying if you can possibly get it.[3]

---

1. "Supernatural Horror in Literature," *Recluse* No. 1 (1927): 48–49.

2. Lovecraft to August Derleth, 22 May [1927] *Essential Solitude* 1.90.

3. Lovecraft to August Derleth, 28 May [1927] *Essential Solitude* 1.91.

Lovecraft accordingly felt obligated to augment his discussion of Shiel when "Supernatural Horror in Literature" was scheduled to appear in a revised version in the *Fantasy Fan* (1933–35):

> In the novel *The Purple Cloud* Mr. Shiel describes with tremendous power a curse which came out of the arctic to destroy mankind, and which for a time appears to have left but a single inhabitant on our planet. The sensations of this lone survivor as he realises his position, and roams through the corpse-littered and treasure-strown cities of the world as their absolute master, are delivered with a skill and artistry falling little short of actual majesty. Unfortunately the second half of the book, with its conventionally romantic element, involves a distinct "letdown".[4]

This is (with one exception) the extent of Lovecraft's public discussions of Shiel, and yet it was sufficient to bring Shiel's work to the attention of his young disciple August Derleth, who would later reissue Shiel's tales under the Arkham House and Mycroft & Moran imprints.

As with several other writers, Lovecraft owed his initial reading of M. P. Shiel (1865–1947) to the generosity of others—in this case, W. Paul Cook, the amateur associate from whose extensive weird library Lovecraft would make many discoveries. In the fall of 1923, Cook lent Lovecraft Shiel's *The Pale Ape and Other Pulses* (1911), containing "The House of Sounds" and other tales that caught his fancy. So taken with that story was he that he immediately wrote what can only be described as a fan letter to Edwin Baird, editor of the recently founded *Weird Tales*:

> Every once in a while I discover some weird masterpiece by an author either wholly unknown or unknown in America, which I wish could be popularised. Just now I am enthusiastic about a tale called 'The House of Sounds', by M. P. Shiel, which occurs in a book of short stories named after the first one, 'The Pale Ape', and published by T. Werner Laurie, Clifford's Inn, London. This is the most haunting thing I have read in a decade—a creeping horror and menace trickling down the centuries in a sub-Arctic island off the coast of Norway, where, amidst the sweep of daemon winds and the ceaseless din of hellish waves and cataracts, a vengeful dead man built a brazen tower of terror. It is vaguely like—yet infinitely unlike—'The Fall of the House of

---

4. *The Annotated Supernatural Horror in Literature* (New York: Hippocampus Press, 2nd ed. 2012), 74. This segment did not actually appear in the *Fantasy Fan*, as the serialisation ended in the middle of Chapter VIII, whereas this passage is included in Chapter IX. It first appeared in print in *The Outsider and Others* (1939).

Usher'. I wish there were a way of getting republication rights from the publisher—for it would surely be a sensation in *Weird Tales*."[5]

The similarity of language between this letter and Lovecraft's subsequent discussion of the story in "Supernatural Horror in Literature" is patent. *Weird Tales* did not in fact reprint the tale, but, as mentioned, a seed may have been planted in August Derleth's mind to do so—first in the anthology *Sleep No More* (1944), then in the Arkham House collection *Xélucha and Others* (1975), the last major assemblage of Shiel's short stories until the present volume.

Lovecraft initially announced his discovery of Shiel in a letter to Frank Belknap Long, in which he wrote:

> Some of the things [in *The Pale Ape*] are mediocre, though all are smooth. One is diabolically clever, though hardly weird. Three or four are superfine—"Huguenin's Wife", "The Bride", "The Great King", and "The House of Sounds". Yes—this last is the masterpiece! How can I describe its poison-grey "insidious madness"? If I say it is very like "The Fall of the House of Usher", or even that one feature mirrors my own "Alchemist", (1908) I shall not even have suggested the utterly unique delirium of arctic wastes, titan seas, insane brazen towers, centuried malignity, frenzied waves and cataracts, and above all hideous, insistent, brain-petrifying, Pan-accursed cosmic SOUND . . . God! but after that story I shall never write another of my own. Shiel has done so much better than my best, that I am left breathless and inarticulate. And yet the man is virtually unknown in America—and almost so in his native Britain.[6]

Lovecraft cannot claim especial acuity in detecting the resemblance of "The House of Sounds" to "The Fall of the House of Usher," for Shiel, profoundly influenced (like Lovecraft) by Poe from an early age, consciously sought to duplicate that fusion of human souls to the fate of a physical structure that is at the core of both stories. It is a bit surprising, in fact, that Lovecraft did not detect the similar parallel between his other favourite, "Xélucha," and Poe's "Ligeia."

Lovecraft manifestly preferred the more subdued, less flamboyantly baroque prose of "The House of Sounds" to its original, "Vaila," first published in Shiel's early collection *Shapes in the Fire* (1896). It is not clear when Lovecraft read the earlier version,[7] but it is likely that he did so at a time when he

---

5. *Weird Tales* 3, No. 1 (January 1924): 88; rpt. in *H. P. Lovecraft in "The Eyrie,"* ed. S. T. Joshi and Marc A. Michaud (West Warwick, RI: Necronomicon Press, 1979), 19.

6. Lovecraft to Frank Belknap Long, 7 October 1923; *Selected Letters 1911–1924*, ed. August Derleth and Donald Wandrei (Sauk City, WI: Arkham House, 1965), 255.

7. In a letter to August Derleth (c. 1933) he writes: "As for Shiel—he is undeniably

was himself in the process of conducting an overhauling and simplification of his own prose style, eschewing the floridity of his earlier work for the scientific realism of his later tales. Lovecraft owned the radically revised edition of *The Purple Cloud* (1929)—it was given to him by Richard Ely Morse in 1932—but it is unclear whether he actually read it.[8] There is lively debate among enthusiasts of weird fiction as to whether these later versions of Shiel's work are in fact superior to the earlier ones, many contending that Shiel's distinctive subject-matter is best suited to the euphuistic prose he cultivated in his early years.

Curiously enough, Lovecraft first read Shiel at the exact time when Shiel's reputation was in the process of undergoing a revival. His career can be neatly divided into two periods—1895–1913, when he published his first twenty books, and 1923–37, when his remaining ten titles appeared. In the interim, Shiel published nothing in book form, although pseudonymous or anonymous publications have long been suspected. In the United States, Shiel was indeed little known until 1929, when Vanguard Press issued the revised *Purple Cloud* and also published the novel *Dr. Krasinski's Secret*, followed the next year by *The Black Box*. Lovecraft also owned Shiel's *The Lord of the Sea* (the edition of 1924, an exhaustive revision of the original edition of 1901); this novel—about a modern-day superman who attempts to control ocean traffic by means of innovative military devices—was given to Lovecraft in 1935 by Richard Ely Morse, and he read it late that year, noting: "'The Lord of the Sea' has a curious power—& its opening chapters sound almost prophetic in these days of Nazidom & sporadic anti-Semitism." (Shiel's novel has also been accused of anti-Semitism.) Samuel Loveman gave Lovecraft a copy of Shiel's early short story collection *Prince Zaleski* (1895), but Lovecraft was unenthusiastic: "I own Shiel's 'Zaleski', but cannot get very deeply excited over it. It consists of three medium length tales—none of which impressed me as 'The House of Sounds' did."[9]

Lovecraft's preference, in consonance with his view that weird fiction

---

clever, but exasperatingly uneven. The florid flamboyancy of some of his prose is painful—& yet at times he becomes virtually peerless. His indubitable masterpiece—"The House of Sounds"—is a revision (made in 1908 [*sic*]) of a vastly weaker & more effusive tale written in 1896. I saw the original (whose title I forget) once, & was certainly glad that the author saw fit to do it over" (*Essential Solitude* 2.573).

8. In a letter to Morse acknowledging the book (30 August [1932]; ms., John Hay Library), Lovecraft speaks of his intention of reading the book, but there is no definitive evidence that he ever did so.

9. Lovecraft to August Derleth, 12 November 1926 (*Essential Solitude* 1.49).

works best in short compass, was manifestly for Shiel's short stories. His letter to Frank Belknap Long of 1923 contains, however, a number of pecularities and ambiguities. What is the "diabolically clever, though hardly weird" tale to which Lovecraft refers? My feeling is that this is "The Case of Euphemia Raphash," a skilful murder mystery with a well-hidden twist at the end. Lovecraft does not specifically note enjoying "The Pale Ape," but it would be difficult to imagine him not relishing this tale of anomalous hybridity, so similar to his own earlier work, "Facts concerning the Late Arthur Jermyn and His Family" (1920), soon to be embalmed in *Weird Tales* under the give-away title "The White Ape" (April 1924). "Huguenin's Wife," another tale of a hybrid monster, accomplished something that Lovecraft had perhaps hoped for much of his career to do: to draw upon the latent weirdness of classical myth. Of the other stories Lovecraft singles out, "The Great King" is an artfully told tale of a revenant, but "The Bride"—never reprinted since its original appearance—is an odd tale for Lovecraft to have enjoyed, being largely a romance, even a melodrama, with a supernatural element slyly inserted only at the very end.

Of *The Purple Cloud* it is difficult to speak in small compass. The novel is the second component of a very loose trilogy—the other volumes being *The Lord of the Sea* (1901) and *The Last Miracle* (1906)—purporting to be visions of the future as transmitted through a psychic, Mary Wilson. Each volume contains a nearly identical introduction recounting this highly contrived premise, but the reader quickly forgets it in Shiel's gripping tale of what appears to be the last man left alive on the earth, following the explosion of a volcano that produces a deadly purple cloud of cyanogen gas. This detail must have amused Lovecraft, for in an early letter he speaks with whimsical misanthropy of his hope that the entire human race "could be mercifully blotted out by a whiff of cyanogen gas in some comet's tail!"[10] Shiel achieves a true sense of cosmicism by his lonely protagonist Adam Jeffson's traversal of entire globe in what appears to be a vain search for any remaining members of his species. Whether the last portion of the book really constitutes a "letdown" will depend upon the temperament of the reader. Lovecraft's comment is of a piece with his general lack of interest in the portrayal of human character in weird fiction, and specifically with any admixture of "romance" that might diffuse the depiction of cosmic horror. In reality, the romance element comprises only the final quarter of the novel (in the 1901 edition); moreover, Shiel's handling of Adam's tortured relationship with the young woman, Leda, is far from conventional, and his gradual shedding of his ferocious cynicism and misanthropy in the face of her naive and winsome optimism is managed with

---

10. Lovecraft to Rheinhart Kleiner, 25 June 1920; *Selected Letters 1911–1924*, 120.

exquisite skill and psychological acuity. But Lovecraft is probably correct in suggesting that the cataclysmic vista of a dead world littered with the suddenly meaningless tokens of humanity's relics—its cities, its art, literature, and science, its religions, its hopes and aspirations all apparently gone for naught—will linger far longer in the reader's mind than Adam and Leda's ultimate decision to renew the human species.

Shiel's revision of *The Purple Cloud* deserves a treatise in itself. In sheer wordage, the novel has shrunk from the 103,000 words of the 1901 edition to 93,000 words in the edition of 1929; but this does not begin to tell the whole story, for scarcely a sentence has been left unaltered. In general, Shiel has pruned what might appear to be excess adjectives and adverbs, in accordance with his echoing, in the essay "On Writing" (1909), of Voltaire's remark that "the adjective is the enemy of the noun, even though it agrees with it in gender and number."[11] Once again, individual temperament will dictate whether the loss of precision and nuance is deemed sufficiently offset by the gain in concision. David G. Hartwell maintains: "This cutting and revision has the subtle and pernicious effect of removing the work from a firm grounding in its own period and casting it adrift as a literary-historical hybrid,"[12] but this criticism seems a bit captious: Shiel was under no obligation to preserve his novel as an historical artifact, and in many ways his revisions do tighten up the work and render it more idiomatic and smooth-flowing. However, since Lovecraft's judgment of it is evidently based upon his reading of the 1901 edition, that is the text that devoted Lovecraftians will wish to read.

It is difficult to detect any clear influence of Shiel upon Lovecraft. Even "The House of Sounds," although it perennially made Lovecraft's lists of his favourite weird tales,[13] may have been of significance only as a stellar example of the sense of the cosmic in literature. One telling detail, however, may be worth noting: its mention of a "door, half a mile wide, flat on the ground" seems highly suggestive of the entrance to Cthulhu's suddenly risen city of R'lyeh, which Lovecraft describes in "The Call of Cthulhu" (1926) as an "immense carved door with the now familiar squid-dragon bas-relief," later remarking: "It was . . . like a great barn-door; and they all felt that it was a door because of the ornate lintel, threshold, and jambs around it, though they could not decide whether it may flat like a trap-door or slantwise like an

---

11. "On Writing," in *Science Life and Literature* (London: Williams & Norgate, 1950), 89.

12. "Introduction" to *The Purple Cloud* (Gregg Press, 1977); rpt. in *Shiel in Divers Hands*, ed. A. Reynolds Morse (Cleveland: Reynolds Morse Foundation, 1983), 115.

13. See "Favourite Weird Stories of H. P. Lovecraft" (*Fantasy Fan*, October 1934); in *The Annotated Supernatural Horror in Literature*, 73.

outside cellar-door."[14] (This detail, however, might also have been derived from the "moon-door" featured in A. Merritt's "The Moon Pool.") Shiel's account of the preparations for the voyage to the North Pole in the opening pages of *The Purple Cloud* may perhaps have had some minimal influence upon Lovecraft's similar description of the preparations of the Miskatonic Expedition to Antarctica, although the parallels are very loose and general.

Suffice it to say that, in Shiel, Lovecraft found a weird writer working along surprisingly similar lines—one who cultivated a mannered, almost *recherché* style to create a kind of incantatory effect upon the reader; one who scorned conventional character portrayal to depict Poe-like protagonists full of quirks, eccentricities, and scorn of mundane morality; and one who looked upon his early work with disfavour and chose to amend it by shearing away some of its grotesqueries of style and incident in light of a newer aesthetic that sought to convey more with less. Lovecraft never got the chance to revise his work in the wholesale manner in which Shiel transformed "Vaila" into "The House of Sounds" or the *Purple Cloud* of 1901 into its leaner version of 1929; but the chances are that, had he been given that chance, he might have pruned away some of the excrescences in his early tales to match the tightly knit rigour of his later ones. Lovecraft in effect performed the same function by taking the core of such plots as those of "Dagon" and "Facts concerning the Late Arthur Jermyn and His Family" and transforming them into "The Call of Cthulhu" and "The Shadow over Innsmouth," respectively. Whether he would have taken a scalpel to those latter works, had he lived another decade or more, is a question that must forever remain unanswered.

---

14. *The Dunwich Horror and Others* (Sauk City, WI: Arkham House, 1984), 151.

May Sinclair: The Spiritual Ghost Story

In a career spanning more than five decades, novelist, poet, and essayist May Sinclair (1863–1946) not only became a leading figure in the literary scene of early twentieth-century Britain, but generated a modest but powerful body of weird short fiction that emphasized her abiding concern with human psychology, the complexities of personal relationships, and the role of the indvidiual within a society whose strict moral codes were being slowly loosened by increasing secularism and the increasing freedom of women to establish their own lives and personalities apart from men. In many ways these weird tales are extensions of her widely acclaimed novels, which address the same issues but without a supernatural or fantastic element.

Mary Amelia St. Clair Sinclair was born on August 24, 1863, in Rock Ferry, Cheshire, a suburb of Liverpool, on the other side of the Mersey—and not far from where the current weird writer Ramsey Campbell resides. She was the youngest of six children (the other five were all boys) of William and Amelia (Hind) Sinclair. William was a once-prosperous shipowner who went bankrupt in 1870 and died in 1881. Upon his death, May and her mother lived apart from the boys. Amelia wished her daughter to be religiously orthodox and conventionally feminine, like herself, but from an early age May resisted what she perceived to be the confining of her mental, spiritual, and personal perspectives. She revealed impressive erudition by learning Greek, German, and French on her own before she entered Cheltenham Ladies College in 1881. Although she stayed at the school for only a single year, it left a lasting impression upon her. She became especially close to the school's principal, Dorothea Beale, who urged her to study philosophical idealism as a way of gaining knowledge of God through reason rather than dogma. May remained in touch with Beale for at least fifteen years after leaving the school, soliciting her judgment on her increasingly ambitious writings.

Sinclair had been experimenting with poetry during this period, and her first published book was a volume of poetry, *Nakiketas and Other Poems* (1886), published under the name Julian Sinclair. But it was in the 1890s that Sinclair, still living with her mother, entered into the first of several fertile periods of her literary career. She had made the acquaintance of Anthony Charles Deane (1872–1946), a poet and clergyman who subjected much of her work to keen scrutiny and helped her to find suitable markets for her writing. During this time she wrote several verse dramas; these were not published, but they served as a bridge between her poetry and her later work in fiction, as they allowed her to develop a facility in narration and character portrayal. She also published articles on Plato and idealism, and translations from Greek and German.

Sinclair's first short story was published in November 1895. Her first novel, *Anthony Craven*, appeared in 1897. It was the first of twenty-four novels she would publish over the next thirty years, along with four collections of stories, three volumes of poetry (including a "novel" in verse), two philosophical treatises, a great deal of literary criticism and reviews, and other matter. *Anthony Craven* is a novel of character and heredity substantially influenced by the work of Thomas Hardy. Her next novel, *Mr. and Mrs. Nevill Tyson* (1898), as described by her biographer, Theophilus E. M. Boll, "treats the sexual relations of man and wife with an almost medical frankness."[1] It was the first of several novels about married life that Sinclair—who never married and who, so far as is known, never had an intimate relationship with either a man or a woman—wrote over the course of her career.

Sinclair, dogged by poverty and worried about the health of her mother, saw Amelia succumb on February 22, 1901. By this time she was living in London, and she quickly became acquainted with many of the leading figures in English literature. This was especially the case after her novel *The Divine Fire* (1904) became a bestseller in both England and the United States. This work is a psychological romance focusing on the life and loves of a classicist poet, Savage Keith Rickman, with a strong emphasis on unconscious states of mind, dreams, and the like. She was particularly cultivated by American publisher Henry Holt, who released several of her novels but was also something of a martinet in regard to her style and content; Sinclair refused to alter her work in light of Holt's comments. *The Divine Fire* was publicly praised by such American critics as Witter Bynner and Jack London, and its success led to an American book tour from November 1905 to January 1906. During this time she attended the seventieth birthday party for Mark Twain and saw Teddy Roosevelt in the White House.

Sinclair was now appearing regularly in leading British and American periodicals ranging from the *Atlantic Monthly* to *Ainslee's* to the *Fortnightly Review* and *Everybody's Magazine*. She met the ageing Thomas Hardy on several occasions in 1908 and, beginning the following year, engaged in a correspondence

---

1. Theophilus E. M. Boll, *Miss May Sinclair: A Biographical and Critical Introduction* (Rutherford, NJ: Fairleigh Dickinson University Press, 1973), 169.

with the young Ezra Pound. She introduced Pound to Ford Madox Hueffer (later Ford Madox Ford), who helped launch Pound's career. Around this time she also began campaigning vocally for women's suffrage; she later wrote the pamphlet *Feminism* (1912), published by the Women Writers Suffrage League.

In a letter written on December 9, 1910, to the American writer Annie Fields, Sinclair confessed: "I am busy writing short stories—stories of all queer lengths and all queer subjects; 'spooky' ones, some of them. I like doing them!"[2] It is not entirely clear what stories were written at this time; the earliest of her weird tales appears to have been a pair of novellas, "The Flaw in the Crystal" and "The Intercessor." The former was written in the spring of 1911 and published separately by E. P. Dutton in 1912; the date of the latter's composition is not known for certain, but it appeared in the July 1911 issue of the *English Review*, so it is possible that it was being worked on as early as late 1910.

Sinclair had developed a strong interest in the Brontë sisters, and she wrote introductions to the Everyman's Library edition of their novels and also wrote the significant treatise *The Three Brontës* (1912). By now a commercially successful and well-regarded writer, Sinclair promoted her interest in psychology not only by writing essays that reveal her study of the work of Freud, Jung, and Adler, but by giving the substantial sum of £500 in 1914 to help establish the Medico-Psychological Clinic of London, the first clinic in England to include psychoanalysis in its thereapeutic methods. It closed in 1922. Sinclair also became interested in avant-garde literary movements such as Imagism and Vorticism. She became acquainted with Richard Aldington and his wife, H. D. (Hilda Doolittle), and also met W. B. Yeats; she later wrote articles on these poets as well as on T. S. Eliot, Ezra Pound, F. S. Flint, and the novelist Dorothy Richardson.

With the outbreak of World War I, Sinclair felt the need to do something to support the war effort. She spent seventeen days in Belgium in late 1914 doing secretarial and other work for the ambulance corps, later recording her experiences in *A Journal of Impressions in Belgium* (1915). She fused many of her interests in the novel *The Tree of Heaven* (1917), which uses the war as a backdrop to explore both literary and political radicalism. *Mary Olivier* (1919), the novel of which Sinclair was most proud, is heavily autobiographical, as its account of a female poet and her struggles with her family keenly reflect Sinclair's own tortured relationship with her mother. She also wrote the first of her two major philosophical treatises, *A Defence of Idealism* (1917).

---

2. Boll 87.

During the years 1914–1919, Sinclair had enlisted the services of Nellie Baltrop as housekeeper and companion. After Nellie's departure, her twin sister Florence took over the role, remaining in that position for the remainder of Sinclair's long life. The 1920s were another period of productivity for her, with eleven novels and much other work to her credit; but it was becoming increasingly evident that Sinclair, while clearly associated with the Modernist writers who were revolutionizing English literature at this time, was not quite as cutting-edge as some of her bolder contemporaries. She had been too thoroughly imbued with Victorian standards of behavior and, consequently, of literary expression; and her spare, elegant, but at times emotionally remote style consigned her to a shadowy middle-ground between more orthodox writers such as Arnold Bennett and Sinclair Lewis (whose novel *Babbitt* [1922] Sinclair reviewed on the front page of the *New York Times Book Review*) and the likes of D. H. Lawrence, Eliot, and Pound.

Nonetheless, Eliot expressed admiration for her work and published several of her weird tales in his periodical, the *Criterion*; one of them, "The Victim," directly followed *The Waste Land* in the October 1922 issue. However, her health began to deteriorate as the decade advanced, and *History of Anthony Waring* (1927) was her last published novel. Although she published two story collections in the early 1930s, the stories themselves had mostly been written earlier. Around 1932 she and Florence moved away from London and settled in a rural region of Buckinghamshire. The exact nature of her malady is not entirely clear; one critic speaks of "the neuromuscular deterioration that was to gradually incapacitate her in both mind and body."[3] May Sinclair lived on until November 14, 1946, when she at her home in Bierton.

The weird work of May Sinclair is confined to two short story collections, *Uncanny Stories* (1923) and *The Intercessor and Other Stories* (1931). But these volumes do not present the stories in anything approaching their chronological sequence. Aside from her two novellas, it would appear that most of these tales were written in the early 1920s.

The extent to which these stories—and her work in general—is governed by her philosophical idealism is unclear, chiefly because that philosophy itself is a trifle opaque. Her idealism was markedly influenced by the nineteenth-century British philosopher T. H. Green, who fashioned his worldview in contrast to the materialism and utilitarianism of such philosophers as Jeremy Bentham and John Stuart Mill. As Hrisey D. Zegger notes:

---

3. Hrisey D. Zegger, *May Sinclair* (Boston: Twayne, 1976), 28.

> Green regarded man's spiritual nature, his consciousness, as primary; he viewed the universe as being divinely ordered and hierarchical, a manifestation of God's consciousness to which man is related by his own consciousness; and he considered the primary ethical category to be man's self-realization, the need for man and for society to help man reach his best and highest nature.[4]

Many of these same concerns would infuse Sinclair's writing, both her novels and her weird work. It becomes clear that Sinclair saw in idealism a means of embracing a quasi-religious view of the world without adopting the rigid dogmas of orthodox Christianity and also of exploring the complexities of mind in a way that subordinates the physical incidents of a narrative to the analysis of those incidents that occur in the minds of her characters.

This is perhaps most evident in "The Flaw in the Crystal," whose "events" take place almost entirely in the psyches of the figures in the story—especially Agatha Verrall, a "spinster" who may be a stand-in for Sinclair and whose ability to heal a married man, Rodney Lanyon, through the power of her own mind is compromised by the presence of the demonic presence of another married man, Harding Powell, who comes close to possessing Agatha's mind and thereby forcing her to confront her hidden carnal desire for Rodney—this being the "flaw in the crystal" that might result in catastrophe for all concerned. The fact that nearly all the central incidents of the tale consist of the shifting psychological and emotional currents in Agatha's mind make the narrative strangely compelling.

More orthodox is "The Intercessor," whose Yorkshire setting is surely influenced by Sinclair's work on the Brontës. Here it becomes evident that the presence of a guest, Garvin, in the home of a rural couple who have suffered the death of a young child causes the child to seek solace with that guest— precisely because he, unlike the child's mother, is unafraid of it. As such, Garvin becomes the "intercessor" who effects a reconcilation between the mother and her dead daughter. There is an intense poignancy in this tale that brings other weird tales of the period—notably Robert Hichens's "The Cry of the Child" (1900)—to mind. And the influence of Henry James's *The Turn of the Screw* is also evident.

Sinclair's weird tales of the 1920s deal chiefly with interpersonal relationships, chiefly between man and woman. The grim tale "Where Their Fire Is Not Quenched" is one of these. The title is of course taken from Jesus' thrice-repeated description of hell (Mark 9:44, 46, 48); and hell is exactly what the central characters—a woman and the man with whom she had, to her own re-

---

4. Zegger 19.

gret, had an affair—find themselves in.[5] Several other tales speak of the complexities of love and sex, such as "The Villa Désirée," where a second wife senses the presence of her husband's first wife in the villa they had occupied before the first wife's sudden death—but she senses other things that reveal to her the true nature of the man she has married. "The Token" tells of a wife, unsure of her husband's love, who learns of it only after her death. Then there is "The Nature of the Evidence," in which the ghost of a first wife haunts her husband's second wife in such a way as to prevent their consummating their love. This and other works lead one to believe that this lifelong virgin may have had some issues regarding physical intimacy.[6]

Two tales feature a dominating mother in a way that may be autobiographical. "Heaven" is a light-hearted fantasy in which a man thinks he has gone to heaven—but it is a very strange place, and not at all what he was expecting. It proves to be only his mother's heaven—a heaven whose features are determined by that mother's narrow, dogmatic view of what such a place should be. "If the Dead Knew" tells of a man, long under the financial and emotional influence of his mother, who upon her death finally gets the chance to seek happiness with the woman he loves; but he is quite literally haunted by the possibility that he had caused his mother's death by wishing it. The uncollected poem "Fright," reprinted here for the first time, is also a plangent vignette about Sinclair's early life with her mother.

Another light-hearted tale is "The Victim," where a man, Mr. Greathead, murdered by his chauffeur comes back from the dead and assures his killer that he is in a much better place and that he should not feel remorse for his

---

5. In a trenchant article on her weird tales, Richard Bleiler believes that this tale is also influenced by Hichens, "particularly *The Garden of Allah*. Hichens's story brings together two characters in the deserts of Northern Africa, establishes them as lovers, then splits them asunder when it is revealed that the man is a Trappist Monk who has fled the monastery. . . . 'Where Their Fire Is Not Quenched' shares with Hichens a refusal to permit the traditional happy ending that would be seen in less original writers." Richard Bleiler, "May Sinclair's Supernatural Fiction," in *May Sinclair: Moving towards the Modern*, ed. Andrew J. Kunka and Michele K. Troy (Aldershot, UK: Ashgate, 2006), 128–29.

6. Boll recounts the testimony of Rebecca West as to whether Sinclair had ever been in love: "As a very young friend and confidante of May Sinclair she [West] learned that May Sinclair had once been in love and might have married but for 'some very obscure grounds of scruple.' It was obvious to her that May Sinclair had felt the renunciation very deeply. The time of the recollection was during the first World War, and the reference was to the very distant past and to a brother-officer of a relative of hers in the service, probably a friend of her brother Frank" (Boll 120).

actions. Sinclair's philosophical predispositions are on display here, as Greathead emphasizes that his murderer's true crime was not the murder itself but the mental state that led to it. "The Finding of the Absolute" is nothing more than a philosophical allegory, once again dealing with what heaven might be like.

Two related stories appear to have been written in the later 1920s, both dealing with the figure of an Indian guru or Mahatma with supernatural powers. In "Jones's Karma" the Mahatma establishes that it is impossible to avoid your karma even if you were granted the power—which the Mahatma grants the hapless Jones—to backtrack along the course of your life and remedy the bad decisions you had made at critical junctures. "The Mahatma's Story" underscores many of the same points in its account of two painters who switch bodies.

In 1923 Sinclair participated in a symposium about "Dreams, Ghosts and Fairies," outlining her views of weird fiction:

> (1) My "attitude" towards ghost stories is one of enthralling interest and admiration if they are well told. I regard the ghost story as a perfectly legitimate form of art and at the same time as the most difficult. Ghosts have their own atmosphere and their own reality, they have also their setting in the everyday reality we know; the story-teller is handling two realities at the same time; he is working on two planes, in two atmospheres, and must fail if he lets one do violence to the other.

> (2) I am not a judge of "popularity," but I should say off-hand that an interest in ghost stories has always existed, and is neither a sign of morbidity nor of "increased belief in spiritual phenomena." The ghost-lover is on the look-out for his own special thrill, which is, or may be, independent of any belief in the supernatural.

> (3) I think Henry James' "The Turn of the Screw" the most perfect and the most convincing ghost story I have read.[7]

What is perhaps of greatest interest here is the second paragraph. The degree to which Sinclair actually believed in ghostly phenomena is a matter of doubt. She was elected as a member of the Society for Psychical Research in 1914, but she did not involve herself very much in its activities. She is on record as being consistently skeptical of claims of ghost-sightings and other spiritualistic phenomena on the part of her friends or other individuals, and little in her weird fiction suggests a literal belief in the supernatual.

---

7. "Dreams, Ghosts and Fairies" [symposium], *Bookman* (London) 65 (December 1923): 144.

And yet, it was precisely this point that led H. P. Lovecraft to make a memorable statement in "Supernatural Horror in Literature":

> May Sinclair's *Uncanny Stories* contain more of traditional occultism than of that creative treatment of fear which marks mastery in this field, and are inclined to lay more stress on human emotions and psychological delving than upon the stark phenomena of a cosmos utterly unreal. It may be well to remark here that occult believers are probably less effective than materialists in delineating the spectral and the fantastic, since to them the phantom world is so commonplace a reality that they tend to refer to it with less awe, remoteness, and impressiveness than do those who see in it an absolute and stupendous violation of the natural order.[8]

This appears to be the somewhat unjust assessment of a thinker whose own atheism and materialism were in stark contrast to Sinclair's idealism and spirituality, for there is very little of the traditionally "occult" in her weird work. And in any number of her tales that sense of the "awe, remoteness, and impressiveness" of ghostly phenomena is in fact present.

Cumulatively, Sinclair's horror tales, with their intense focus on the shifting psychological states of her sensitive and pensive characters, are far indeed from the weird fiction of Lovecraft, Hodgson, and even Machen; perhaps they are more closely allied to the tales of Algernon Blackwood, who from a very different perspective (that of a kind of Buddhist-inspired pantheism) was similarly concerned with human psychology and utilized the weird to explore its complexities. There is of course considerably more of the cosmic in Blackwood than in Sinclair, but her emphasis on the human should be regarded as a virtue, not a drawback. Even if her use of the supernatural is in itself largely conventional, she was supremely skilled in using ghostly phenomena to underscore the manner in which human beings confront—or find themselves incapable of confronting—the tangled network of relationships that can make daily life baffling, perplexing, and at times terrifying.

---

8. *The Annotated Supernatural Horror in Literature*, ed. S. T. Joshi (New York: Hippocampus Press, 2nd ed. 2012), 77.

H. B. Drake's *The Shadowy Thing*

Henry Burgess Drake (1893–1964) is a mystery man in Anglo-American letters. He was the author of nine weird and adventure novels, a children's story, a travel book, and several English textbooks, but aside from his dates of birth and death only a single biographical fact about him has emerged: at some point he served as a professor of English at the preparatory school of Keijo Imperial University in Seoul, Korea (an experience that led to his writing of his travelogue, *Korea of the Japanese* [1930]). His first published book dates to 1925, his last to 1959. But today he is known, if at all, for a single work: the weird novel *The Shadowy Thing* (1928).

This work itself was first published in England under the title *The Remedy* (1925), and constituted Drake's first novel. Several adventure novels followed in the 1920s: *The Schooner California* (1926), *Cursed Be the Treasure* (1926), *The Children Reap* (1929), and *Shinju* (1929), the last two of which are set in the Orient and apparently draw further upon Drake's years spent there. Although *The Children Reap* has some elements of weirdness, these novels are rousing adventure tales that evoked reviewers' comparisons with Robert Louis Stevenson and even Joseph Conrad.

In the 1930s Drake was literarily quiescent, issuing only his book on Korea and another novel (*The Captain of the Jehovah*, 1936), and commencing a five-book series, *An Approach to English Literature for Students Abroad*, published by Oxford University Press between 1938 and 1950. In the 1940s all we have is a further textbook, *Foundation Exercises in English*, published by Macmillan in two books in 1941.

In the 1950s Drake resumed fiction writing, producing a children's story, *The Book of Lyonne* (1952), that had the distinction of being illustrated by Mervyn Peake, and three further novels, *Chinese White* (1950), *Hush-a-by Baby* (1952; published in the U.S. as *Children of the Wind*), and *The Woman and the Priest* (1955). *Hush-a-by Baby* is manifestly a weird novel, about a woman haunted by the spirits of her twin unborn babies. I have not read it, but it received good reviews upon its appearance. Drake also produced *The Oxford English Course for Secondary Schools* in three books (1957–59); a fourth book written by another author appeared in 1963, leading one to believe that Drake was dead by this time.

But if Drake had done nothing but write *The Shadowy Thing*, he would deserve to be remembered. Not only is this a strangely compelling supernatural novel, but it clearly influenced H. P. Lovecraft's "The Thing on the Doorstep" (1933), as both works deal with characters who display anomalous powers of hypnosis and mind-transference. In the revised version of "Supernatural Horror in Literature" he states somewhat vaguely: ". . . H. B. Drake's *The Shadowy Thing* summons up strange and terrible vistas."

An entry in Lovecraft's commonplace book (#158) records the plot-germ of his story:

> Man has terrible wizard friend who gains influence over him. Kills him in defence of his soul—walls body up in ancient cellar—BUT—the dead wizard (who has said strange things about soul lingering in body) *changes bodies with him . . .* leaving him a conscious corpse in cellar.

This is not exactly a description of the plot of *The Shadowy Thing*, but rather an imaginative extrapolation based upon it. In Drake's novel, a man, Avery Booth, does indeed exhibit powers that seem akin to hypnosis, to such a degree that he can oust the mind or personality from another person's body and occupy it. Booth does so on several occasions throughout the novel, and in the final episode he appears to have come back from the dead (he had been killed in a battle in World War I) and occupied the body of a friend and soldier who had himself been horribly mangled in battle. Lovecraft has amended this plot by introducing the notion of *mind-exchange:* whereas Drake does not clarify what happens to the ousted mind when it is taken over by the mind of Booth, Lovecraft envisages an exact transference whereby the ousted mind occupies the body of its possessor. Lovecraft then adds a further twist by envisioning what might happen if the occupier's body were killed and a dispossessed mind was thrust into it. The significant difference between the story and the plot-germ as recorded in the commonplace book is that the "wizard friend" has become the man's wife—a feature that may have been derived from Barry Pain's *An Exchange of Souls* (1911), which Lovecraft had in his library. This element also points to highly revealing autobiographical connexions (for Asenath Waite is clearly a compendium of Lovecraft's wife and his mother) that we cannot pursue here.

Otherwise, much of Lovecraft's story can be found directly in *The Shadowy Thing*. Avery Booth first possesses a weak-willed schoolmate, Gaveston, who is forced into an insane asylum as a result of his aberrant behaviour, just as Asenath Waite (in Edward Derby's body) is confined to the Arkham Sanitarium. Later Gaveston escapes, and the narrator of the novel is forced to shoot him, just as the narrator of "The Thing on the Doorstep" goes to the sanitarium to shoot the body of Edward Derby. When he does so he maintains that he has "purged the earth of a horror whose survival might have loosed untold terrors on all mankind"; in *The Shadowy Thing* the narrator's sister, Blanche, says of Gaveston, "If he goes under, a power of evil will be let loose in the world that none of us can estimate."

And yet, it would be unfair to claim that *The Shadowy Thing* is solely of interest for its relation to a major Lovecraft story. It is a worthy novel in its own right. Although Lovecraft would probably have discounted it, the romance between the narrator, Dick Bellew, and Katrina Guthrie is delicately handled and integral to the plot; the etching of the other characters—Blanche Bellew, Olave Guthrie, Gaveston, and in particular Avery Booth, who hovers like a dark shadow behind all the events of the novel—is deft and skilful. The work's excellence should lead us to seek out Drake's other weird novel, *Hush-a-by Baby*, and to regret that he did not receive more encouragement to continue in this vein. Although *The Shadowy Thing* garnered relatively cordial reviews, it took three years to receive an American edition—a fact that perhaps led Drake to work in what he felt to be the more lucrative vein of the adventure story. It has been the fate of most weird writers to labour in obscurity, and the result is that minor masterworks like *The Shadowy Thing* must be resurrected by devotees and presented for the delectation of a select audience. Even if Drake's novel must ride Lovecraft's coattails to achieve a tenuous immortality, it is a more welcome fate than many other worthy contributions to our field have endured.

Carl Jacobi: The Life of a Pulpsmith

The long literary career of Carl Jacobi (1908–1997) makes him a key transitional figure between the classic weird writers of the early twentieth century and the best-selling authors of the 1970s and 1980s. His extensive involvement in the horror, fantasy, detective, adventure, and science fiction pulp magazines demonstrated that he was the consummate professional, capable of tailoring his stories to specific markets; but his meticulous craftsmanship and careful attention to the conception, execution, and style of each of his stories allowed him to transcend hackneyed pulp conventions and produce work of lasting merit.

Carl Richard Jacobi was born on July 10, 1908, in Minneapolis, Minnesota, where he spent nearly his entire life. He was the only child of Richard Cleveland Jacobi and Meta Todell Hoffman. His parents were of German ancestry, although Carl never became fluent in the language. His father, a stockbroker, was a boisterous, larger-than-life figure who cast a heavy shadow over his rather shy and introverted son. As a boy Carl became an avid reader of adventure stories, and he anticipated his future career by producing handwritten "dime novels" that he would distribute to friends in junior high school. While attending Central High School in Minneapolis, he contributed an array of stories to the student magazine, *The Quest*. These stories ranged from humorous sketches to adventure tales, but at least a few ventured close to fantasy and weirdness. It was in high school that he began reading *Weird Tales*.

In 1927 he began attending the University of Minnesota, where he contributed to the student-run literary magazine, the *Minnesota Quarterly*. This well-produced periodical also featured essays and stories by another devotee of the weird who was attending the university at that time, Donald Wandrei (1908–1987). Jacobi and Wandrei became lifelong friends during their college years. Jacobi contributed not only his early triumph, "Mive," to the *Quarterly* (Fall 1928), but also detective tales during the period 1929–30. It was through Wandrei that Jacobi came into contact with August Derleth, then a student at the University of Wisconsin; Jacobi remained a colleague and correspondent of Derleth until the latter's death in 1971.

Graduating from the University of Minnesota with a degree in English literature and composition and a minor in journalism, Jacobi began working for the *Minneapolis Star* as a reporter, but after a few months gave up the work to try his luck at being a full-time freelance writer. He had already had his first professional sale, "Rumbling Cannon," by this time; the story appeared in *Secret Service Stories* for September 1928. But Jacobi knew that, in order to make an actual career as a pulp writer, he would have to work in a multiplicity of genres; that goal came naturally to him, as his literary tastes were broad and his interest and ability to work in a variety of literary modes correspondingly wide. His biographer, R. Dixon Smith, gives some idea of the breadth of Jacobi's output during the 1930s:

> His stock of available manuscripts included adventure stories, historical romances, mysteries, detective thrillers, and an occasional railroad yarn or western, and they were published by the dozens; but his efforts in the genre of fantasy—weird, macabre, supernatural and science fiction—held more promise of literary durability.[1]

Jacobi broke into *Weird Tales* with "Mive" in the January 1932 issue. The tale was appreciated by no less a figure than H. P. Lovecraft. Their mutual colleague August Derleth had evidently asked Lovecraft to convey his fondness for the story to the magazine's editor, Farnsworth Wright, and Lovecraft expressed an eagerness to do so:

> About "Mive"—of course I'd have been glad to say a good word whether I liked it or not, but fortunately I am really quite enthusiastic about the tale! It has the pervasive, insidious atmosphere so discouragingly lacking in almost all cheap weird fiction; & I gave it a puff on a postal sent [to Wright].[2]

Around this time, a correspondence between Lovecraft and Jacobi sprang up. Only one letter (dated February 27, 1932) by Lovecraft survives. Here he reiterates his praise of "Mive" and adds a good word for "The Coach on the Ring." He passes on the address of Robert E. Howard, and Jacobi did indeed correspond briefly with the creator of Conan as well as with Clark Ashton Smith; but Jacobi's most enduring associations were with such other pulpsmiths as Hugh B. Cave, E. Hoffmann Price, and Mary Elizabeth Counselman.

Jacobi's versatility extended well beyond writing for *Weird Tales*. He pub-

---

1. R. Dixon Smith, *Lost in the Rentharpian Hills: Spanning the Decades with Carl Jacobi* (Bowling Green, OH: Bowling Green State University Popular Press, 1985), 18.

2. *Essential Solitude: The Letters of H. P. Lovecraft and August Derleth*, ed. David E. Schultz and S. T. Joshi (New York: Hippocampus Press, 2008), 1.433.

lished "weird menace" stories (stories that suggest the supernatural but explain it away naturalistically, usually as a result of machinations by some crafty villain) in *Thrilling Mystery*, *Terror Tales*, and *Thrilling Adventures*; science fiction tales in *Thrilling Wonder Stories*; and adventure tales in *Complete Stories* and *Dime Adventure*. His enthusiasm for railroads led not only to the publication of the weird tale "Phantom Brass" in *Railroad Stories* (August 1934) but also of the adventure story "Train Kidnap" in the *Toronto Star Weekly* (December 21, 1935) and, most impressively, of "Loaded Coupling" in the well-paying Canadian "slick" magazine *Maclean's* (February 1, 1936). Otherwise, however, Jacobi published few stories outside the pulp magazines.

In 1940 Jacobi became an early member of the Minneapolis Fantasy Society, established by Clifford D. Simak. He would later collaborate on two stories with Simak. By this time, however, Jacobi's father had lost his job as a result of the ongoing worldwide depression, and Jacobi had to become the family's sole breadwinner—much as, at a slightly earlier date, Clark Ashton Smith had to begin churning out weird, fantasy, and science fiction tales for the pulp magazines to support his aging parents. Jacobi's relative slowness in literary production, however, meant that he could not rely on pulp writing for a steady income. His fascination with exotic locales led to the writing of a textbook, *Paths to the Far East* (1940), for the Minnesota public school system. In 1941 he became the editor of *Midwest Media*, a trade magazine, but lost the job after only a few months. With the advent of World War II and of the United States' entry into it, Jacobi took a job with the Honeywell defense plant; he began work there in the fall of 1942 and remained there for the next twenty-three years. The job severely restricted his ability to write, and his output radically dwindled. Accordingly, a substantial number of the tales for which he is remembered today were written during his first decade or so as a professional writer.

It was at this very time that Jacobi's overall reputation was in the process of being substantially augmented. In 1944, taking advantage of his long association with August Derleth—who had co-founded Arkham House in 1939, initially to publish the work of H. P. Lovecraft, but who quickly issued books by other writers of pulp fiction—and proposed a volume of his tales. He suggested a book of his Borneo adventure stories, but such a volume would not have been in harmony with the Arkham House list as it was then evolving, and Derleth told Jacobi he preferred a collection of his tales of horror and the supernatural.

The resulting volume—*Revelations in Black* (1947)—did indeed include some of Jacobi's finest work during his first decade as a professional writer. Jacobi performed significant revisions on a number of the tales, and the result is a book that not only contains such classics as "Mive" and the title story, but features dust jacket art by Ronald Clyne. A total of 3082 copies were printed. The book may not have been quite as revolutionary as its immediate predecessor on the Arkham House's list—Ray Bradbury's *Dark Carnival* (1947)—but it was a highly creditable contribution to weird fiction. Not surprisingly, it was favorably reviewed by Robert Bloch in the *Arkham Sampler*. In some senses the review is nothing more than a "puff," given that it was a review of an Arkham House book by another Arkham House author in a magazine published by Arkham House; nevertheless, Bloch makes some insightful comments, providing an accurate impressionistic account of the essence of Jacobi's weird work:

> Carl Jacobi's concept is, at first glance, the velvet pall, the midnight moor, the unlit house, the *mysterioso* chord on the piano—in a word, the conventional, almost traditional "stage effect" or backdrop for the saga of the supernatural. It is the inevitable background for the mysterious veiled woman in "Revelations in Black," the genius recently released from the asylum in "The Satanic Piano," and the diabolical stranger of "The Coach on the Ring." Yet one cannot dismiss the Jacobi gambit quite this easily. On the surface, his use of "black" is proper to the atmosphere of "manors" and "lodgings" and "laboratories" so familiar to readers of the standard weird tale. But on closer examination of thematic material, one notes the peculiar correspondence of darkness in the background and mental disorder in the characters who emerge from that background.[3]

During the rest of the decade, Jacobi continued to write and publish pulp fiction as much as time allowed: he had four stories in *Weird Tales* during the period 1947–50 and also continued to publish adventure, weird menace, and science fiction stories in other venues. He even tried his hand at mainstream and romance tales, publishing one of the latter ("Her Impulse Day") in the *Toronto Star Weekly* (May 21, 1949). Subsequently reprinted in New Zealand and also translated into French, this single story "has brought in to date more money than anything I've written."[4]

But the market for pulp fiction was dying. Increased paper costs and the rise of the paperback book were spelling doom for many pulp magazines, and

---

3. Robert Bloch, "Through a Glass, Darkly," *Arkham Sampler* 1, No. 1 (Winter 1948): 84.

4. Letter to August Derleth (March 26, 1956); quoted in R. Dixon Smith, *Lost in the Rentharpian Hills: Spanning the Decades with Carl Jacobi* (Bowling Green, OH: Bowling Green State University Popular Press, 1985), 40.

the flagship journal of supernatural fiction, *Weird Tales*, finally ceased publication in 1954 after thirty-one years. Its demise led to Jacobi's plangent comment: "I simply don't know what to write or whom to write for."[5]

But he soldiered on. If weird fiction no longer had a prominent periodical, the burgeoning field of science fiction might still be open to the kind of work Jacobi wanted to write. He published several tales in *Fantastic Universe* in the 1950s and also landed stories in *Fantastic Story Magazine*, *Imagination*, *Cosmos Science Fiction and Fantasy*, and Donald A. Wollheim's anthology series, *The Avon Fantasy Reader*; he even published a few detective stories in the *Saint Detective Magazine*. But numerous other stories were rejected or abandoned before completion.

Jacobi had suggested a second volume of his stories to Derleth as early as 1953; but this was the very time when Arkham House, itself facing difficulties because of the shrinking market for purely weird fiction and competition from other small presses in the fantasy field, was going through a virtually moribund period. In that entire decade it published only fourteen titles, several of which were slim poetry volumes. Things picked up for Arkham House in the 1960s, in part through the fees generated from licensing film versions of some Lovecraft stories. Jacobi's second volume, *Portraits in Moonlight*, appeared in 1964, with dust jacket art by Frank Utpatel. It was a slimmer volume than *Revelations in Black* and, in spite of its modest print run (1987 copies), it remained in print well into the 1970s. As with its predecessor, Jacobi meticulously revised his stories for the book appearance.

In the 1960s Jacobi's work appeared in several of the original anthologies that Derleth prepared for Arkham House, from *Dark Mind, Dark Heart* (1962) to *Dark Things* (1971). He had only three stories in magazines in the 1960s and four in the 1970s. One of the former was a reprint ("Moss Island," in *Amazing Stories*, February 1966); but one of the latter, "The Music Lover," appeared in Sam Moskowitz's revival of *Weird Tales* (Summer 1974).

Changes were occurring in Jacobi's personal life as well. His father had died on March 4, 1955. Then, in a matter of weeks, his aunt, Laura Emilie Jacobi, died on October 13, 1965, followed by his mother on October 22. August Derleth's death on July 4, 1971, was also a blow. By this time Jacobi, no longer faced with the need to support his parents, gave up his job at Honeywell. He carried on with writing, this time focusing on longer narratives. He had made several attempts to write a full-length novel—either adventure or historical or science fiction—throughout the 1940s and 1950s, but could never hit upon a plot that would allow for extended development. Then, in

---

5. Letter to August Derleth (March 26, 1956); quoted in Smith, 42.

1967–69, he managed to complete a 50,000-word juvenile mystery/adventure novel, *The Jade Scorpion;* but although it was sent to his agent, Kirby McCauley, it did not find a publisher and remains in manuscript.

Health difficulties plagued Jacobi in the 1970s; and to add insult to injury, his house was burgled while he was in the hospital, and many of his pulp magazines and other paraphernalia were taken. But Jacobi was surely cheered by the appearance of his third Arkham House volume, *Disclosures in Scarlet* (1972). The book had been planned in consultation with Derleth, and it was one of the first to see print after the latter's death. It featured another dust jacket by Frank Utpatel, and its print run was 3127 copies. This volume contained a much greater proportion of science fiction than its two predecessors, reflecting Jacobi's shift to that genre in recent decades.

While he continued publish tales in professional venues in the 1980s, ranging from Lin Carter's paperback *Weird Tales* volumes to Stuart David Schiff's *Whispers* anthologies, Jacobi was also reduced to publishing supernatural and weird menace stories in fanzines edited by Robert M. Price, from *Crypt of Cthulhu* to *Shudder Stories.* He was no doubt gratified to see the publication of an array of his earlier tales in the volume *East of Samarinda* (1989), edited by R. Dixon Smith, who had become his leading biographer and critic; *Smoke of the Snake* (1994), also edited by Smith, contained more recent work, including several unpublished stories.[6] His final years were marred by serious illness, and he died on August 25, 1997.

Jacobi's early weird tales exhibit not only an ability to rework traditional supernatural motifs but also to expand the scope of the weird by the use of innovative subject-matter and treatment. "The Coach on the Ring" is one of the earliest and most effective of his tales using the tried-and-true supernatural revenge motif. Here a goldsmith whose daughter was killed by a haughty nobleman exacts his vengeance long after his death. A somewhat similar revenge traversing the centuries is the focus of "The King and the Knave."

Somewhat more conventional, both in motif and in setting, are "The Cane," an effective psychic possession narrative, and "The Spectral Pistol," a skillful tale of a werewolf. There is a vague trace of the morbidity of Ambrose Bierce in "The Last Drive," where the loathsomeness of being in proximity with a corpse is etched; and Jacobi mingles weirdness with the historical tale in "A Pair of Swords."

---

6. As early as 1971, Jacobi had begun depositing manuscripts of his published and unpublished stories in the Special Collections division of the University of Minnesota Library.

"Revelations in Black"—the title story of Jacobi's first collection of tales with Arkham House (1947)—is a deftly executed vampire tale. Initially it appears to focus on an antique dealer, Giovanni Larla—reprised from an earlier hard-boiled detective story, "The Masked Orange," where Larla is ultimately identified as a murderer—who is in possession of a trilogy of books written by his dead brother; but the focus gradually shifts to the first-person narrator's increasing obsession with a woman in black whom he meets in a secluded garden, and who proves to be a vampire. Jacobi later gave an account of the tale's inspiration:

> . . . I was driving down the Rockford road west of Minneapolis; it was a beautiful moonlit night and the countryside was bright as day. Suddenly I came upon a farm which riveted my attention. Three life-sized statues stood at attention by the roadside. In the farmyard was what appeared to be an old stone fountain with images carved on its sides. And on either side of the farmhouse door like silent sentries stood two more life-sized statues. Extending to the west end of the property for apparently no reason at all was a brick wall, the top of which was ornamented with more carvings. In the moonlight the scene made a profound impression on me, and I gave no thought to the fact that the farm in all probability had been taken over by someone whose former occupation had been a stonecutter. I only know that the scene served as the germ for what was to be perhaps my most successful fantasy story "Revelations in Black."[7]

"Revelations in Black" may well be Jacobi's most successful tale in the old-time Gothic mode, but "Mive" is unquestionably a superlative example of the pure "weird tale," where the focus is strictly on the weird phenomenon, with relatively little focus on the human characters or on the development of an elaborate narrative. This account of an enormous, carnivorous butterfly—a creature ordinarily associated with ethereal beauty—is grimly effective as a tale of topographical horror:

> A wave of warm humid air, heavy with the odor of growth, swept over me as though I had suddenly opened the door of some monstrous hothouse. Great masses of vines with fat creeping tendrils hung from the cypress trees. Razor-edged reeds, marsh grass, long waving cattails, swamp vegetation of a thousand kinds flourished here with luxuriant abundance. I went on along the shore; the water lapped steadily the sodden earth at my feet, oily-looking water, grim-looking, reflecting a sullen and overcast sky.

---

7. Jacobi, "The Derleth Connection" (1981); quoted in Smith, 16–17.

Not entirely dissimilar is "Moss Island," where a researcher conducting a geological survey comes upon a substance found in a rare moss that has the ability to induce spectacularly rapid growth; and the protagonist is horrified by the result: "Like an octopus the tentacles were clawing the sky, engulfing the whole island."

"The Satanic Piano" is one of several tales that seek to embody weirdness in music. Here Jacobi devises the notion of a piano that can automatically translate a composer's thoughts into notes. The piano's inventor provides a quasi-scientific rationale for the instrument:

> "Call it telepathy, if you need a term, but my postulation was that each thought, each idea, and particularly each strain of melody which passes through the brain sets up a distinct field of motion as existent as the field of an electro magnet, and that if an instrument could be made delicate enough, it would seize those waves and transform them into their actual sound."

"A Study in Darkness" makes use of a "color-music" machine; but the true focus of this tale is the metaphysical and moral overtones of colors, as a crazed researcher believes that black is the essence of all evil.

"Mive" introduces us to the "Rentharpian hills," an imaginary realm whose precise location in the United States is never clarified. In "Moss Island" we find that there is a University of Rentharp. It is unclear whether Jacobi was attempting to establish a recurring cycle of tales in the manner of Lovecraft's Arkham, Innsmouth, and Dunwich, as this "Rentharpian mythos" is never truly fleshed out in the stories where the locale is mentioned. It is also peculiar that Jacobi set so many tales in England, which he apparently never visited; but it is likely that he was seeking to draw upon a civilization exponentially older than what could be found in his native country, as in "The Face in the Wind," a gripping tale that not only is set in an old English manor house but that succeeds in evoking terror from the Greek myth of the harpy.

Given his interest in exotic locales, it is no surprise that Jacobi often set his tales in the East, which for Western readers of that era still constituted a land of sinister mystery. The non-weird terror tale "Smoke of the Snake" is prototypical, with its evocation of Chinese opium dens and the ancient wisdom of the East. Borneo became a particular obsession with Jacobi, to the extent that he actually corresponded with officials on that remote island, receiving "geographic information, ethnic lore and a wealth of detail"[8] after many months. Borneo plays a significant role in "The Tomb from Beyond,"

---

8. Smith, 23.

where an ancient civilization, named Dras, is the focus. The telescope featured in "Sagasta's Last" has apparently gained its peculiar qualities by virtue of its being constructed from sand taken from the Middle Eastern realm of Kurdistan.

A number of Jacobi's tales feature imaginary books, either printed or in manuscript. It is not entirely clear whether this motif is derived from Lovecraft and his disciples, who made liberal use of such fictitious tomes of occult lore as the *Necronomicon* and *De Vermis Mysteriis*. Jacobi stated late in life that "I suppose most fantasy writers have at one time or another created the title of a book to promote some theory of witchcraft or supernatural postulation,"[9] and on occasion he cited a book invented by some member of the Lovecraft circle. But his imaginary books are indeed devised for specific purposes in the tales in which they are cited. One of the books most often cited is Richard Verstegan's *Restitution of Decayed Intelligence*—which sounds like a clever creation indeed! But this is in fact an actual book, although Jacobi has misspelled the author's name.[10] The title of the manuscript book cited in "Revelations in Black," *Five Unicorns and a Pearl*, is strikingly evocative.

Jacobi exhibits impressive erudition in all the subjects that serve as the basis of his tales, ranging from the different kinds of moss in "Moss Island" to the historical weapons in "A Pair of Swords" and "The Spectral Pistol." His lifelong devotion to classical music yields impressive results in "The Satanic Piano" and other tales.

Jacobi's later stories reflect his abiding fascination with exotic locales as well as with traditional weird motifs—but are also leavened by his increasing interest in the motifs and conceptions of science fiction, lending them a distinctiveness that sets them apart from his earlier work. "Carnaby's Fish" is a vivid recounting of the lorelei myth, as Jacobi effectively brings out both the seductiveness and the baleful nature of these sirenlike female entities. "The Corbie Door" mingles the haunted house motif with that of psychic possession—and may also reflect Jacobi's fondness for Lovecraft's "The Rats in the Walls," as it echoes that story's English setting, its focus on a sinister family history, and other elements.

The theme of supernatural revenge finds powerful expression in "The Lorenzo Watch" as well as in "The Spanish Camera." In the latter tale it is that camera that appears to possess the power of killing any person whose picture

---

9. Letter to R. Dixon Smith (May 23, 1982); quoted in Smith, 62.

10. Richard Verstegen (1550?–1640), *Restitution of Decayed Intelligence, in Antiquities* (1605). Some editions actually spell the author's name (a pseudonym of Richard Rowland) as "Verstegan."

it takes, as the unwitting owner of the camera discovers to her dismay. A revenant appears in hideous fashion to seek revenge on her murderer in "The Digging at Pistol Key." This story is one of several that draw upon the residue of weirdness that Jacobi found in the Caribbean with its legends of *obeah* (witchcraft) and voodoo. "Incident at Galloping Horse" is set on Tortola, one of the British Virgin Islands. On the surface this tale also seems to be an account of a revenant—a woman whose death was caused by jealousy reappears, riding a horse and leaping over a cliff—but there is a further twist in that her appearance triggers an analogous event in the present day.

"Matthew South and Company" is another tale set in the Caribbean, this time on Trinidad; but its focus is on the title character, who has adopted that name because he dislikes his given name, Henry Walters. When he encounters other men at a club with such names as Philip Spayne and James K. Vermont—names that Walters had also created as possible pseudonyms (these were, in fact. names that Jacobi had considered using as pseudonyms for some of his tales)—the weirdness begins. In the end the tale is chiefly one of psychological terror, although Jacobi suggests voodoo as the source of Walters's mental aberration.

A difference in tone can be detected in "The La Prello Paper," where a man who scorns the present finds himself drifting increasingly into the past. There is a wistful pathos in the story that contrasts sharply with the general run of Jacobi's weird tales. The same can be said for the much later tale "The Unpleasantness at Carver House." This brooding, atmospheric narrative suggests an unthinkable psychological anomalies in its central character, bringing to mind such works as William Faulkner's "A Rose for Emily" or Robert Bloch's *Psycho*. This tale is set in Minnesota (the title character's name comes from Carver county, a region west of the Twin Cities), and we can see Jacobi using his native land in several other stories. The actual locale of "Witches in the Cornfield" is not specified; but this evocative tale of scarecrows, set up on properties on either side of a county road, reflects Jacobi's actual witnessing of this scenario in rural Minnesota. "The Singleton Barrier" also has a Minnesota setting, although it is essentially a tale of gypsy witchcraft. "Kincaid's Car," like "The La Prello Paper," has something of a Bradburyesque atmosphere of nostalgia and pathos, but resolves into a cynical tale expressing scorn of the moral and intellectual capacities of the entire human race.

Two tales of sea horror are of note. "The Aquarium" tells of a house in England that has an enormous aquarium in the library—a relic of the previous owner's fascination with deep-sea shells. The original version of this tale had explicitly Lovecraftian elements, but August Derleth had Jacobi remove them for its appearance in *Dark Mind, Dark Heart*.[11] "Hamadryad" takes us on board a vessel where a Malay woman may have the power to control cobras and make them carry out her murderous wishes.

Jacobi's abiding love of music is reflected in "The Music Lover," although here the focus is on the possible supernatural manifestations caused by vibrations from a highly advanced stereo system. "Chameleon Town" is a grim tale of topographical horror posing the question of whether the town in question actually exists or only its "psychic residue." Finally, "The Elcar Special" proposes the notion of a supernatural car—anticipating by several years Stephen King's extensive working out of this idea in *Christine* (1983).

Several of these tales return obsessively to the notion of forbidden books, and Jacobi increasingly draws upon Lovecraft—or his disciples—for inspiration. "The Corbie Door" provocatively cites "*Loreleysage in Dichtung und Musik, Mysteries of the Sea*, by Cornelius Van de Mar. *The History of Atlantis*, by Lewis Spence"—in other words, two imaginary books and one real one. In "The Corbie Door" we find, in addition to one more citation of Richard Verstegan's *Restitution of Decayed Intelligence* (a real book), "Herzog's *Furchtbare Kulte*, [and] an incomplete and heavily expurgated edition of deKorlette's *Cultes des Goules*." The author of the latter is usually cited in Lovecraftian fiction as the Comte d'Erlette, a clear reference to the founder of Arkham House.

Jacobi's greatest innovation as a weird writer is the gradual way in which he introduces the weird in a meticulously depicted locale and the almost blandly realistic characters with which he populates his tales. A late essay articulates this principle:

> To me there is one unbreakable rule in successful fiction writing. If your chief character's actions are fantastic or removed from reality, then your background should be commonplace. If your backdrop is a strange world, a far distant planet, or an antediluvian period of the Earth's past, then your protagonist should be an ordinary fellow with ordinary traits and characteristics. If you have both in the same story (as some sword and sorcery tales do), it is difficult for your reader to have something which he can relate to.[12]

This focus on the "ordinary fellow" demonstrates how Jacobi anticipated the work of Ray Bradbury, Richard Matheson, and Charles Beaumont, whose work of the 1940s through the 1960s laid the groundwork for the bestselling

---

11. The original version, with the Lovecraftian elements retained, appeared in *Fantasy Crossroads* No. 7 (February 1976): 18–22.

12. Jacobi, "The Derleth Connection"; quoted in Smith, 66–67.

horror novels of the 1970s and 1980s. It is precisely in this aspect that Jacobi constitutes the link between Lovecraftian cosmic horror and the mundane realism of Stephen King and his followers.

A random line in "The Unpleasantness at Carver House"—"What a strange creature man is, I thought, to create terrors and set them upon himself"—vividly conveys the essence of Carl Jacobi's weird work, where the simplest objects of ordinary life can become objects of horror and strangeness. But the supernatural phenomena in his tales almost always serve a broader aesthetic purpose, underscoring human weakness, hypocrisy, treachery, and greed. Along with his meticulous craftsmanship, it is this emphasis on the symbolic function of the supernatural that sets Jacobi's work apart from its now largely forgotten congeners in the realm of pulp fiction. And it is these qualities that will allow his work to endure well into the future.

III. H. P. Lovecraft and His Disciples

Lovecraft and the Gothic

In *The Supernatural in Fiction* (1952), Peter Penzoldt stated that Lovecraft was "too well read." By this he meant that on occasion Lovecraft's tales were so heavily reliant on their literary antecedents that it was sometimes difficult to detect what was genuinely "Lovecraft" and what was some deliberate or unconscious pastiche. Penzoldt's formulation is considerably overstated: most of Lovecraft's borrowings from his predecessors consist in surface details and rarely affect the thematic or philosophical essence of the tales, which remain emphatically "Lovecraftian" even when he is being most derivative.

Those who contend that Lovecraft was too influenced by the literary heritage of Gothic fiction have to contend with the fact that in many instances, he did not read many celebrated authors and works of Gothic literature until a surprisingly late stage in his career. Lovecraft came upon Ambrose Bierce and Lord Dunsany only in 1919; Arthur Machen in 1923; Algernon Blackwood in 1924; and M. R. James in 1925. Many older works of Gothic fiction were somewhat hastily and incompletely absorbed in 1925–26 while he was doing research for his landmark treatise "Supernatural Horror in Literature" (1927). In one striking instance, Lovecraft devoted several pages of this book to a discussion of Charles Maturin's *Melmoth the Wanderer* (1820), but later admitted that he had never read the whole of this immense novel, but only two extracts of it found in anthologies. The dominant literary influence on Lovecraft's creative work is Edgar Allan Poe, his "God of Fiction," whom he read as early as the age of eight. It could well be said that Lovecraft spent a good part of his career in absorbing—perhaps even overcoming or surmounting—the Poe influence; he may never have fully done so.

Lovecraft was, therefore, among the most diligent Gothic writers in ferreting out the meritorious work of his predecessors. From childhood onward he read all manner of weird writing, from dime novels to the pulp magazines (beginning with the Munsey magazines of the turn of the century and moving on to *Weird Tales*, *Strange Tales*, and even such crude specimens as *Ghost Stories* and *Terror Tales*) to the loftiest contributions of Poe, Machen, and Dunsany. A variety of little-known works—ranging from Irvin S. Cobb's "The Unbroken Chain" (1923) to H. B. Drake's *The Shadowy Thing* (1928) to Hans Heinz Ewers's "The Spider" (1931)—demonstrably influenced some of Lovecraft's great-est tales, although again usually in superficial details of plot.

Lovecraft, then, approached the writing of Gothic fiction with the atti-tude of both an appreciator and a critic. Perhaps he felt that some themes, elements, and plot devices had not been used to full advantage in prior work, although with his habitual modesty he rarely said so explicitly. What he did say, repeatedly, was that many of the conventional staples of Gothic fiction—the ghost, the vampire, the haunted house—had, by his day, become stale and void of imaginative resonance because modern advances in science had shown them to be merely the delusions of ignorance. Some of these elements might still retain a residual power because they drew upon the deepest fears of the human psyche, but they would have to be updated—or, at the very least, expressed more subtly—if they were to be effective in the age of Einstein, Freud, and Bertrand Russell. It was to this kind of updating that Lovecraft devoted the bulk of his career. In so doing, he pushed the envelope of Gothi-cism so far that it approached the realm of science fiction, but at the same time it remained true to the Gothic impulse that gave it birth. Three domi-nant themes drawn from Gothic fiction used frequently by Lovecraft, the haunted castle, the Faustian man, and psychic possession, can perhaps most fruitfully be studied here to display Lovecraft's expansion of the form.

The very first tale of Lovecraft's maturity, "The Tomb" (1917), exhibits not one but two haunted dwellings, the tomb itself, which the protagonist, Jervas Dudley, finds insidiously fascinating, and the lavish eighteenth-century mansion that he believes himself to be occupying during his dreams or hallu-cinations. In the end, this tale proves to be one of psychic possession: Dudley is the virtual twin of an eighteenth-century ancestor, Jervas Hyde, who had perished in the mansion and was therefore denied the chance to be buried in his ancestral tomb.

"The Picture in the House" (1920) finds horror in a lonely house in the remote backwoods of New England, where an ignorant, unkempt individual has prolonged his life unnaturally by means of cannibalism. Perhaps proto-typically Gothic is the celebrated "The Outsider" (1921), in which the hapless protagonist strives valiantly to escape from what he fancies to be the dark, dismal, mirrorless castle of his birth and to reach the brilliantly lighted man-sion where a lavish party is being held. Although the story borrows heavily from Poe's "Berenice" and "The Masque of the Red Death," it nevertheless plays effectively upon the standard contrast of darkness (ignorance) and light (knowledge): the self-knowledge the outsider gains when he sees his hideous form in a mirror is not the sort he had hoped to obtain. Interesting as these early tales are, they do little to expand the bounds of traditional Gothicism, offering only dim hints of future development.

It is therefore something of a surprise that as early as 1923, Lovecraft wrote one of his most artistically finished tales, "The Rats in the Walls," which might be thought of as a kind of combined homage to Poe's "Fall of the House of Usher" and Hawthorne's *House of the Seven Gables*, which Lovecraft believed to be "New England's greatest contribution to weird literature." Lovecraft still looks to the past, but he does so as much as a scientist as an antiquarian. The call of ancestry is at the heart of the tale: when Walter de la Poer discovers that his ancestors had been a band of cannibals, he immediately descends the evolutionary scale and becomes a cannibal himself. This climax could not have been conceived by one who did not know of Darwin.

"The Shunned House" (1924) is even more interesting from this perspective. It too, on the surface, seems conventional: the death of a werewolf's descendant in the seventeenth century leads to two centuries of mysterious deaths in a house in Providence, Rhode Island, until the narrator and his uncle eventually put an end to the horror. But consider how Lovecraft makes clear that "the house was never regarded by the solid part of the community as in any real sense 'haunted'"; it was merely thought to be "unlucky." Consider, too, how the entity is dispelled—not by an incantation, but by being doused with acid. But most remarkable is a striking passage in the middle of the tale in which the narrator ponders the true causes of the entity's pervasive influence. "Such a thing was surely not a physical or biochemical impossibility in the light of a newer science which includes the theories of relativity and intra-atomic action." Here is Lovecraft appealing to Einstein and Planck to account for a gelatinous vampire in the cellar of a New England wood-frame house.

The Case of Charles Dexter Ward (written in 1927, but not published during his lifetime), Lovecraft's greatest homage to the heritage of the Gothic, is considerably more conventional, and in terms of setting—the bungalow where the seventeenth-century wizard Joseph Curwen conducts his nameless experiments—we are not very far from the Gothic castle of tradition. But the novel's interest clearly lies elsewhere. It was shortly after writing this tale that Lovecraft began that exhaustive exploration of the terrors and wonders of his native region—fleetingly hinted at in "The Picture in the House" and "The Festival" (1923)—that would represent his ultimate treatment of the topos of the "haunted locale." In tale after tale—for example, "The Colour out of Space" (1927), "The Dunwich Horror" (1928), "The Whisperer in Darkness" (1930), "The Shadow over Innsmouth" (1931), and "The Thing on the Doorstep" (1933)—it is not a single dwelling that is haunted, but an entire city or countryside. Again, the haunting is not the product of mere ghosts or ghouls, but of entities from "outside": the meteorite that lands on a hapless farmer's land in "The Colour out of Space," producing effects strikingly similar to radiation poisoning; the twin offspring of a backwoods farm girl and the cosmic entity Yog-Sothoth, who strew death and madness in "The Dunwich Horror"; the "fungi from Yuggoth," dwelling on the farthest planet in the solar system, who have established an outpost in Vermont in "The Whisperer in Darkness"; and the unholy unions between hybrid fish-frogs and local residents that corrupt the entire town of Innsmouth in "The Shadow over Innsmouth." "The Dreams in the Witch House" (1932) perhaps signalises Lovecraft's attempt to have his cake and eat it too: in this relatively unsuccessful tale, we see the tug-of-war that was continually waged in the mind of a man who nurtured himself on the historic and aesthetic fruits of the past (colonial architecture, the literature of Greece, Rome, and Augustan England) but who also sought to keep abreast of the newest advances in science and philosophy. In this tale, we seem to be presented with a conventional haunted house and a conventional witch; but the witch, it proves, can traverse the fourth dimension by her mastery of mathematics. Lovecraft's depiction of "hyperspace" as a "bewildering succession of geometrical forms" is a triumph of the imagination, but he lapses into conventionality (particularly curious in an atheist) by having the witch frightened off by a crucifix. Lovecraft cannot decide whether he is writing a typical Gothic tale or a tale of science fiction. As a result, neither facet of the story rings true.

The age-old theme of the individual who strives to break the barriers of human limitations was of compelling fascination for Lovecraft, since in many ways this quest echoed his own goals as a writer of weird fiction. In "Notes on Writing Weird Fiction" (1933), he maintained, "I choose weird stories because they suit my inclination best—one of my strongest and most persistent wishes being to achieve, momentarily, the illusion of some strange suspension or violation of the galling limitations of time, space, and natural law, which forever imprison us and frustrate our curiosity about the infinite cosmic spaces beyond the radius of our sight and analysis." It is scarcely to be wondered, then, that Lovecraft reacts with a mixture of horror and fascination to his own depictions of those lonely seekers after unholy knowledge.

Almost a caricature of the mad scientist is Crawford Tillinghast in "From Beyond" (1920), whose histrionic utterances make him a parody of himself. Nevertheless, his quest to harness all space and time by means of a machine that expands the bounds of human sense perception is typical. More subtle is the nebulous figure (whether a figment of the narrator's imagination or not) in "Hypnos" (1923), who appears to have "designs which involved the rulership of the visible universe and more; designs whereby the earth and the stars would move at his command, and the destinies of all living things be his." Such an appalling quest carries its rightful doom.

The Case of Charles Dexter Ward presents two such figures in the baleful seventeenth-century alchemist Joseph Curwen and the guileless twentieth-century student Charles Dexter Ward, Curwen's lineal descendant. Curwen's plan, it transpires, is to capture the "essential saltes" of the great minds of human history, and with this combined knowledge Curwen hopes to gain such power as might endanger "all civilisation, all natural law, perhaps even the fate of the solar system and the universe." Ward, for his part, represents a benign pursuit of knowledge: he has unwittingly been drawn into following Curwen's footsteps to the point of resurrecting Curwen himself from his own essential saltes, but Lovecraft holds him blameless. When Ward writes, "I have brought to light a monstrous abnormality, but I did it for the sake of knowledge," it is Ward's (and Lovecraft's) fully adequate moral justification for his actions. Curwen himself, although he seems cut from the standard Gothic mould, proves to be more a scientist than a wizard: we are led to believe that the perfecting of these "essential saltes" is really more a matter of implementing the proper chemical and biological formulas than of muttering the proper spells.

The kind of unintentional gathering of information engaged in by Ward, what the narrator of "The Call of Cthulhu" (1926) terms "the piecing together of dissociated knowledge," is exhibited by several Lovecraft protagonists, from Henry Akeley in "The Whisperer in Darkness" (who stumbles, to his peril, upon evidences of the fungi from Yuggoth) to Walter Gilman, the student in "The Dreams in the Witch House," of whom Lovecraft rather wryly states, "Possibly Gilman ought not to have studied so hard." Quite otherwise is the Whateley family in "The Dunwich Horror," who pore through tomes like the *Necronomicon* in search of the formulas that will bring down alien entities from another dimension to plague this earth. Asenath Waite in "The Thing on the Doorstep" is similarly motivated; incensed at being in a woman's body, she uses some kind of witchcraft to usurp the body of her husband Edward Derby and fulfil her ill-defined but clearly nefarious goals.

To Lovecraft, the perennial student, knowledge is power. Whether it is used for good or ill depends upon the morality of the individual. But in nearly every case, that knowledge is knowledge of the hard sciences—mathematics, physics, chemistry. In his early stories, Lovecraft's protagonists pursue knowledge or other activities in histrionic ways that point to their own mental aberration: the "neurotic virtuosi" who rob graves for aesthetic pleasure in "The Hound" (1922) and the unnamed narrator of "The Lurking Fear" (1922) who seeks out horrors because of a "love of the grotesque and the terrible" are virtual caricatures of this character type. But his later protagonists—

all sober, sceptical men of science—augment the horror of the scenario by their very reluctance to accept the implications of their meticulously researched findings. In this sense, Lovecraft's Antarctic novel *At the Mountains of Madness* (1931) is the pinnacle of his achievement.

Possession by the devil is something that the unbeliever Lovecraft could scarcely credit, so he had to employ this topos in more ingenious, and more modern, ways. In some ways, this trope fuses with that of the Faust figure in that it is ordinarily a man (or, in rare instances, a woman) of exceptional strength of will who is able to exert his or her psychological dominance over another. Straightforward psychic possession occurs in "The Tomb" and, perhaps, in *The Case of Charles Dexter Ward*, in which Curwen may have exercised some kind of influence that led Ward to follow in his footsteps. But a more interesting kind of possession occurs in two other stories, "The Thing on the Doorstep" and "The Shadow out of Time" (1934–35). In the former, Asenath Waite can effect a kind of mind exchange by hypnosis; indeed, she herself is actually the mind of her father, Ephraim Waite, occupying his own daughter's body. Far more interesting is the mind exchange performed by the supremely rational alien entities called the Great Race in "The Shadow out of Time," who spend their entire existence in casting their minds forward and backward in time, temporarily occupying the bodies of a variety of other species throughout the cosmos and thereby learning all they can about the civilisations of their mental captives. In turn, the minds of these individuals are lodged in the bodies of the Great Race, where they write accounts of their own times for the Great Race's immense archives. Although this mental exchange is presented as initially traumatic, it is ultimately seen as benign and even imaginatively liberating. Who would not wish to be able to scan the entire history of the cosmos, written from the vantage point of all the different species that have occupied and will occupy it in the past and future?

Lovecraft may have said, as late as 1930, that "the past is *real*—it is *all there is*," but he also looked forward to a time when science had definitively overthrown primitive superstition. As a writer of weird fiction, he knew that he could not entirely jettison the rich heritage of Gothic literature, but he also felt that in the light of modern advances in science, "the time has come when the normal revolt against time, space, and matter must assume a form not overtly incompatible with what is known of reality—when it must be gratified by images forming *supplements* rather than *contradictions* of the visible and mensurable universe." Throughout the twenty years of his literary career, he sought as best he could to achieve this difficult goal and in so doing transformed Gothic fiction into something that could be both imaginatively and intellectually satisfying in the modern age.

Poe and Lovecraft

Edgar Allan Poe (1809–1849) and H. P. Lovecraft (1890–1937) are the two leading writers of weird or supernatural fiction in American literature, and perhaps in all literature. Both emerged at critical junctures in the history of the genre. Poe's earliest writings in the 1830s were published during the waning stages of the Gothic movement, initiated when Horace Walpole wrote *The Castle of Otranto* (1764) and inspired legions of imitators and successors, including Ann Radcliffe, Matthew Gregory Lewis, Charles Robert Maturin, and Mary Shelley. Poe either discarded or radically refashioned the cumbersome "dramatic paraphernalia" (as Lovecraft called it)[1] of the Gothic novel and focused intensely on the psychology of terror. He also sensed that fear is best conveyed in short compass, and all but invented the short story as a literary mode, focusing on the "unity of effect" and emphasizing the importance of every episode, every paragraph, even every word for the story's dénouement.

Lovecraft, beginning his career almost seventy years after Poe's death, and after weird fiction had definitively established itself as a viable genre in the work of such writers as J. Sheridan Le Fanu, Ambrose Bierce, Arthur Machen, Lord Dunsany, Algernon Blackwood, M. R. James, and many others, came to the realization that weird fiction must strike a new path away from the already stale vampires, werewolves, and ghosts that had populated the field for generations. Contemporary findings in science—especially physics, biology, chemistry, and anthropology—had rendered many of these tropes so implausible that, in Lovecraft's view, they had become unusable in serious literature. Accordingly, Lovecraft felt that only the boundless universe—the nature and extent of which had barely begun to be charted by the human intellect—contained sufficient reservoirs of mystery that it could serve as the aesthetic foundation of a weird tale. In the course of his brief literary career, Lovecraft definitively established the tale of "cosmic horror" as a central component of the weird tale, and it remains his signature contribution to literature.

---

1. H. P. Lovecraft, "Supernatural Horror in Literature" (1927), in *The Annotated Supernatural Horror in Literature*, ed. S. T. Joshi (New York: Hippocampus Press, 2nd ed. 2012), 34.

Poe and Lovecraft share a number of common features, some superficial and some much more profound. Both their careers lasted less than two decades; both produced a relatively slim body of fiction, confined almost entirely to the short story; both devoted much time to essays and criticism, and in their essays and reviews they laid down important principles for the kind of literature they wished to write. In their personalities, they tended to be solitary, withdrawn, and not entirely comfortable with women; they both claimed extensive but largely self-taught learning; and poverty dogged both their lives, manifestly contributing to their early deaths. Perhaps as a result of their distinctive personalities, as well as the compelling nature of their literary work, both have become recognizable icons who appeal to a wide array of readers throughout the world.

Lovecraft had a deep and abiding respect for Poe, referring to him famously as his "God of Fiction."[2] His initial reading of Poe at the age of eight effected a revolution in his aesthetic interests. Having previously become enamored of such things as Greek mythology and the *Arabian Nights*, he stumbled upon Poe and was never the same again: "Then I struck EDGAR ALLAN POE! It was my downfall, and at the age of eight I saw the blue firmament of Argos and Sicily darkened by the miasmal exhalations of the tomb!"[3] As late as 1935, Lovecraft was admitting the Poe influence, although interestingly enough he denied a correspondent's assertions that his prose style was exclusively modeled on Poe's. In commenting on a story by Richard F. Searight that some had felt was written in Lovecraft's idiom, Lovecraft stated:

> . . . I can't see this in any marked degree. Rather would I say that you have simply chosen the same general cast of language which I prefer—but which hundreds of others, long before I was born, have preferred. Many think I have derived this style exclusively from Poe—which (despite the strong influence of Poe on me) is another typical mistake of uninformed modernism. This style is no especial attribute of Poe, but is simply *the major traditional way of handling English narrative prose.* If I picked it up through any especial influence, that influence is probably the practice of the 18th century rather than Poe . . .[4]

---

2. H. P. Lovecraft, letter to Rheinhart Kleiner (2 February 1916); *Selected Letters*, ed. August Derleth, Donald Wandrei, and James Turner (Sauk City, WI: Arkham House, 1965–76; 5 vols.), 1.20.

3. H. P. Lovecraft, letter to Bernard Austin Dwyer (3 March 1927); *Selected Letters*, 2.109.

4. H. P. Lovecraft, letter to Richard F. Searight (4 November 1935); *Letters to Richard F. Searight*, ed. S. T. Joshi and David E. Schultz (West Warwick, RI: Necronomicon

Lovecraft may be protesting a bit too much: it is difficult to deny that his earlier work in particular manifestly echoes the overheated rhetoric and occasionally esoteric language that render Poe's prose instantly recognizable. It might well be said that Lovecraft, initially overwhelmed by the Poe influence, both in prose and in many other elements of plot and motif, worked hard to overcome that influence and become, as it were, his own writer. That he had done so by the 1930s, creating a distinctive fusion of Poesque prose and scientific precision while at the same time effecting a fusion between traditional weird fiction and the burgeoning genre of science fiction, is undeniable.

It is remarkable that a volume treating of the interrelations between these two giants of weird fiction has not been assembled before now. The influence of Poe on Lovecraft is of course unmistakable and has been discussed in a scattered and unsystematic manner by many critics; but it perhaps required Lovecraft's definitive ascent into the American and world literary canons to underscore the point that Lovecraft was not merely a perennial student of his great predecessor but one who—however much he himself, in his excessive humility, would deny it—in many ways has achieved equal standing with Poe as a literary figure. Indeed, the opening essay in this book, by Brian Johnson, focuses precisely on Harold Bloom's concept of the "anxiety of influence" as it applies to these two writers, asserting that some of the early tales of Lovecraft that have been criticized as being slavishly Poesque, such as "The Tomb" and "The Outsider," feature considerably more originality than even their author was prepared to admit.

Lovecraft readily adopted Poe's critical theory of the "unity of effect," extending it not merely to the short story but even to the novella and the short novel. This fruitful subject is treated perceptively in Dan Clinton's essay in this book. Many readers who come upon these two writers for the first time are struck with the numerous parallels in their treatment of weird motifs. Here, Juan L. Pérez-de-Luque examines the use of "vertical spaces" in Poe and Lovecraft—their use of attics, cellars, and dungeons to create a kind of architecture of terror in enclosed spaces. Robert H. Waugh examines both authors' incorporation of the feline species in some of their most noteworthy tales.

"Cosmic horror" is the one area where Lovecraft might seem to have surpassed his master. Michael Cisco's essay examines the extent to which this element also found its antecedent in Poe. For all the respect, even adulation, that Lovecraft evinced for Poe, there are signs that former felt that in the area of "cosmicism" he might be able to assert a kind of declaration of independ-

---

Press, 1992), 66.

ence from his predecessor. Although he wrote in 1930 to Clark Ashton Smith (another writer whose sense of the cosmic was very acute) that "In literature we can easily see the cosmic quality in Poe, Maturin, Dunsany, de la Mare, & Blackwood,"[5] a letter written only a few months before his death tells a somewhat different story: "What I miss in Machen, James, Dunsany, de la Mare, Shiel, and even Blackwood and Poe, is a sense of the *cosmic*. Dunsany—though he seldom adopts the darker and more serious approach—is the most cosmic of them all, but he gets only a little way."[6]

Lovecraft's most cosmic story is probably *At the Mountains of Madness*, a short novel of breathtaking scope that hints at the infinity of both space and time. The fact that it is set in Antarctica has drawn inevitable comparisons to Poe's only novel, *The Narrative of Arthur Gordon Pym*—a comparison that Lovecraft himself highlights by mentioning the work by name in his tale. Jeffrey Andrew Weinstock focuses on the possible racial elements underlying both works in his sensitive analysis. (I myself, however, have doubts as to whether racialism is a dominant feature in either Lovecraft's philosophical thought or his fiction. A fair reading of the totality of his work seems, in my mind, to militate against such a judgment.)

The one area where Lovecraft cannot be said to have come close to his mentor is poetry. Although Lovecraft's collected poetry dwarfs Poe's in output, few critics would place even the celebrated *Fungi from Yuggoth* sonnet series on a par with such imperishable works as "The Raven" or "Annabel Lee." Two papers here, however, find more virtues in Lovecraft's poetry—and greater parallels to Poe's—than many previous critics have done. Sławomir Studniarz conducts a sophisticated examination of the "crucial relation between sound and sense" in the poetry of the two writers, while Miles Tittle examines Lovecraft's "The Poe-et's Nightmare" in an effort to see exactly how the work of Poe might stand behind this long poem.

If there is any area in which both Poe and Lovecraft can be said to excel, it is in their all-pervasive influence on both the literature of the weird and its extensive expansion into the media. Four papers shed light on this broad issue. Murray Leeder studies Roger Corman's film *The Haunted Palace* (1963) for its fusion of Poesque and Lovecraftian elements; Alissa Burger dissects the unreliable narrator in Poe, Lovecraft, and Stephen King; Lee Woodard examines the use of crowds and cities in Poe, Lovecraft, and Thomas Ligotti; and Sean Moreland keenly ruminates on the influence of Poe and Lovecraft on a

---

5. H. P. Lovecraft, letter to Clark Ashton Smith (17 October 1930); *Selected Letters*, 3.196.

6. H. P. Lovecraft, letter to Fritz Leiber (9 November 1936); *Selected Letters*, 5.341.

writer who may well be their most distinguished contemporary disciple, Caitlin R. Kiernan.

The Swiss critic Peter Penzoldt famously wrote that Lovecraft was "too well read."[7] By this he meant that Lovecraft had read so much weird fiction that it was at times difficult to determine what was genuinely his and what was a dim and perhaps unconscious recollection of something he had read. While there is some superficial justice in this remark, it should now be evident that the core elements of Lovecraft's work—cosmicism, psychic transference, a deep sense of the cumulative weight of history and topography upon human character—are highly original and are largely outgrowths of the materialist and atheistic philosophy he evolved over his lifetime. That said, the influence of Edgar Allan Poe remained pervasive in his fiction, and this book establishes significant markers of the depth and extent of that influence. And whatever we may think of the relative merits of these two writers, they are likely to be permanently conjoined as towering pioneers in the literature of the weird.

---

7. Peter Penzoldt, *The Supernatural in Fiction* (1952); extracted in *H. P. Lovecraft: Four Decades of Criticism*, ed. S. T. Joshi (Athens: Ohio University Press, 1980), 64.

Lovecraft and the Titans: A Critical Legacy

Edmund Wilson's hostile review of Lovecraft, "Tales of the Marvellous and the Ridiculous" (*New Yorker*, November 24, 1945), chiefly focused on the perceived deficiencies in Lovecraft's fiction, including the notorious put-down, "The only real horror in most of these fictions is the horror of bad taste and bad art."[1] Wilson's prejudice against genre fiction (he condemned both the detective story and Tolkien's *Lord of the Rings* in terms scarcely less censorious) largely accounts for his blind eye toward Lovecraft, but what is curious about his review is the frequency with which Wilson finds himself grudgingly praising various aspects of Lovecraft's work. In regard to "Supernatural Horror in Literature" (which Wilson read in the Ben Abramson edition of 1945), he notes: "his long essay on the literature of the supernatural horror is a really able piece of work. He shows his lack of sound literary taste in his enthusiasms for Machen and Dunsany, whom he more or less acknowledged as models, but he had read comprehensively in this special field—he was strong on the Gothic novelists—and writes about it with much intelligence."[2]

There is at least one inaccuracy here—Lovecraft was not in fact "strong" on the Gothic novelists, having read them fairly cursorily and deriving much of his information about them from Edith Birkhead's treatise *The Tale of Terror* (1921)—but the suggestion that Lovecraft overvalued Machen and Dunsany, on the grounds that he was significantly influenced by them, is an accusation made even by more sympathetic critics. In a review of the first omnibus of Lovecraft's tales, *The Outsider and Others* (1939), T. O. Mabbott, the leading Poe scholar of his generation, remarks in passing that Lovecraft "tends to underrate Stevenson, and overrate Dunsany."[3]

---

1. Edmund Wilson, "Tales of the Marvellous and the Ridiculous" (1945), in *H. P. Lovecraft: Four Decades of Criticism*, ed. S. T. Joshi (Athens: Ohio University Press, 1980), 47.

2. Wilson, 48.

3. T. O. Mabbott, Review of *The Outsider and Others* (*American Literature*, March 1940, in *A Weird Writer in Our Midst: Early Criticism of H. P. Lovecraft*, ed. S. T. Joshi (New York: Hippocampus Press, 2010), 183.

These comments may have more to do with the declining reputations of Machen and Dunsany in the mid-twentieth century than with any flaws in Lovecraft's critical judgment. For I maintain that the bulk of literary scholarship on weird fiction in the ninety years following the first publication of "Supernatural Horror in Literature" emphatically endorses the prescience of Lovecraft's identification, in the tenth and final chapter of his treatise, of the four "modern masters" of the weird tale in his era: Arthur Machen (1863–1947), Lord Dunsany (1878–1957), Algernon Blackwood (1869–1951), and M. R. James (1862–1936). Lovecraft's judgments on these writers are the more remarkable given how relatively late in his own life he first read them—in one case, only a few months before beginning the initial composition of the essay itself.

Lovecraft Reads the Titans

Peter Penzoldt may have been right in remarking, in *The Supernatural in Fiction* (1952), that Lovecraft was "too well read," meaning that "he was influenced by so many authors that one is often at a loss to decide what is really Lovecraft and what some half-conscious memory of the books he has read";[4] but recent scholarship has found repeated instances of Lovecraft coming upon a particular motif or image independently of a perceived literary influence, or years before he read the author in question. This is strikingly the case with Lord Dunsany, whom Lovecraft idolized for several years after first encountering his work in the fall of 1919. More than a year previously, he had written "Polaris," a tale that seems strikingly "Dunsanian" in its use of a dream-setting and prose-poetic language; but no such influence is possible. Lovecraft went on to read the bulk of Dunsany's bejeweled early story collections, from *The Gods of Pegāna* (1905) to *Tales of Three Hemispheres* (1919), as well as his early collections of fantastic plays; and he cites or alludes to all these works in his discussion of Dunsany in "Supernatural Horror in Literature."

Lovecraft's ignorance of Dunsany until 1919 is explicable only by assuming that he thought Dunsany's work was of a whimsically fantastic sort that left little room for the cosmic horror he preferred. In 1929, commenting on his first reading of *A Dreamer's Tales* (1910), he noted that "I had never read anything of Dunsany's [before 1919], though knowing of him by reputation. The book had been recommended to me by one whose judgment I did not

---

4. Peter Penzoldt, *The Supernatural in Fiction* (1952), excerpts in *H. P. Lovecraft: Four Decades of Criticism*, 64.

highly esteem."[5] This person was Alice M. Hamlet, a woman associated with the amateur journalism movement in which Lovecraft was involved. Hamlet apparently urged Lovecraft to read the book in anticipation of hearing Dunsany lecture in Boston in October 1919. The effect was immediate: "The first paragraph arrested me as with an electric shock, & I had not read two pages before I became a Dunsany devotee for life."[6]

Lovecraft came upon Arthur Machen around 1923. Here too his discovery is anomalously late, for Machen had become celebrated—indeed, notorious—as one of the more daring writers of the "Yellow Nineties," when his novella "The Great God Pan" (1894) was condemned in reviews as the outpouring of a diseased mind. Machen produced much of the work for which we remember him today in what has been called his "great decade" of writing (roughly 1890–1901), although it is true that some of the works written during this period—such as the sensitive novel *The Hill of Dreams* (1907)—were only published years later. But by 1925, when Lovecraft began writing his essay, Machen was a fully established figure in general literature—indeed, in some literary circles he was already coming to be regarded as somewhat passé. Lovecraft had no excuse for not reading Machen earlier; unlike Dunsany, Machen wrote exactly the kind of documentary-style supernatural horror that Lovecraft himself would spend his entire career refining.

As with Dunsany, Lovecraft's discovery of Machen occurred through the recommendation of a friend—in this case, his fiery young colleague Frank Belknap Long (1901–1994), who was urging Lovecraft to get out of his fixation with the eighteenth century and read all manner of contemporary writers, from T. S. Eliot to Sherwood Anderson. And yet, one of Lovecraft's earliest comments on Machen, in a letter to Long, is of interest:

> And I have read *The Hill of Dreams!!* Surely a masterpiece—though I hope it isn't quite as autobiographical as some reviewers claim. I'd hate to think of Machen himself as that young neurotic with his sloppy sentimentalities, his couch of thorns, his urban eccentricities, and all that! But Pegāna, what an imagination! Cut out the emotional hysteria, and you have a marvellously appealing character—how vivid is that exquisite Roman day-dreaming! . . . even if the *spirit* is sadly un-Roman. Machen is a Titan—perhaps the greatest living author—and I must read everything of his. But *Dunsany* is closer to my own personality and understanding. Machen has an hysterical intensi-

---

5. H. P. Lovecraft, Letter to Clark Ashton Smith (April 14, 1929); in *Selected Letters 1911–1937*, ed. August Derleth, Donald Wandrei, and James Turner (Sauk City, WI: Arkham House, 1965–76), 2.328.

6. *Selected Letters* 2.328.

ty which I neither experience nor understand—a seriousness which is a philosophical limitation. But Dunsany *is myself*, plus an art and cultivation infinitely greater. His cosmic realm is the realm in which I live, his distant, emotionless vistas of the beauty of moonlight on quaint and ancient roofs are the vistas I know and cherish.[7]

This statement is of intense interest, and I shall return to some aspects of it later; but here we can say that Lovecraft immediately recognized that Machen's "hysterical intensity" (a code word for Machen's devout Anglo-Catholicism) was antipodal to the lofty "indifferentism"[8] toward human affairs and all human life that he and Dunsany, both atheists, shared.

Lovecraft's response to Algernon Blackwood is very curious. It had previously been thought that he first encountered Blackwood only in 1924, when he waxed enthusiastic about reading "The Willows" (which he later declared the finest weird tale in all literature) in *The Listener and Other Stories* (1907): "One of the tales in this book, 'The Willows', is perhaps the most devastating piece of supernaturally hideous suggestion which I have beheld in a decade."[9] But recently a letter dating to 1920 has surfaced in which Lovecraft expresses a much more mixed view of Blackwood. Having received a copy of *Incredible Adventures* (1914) from his friend James F. Morton, Lovecraft writes: "I can't say that I am very much enraptured, for somehow Blackwood lacks the power to create a really haunting atmosphere. He is too diffuse, for one thing; and for another thing, his horrors and weirdness are too obviously symbolical—symbolical rather than convincingly outré."[10]

The remarkable thing is that *Incredible Adventures* is the very volume that Lovecraft later singled out as the pinnacle of Blackwood's achievement. In "Supernatural Horror in Literature" he states (in direct contradiction to his comment of 1920): "Some of these accounts are hardly stories at all, but rather studies in elusive impressions and half-remembered snatches of dream. Plot is everywhere negligible, and atmosphere reigns untrammelled."[11] In a later letter he elaborates: "A weird story, to be a serious aesthetic effort, must form primar-

---

7. Lovecraft, Letter to Frank Belknap Long (June 5, 1923); *Selected Letters* 1.233-34.

8. Lovecraft, Letter to James F. Morton (October 30, 1929); *Selected Letters* 3.39.

9. Lovecraft, Letter to Lillian D. Clark (September 29–30, 1924); in *Letters from New York*, ed. S. T. Joshi and David E. Schultz (San Francisco: Night Shade, 2005), 63.

10. Lovecraft, Letter to the Gallomo ([April 1920]); in *Letters to Alfred Galpin*, ed, S. T. Joshi and David E. Schultz (New York: Hippocampus Press, 2003), 73.

11. H. P. Lovecraft, *The Annotated Supernatural Horror in Literature*, ed. S. T. Joshi (New York: Hippocampus Press, 2nd ed. 2012), 88. Further references will occur in the text.

ily a *picture of a mood*—and such a picture certainly does not call for any clever jack-in-the-box fillip. There *are* weird stories which more or less conform to this description . . . especially in Blackwood's *Incredible Adventures.*"[12] Lovecraft's less than enthusiastic response to Blackwood in 1920 may stem from his enrapturement with Dunsany at that juncture: it becomes evident that he was so taken with Dunsany's exquisite prose-poetry (which he himself attempted, unsuccessfully, to duplicate in some of his own tales) that Blackwood's somewhat workmanlike prose did not evoke a chord with him. Later Lovecraft recognized that Blackwood's keen portrayal of an individual's psychological response to fear, terror, wonder, and awe is his greatest literary strength.

Lovecraft came upon M. R. James as late as mid-December 1925, several weeks *after* he had received the offer from W. Paul Cook to write "Supernatural Horror in Literature," in November. The earliest known mention of James in Lovecraft's correspondence occurs in a letter to his aunt, Lillian D. Clark, dated December 13, 1925, when he speaks of going to the New York Public Library to "read the ghost stories of Montague Rhodes James."[13] The reference is apparently to *Ghost-Stories of An Antiquary* (1904), although Lovecraft quickly read James's three subsequent volumes of ghost stories, concluding with *A Warning to the Curious* (1925). By late January he was conducting a vigorous course of reading and re-reading the classics of weird fiction in preparation for writing the various chapters of his essay, and he refers to "my new idol of idols, the erudite Montague Rhodes James . . . James' mastery of horror is almost unsurpassable." He goes on say: "I am eager to get hold of . . . his very recent (just reviewed) new volume for grown-ups—'A Warning to the Curious'. I shall give James very prominent mention in my article."[14]

I do not wish to examine Lovecraft's actual discussion of the four "modern masters" in "Supernatural Horror in Literature," except to note a few peculiar features. The segment on Arthur Machen begins grandly: "Of living creators of cosmic fear raised to its most artistic pitch, few if any can hope to equal the versatile Arthur Machen" (81). This may be one of several instances where Lovecraft uses the word "cosmic" almost ornamentally, or as a general term of praise. For in fact Machen's work is not notably "cosmic" in the sense that Lovecraft understood the term, at least as applied to his own work—the depiction of the vast gulfs of space and time and the resultant insignificance, physical and moral, of the human race within those gulfs. This is not at all the focus of Machen's writing. As a devout Christian whose hostility to science as

---

12. Lovecraft, Letter to R. H. Barlow (May 11, 1935); *Selected Letters* 5.160.

13. Lovecraft, Letter to Lillian D. Clark (December 13, 1925); *Letters from New York* 253.

14. Lovecraft, Letter to Lillian D. Clark (January 26, 1926); *Letters from New York* 275.

the destroyer of mankind's comforting illusions of self-importance was unremitting, Machen was the very last person to be a proponent of cosmicism. Much of his work—and this applies not only to "The Great God Pan" but also to "The White People," which Lovecraft decreed the second-greatest weird tale in literature, after "The Willows"—is focused on departures from religious orthodoxy (especially in sexual matters), which he was able to depict as symbols for both physical and psychological aberration. A later letter, written in 1932, shows Lovecraft's grasp of this point:

> I'd a great deal rather have Machen as he is than not have him at all! What Machen probably likes about perverted and forbidden things is their departure from and hostility to the commonplace. To him—whose imagination is not cosmic—they represent what Pegāna and the River Yann represent to Dunsany, whose imagination *is* cosmic. People whose minds are—like Machen's—steeped in the orthodox myths of religion, naturally find a poignant fascination in the conception of things which religion brands with outlawry and horror. Such people take the artificial and obsolete concept of "sin" seriously, and find it full of dark allurement.[15]

This letter is actually a far more acute analysis of the essence of Machen's weird work than the fulsome praise we find in "Supernatural Horror in Literature."

As for Dunsany, Lovecraft admits to his admiration of the "sorcery of [his] crystalline singing prose," going on to say with considerable hyperbole: "His point of view is the most truly cosmic of any held in the literature of any period" (89). Stating rather tritely that "Beauty rather than terror is the keynote of Dunsany's work" (90), Lovecraft nonetheless emphasizes the horrific undercurrent inherent in Dunsany's prodigal creation of fantastic cities, gods, and monsters.

Blackwood, in many ways, becomes for Lovecraft the model for weird writing; and although he still harps on Blackwood's lack of "notable command of the poetic witchery of mere words," he realizes the English writer's *approach* to the weird is exemplary:

> no one has ever approached the skill, seriousness, and minute fidelity with which he records the overtones of strangeness in ordinary things and experiences, or the preternatural insight with which he builds up detail by detail the complete sensations and perceptions leading from reality into supernormal life or vision. . . . Above all others he understands how fully some sensitive minds dwell forever on the borderland of dream, and how relative-

---

15. Lovecraft, Letter to Bernard Austin Dwyer (1932); *Selected Letters* 4.4.

ly slight is the distinction betwixt those images formed from actual objects and those excited by the play of the imagination. (87)

As for James, what is remarkable in Lovecraft's analysis is that a substantial proportion of it is spent on a plot synopsis of a single story, "Count Magnus." This is because what Lovecraft truly admired in James was what might be called the *architecture* of his tales: the extraordinarily complex structure of some of his longer narratives, resulting in an extreme disjunction between the events as they occur in chronological sequence and the events as they are recounted in the story. This disjunction, indeed, is something Lovecraft himself adopted in his later novelettes and novellas, and it is highly likely that James provided a kind of working model of how it could be done. Later, Lovecraft made this feature a central component of his theory of weird fiction writing; in the essay "Notes on Writing Weird Fiction" (1933) he advised writers to prepare *two* synopses for a story, one portraying "events in the order of their absolute occurrence" and the other portraying events "in order of *narration* (not actual occurrence)."[16] Indeed, the extent to which these two synopses diverge is a key to the structural complexity of a given tale.

This emphasis on James as literary architect is not at all surprising, because the actual content of James's writing is about as far from Lovecraftian cosmic horror as it is possible to get. While it is true that some of James's "ghosts" are more or less material—as Lovecraft memorably observed in his essay, "the average James ghost is lean, dwarfish, and hairy—a sluggish, hellish night-abomination midway betwixt beast and man" (92)—others are of the more conventional immaterial sort, embodying a philosophical dualism that Lovecraft the mechanistic materialist would have rejected. And James was also the culmination of the British ghost story tradition—a tradition Lovecraft appreciated with no great enthusiasm, as a letter of 1933 suggests: "the Victorians went in strongly for weird fiction—Bulwer-Lytton, Dickens, Wilkie Collins, Harrison Ainsworth, Mrs. Oliphant, George W. M. Reynolds, H. Rider Haggard, R. L. Stevenson and countless others turned out reams of it."[17]

Lovecraft's Later Views of the Titans

It is of some interest to note what Lovecraft thought of the work of the "modern masters" subsequent to the publication of his essay. On the surface it may seem remarkable—given that three of the four "modern masters"

---

16. "Notes on Writing Weird Fiction," in *Collected Essays*, ed. S. T. Joshi (New York: Hippocampus Press, 2004–06), 2.176.

17. Lovecraft, Letter to Elizabeth Toldridge (August 28, 1933); *Selected Letters* 4.239.

outlived Lovecraft by ten, fourteen, and twenty years—that Lovecraft did not revise this tenth chapter to any significant degree for the *Fantasy Fan* serialization of 1933–35 (in the event, the serialization had proceeded only to the middle of chapter eight when the magazine folded); but a study of these writers' subsequent work—and, more relevantly, Lovecraft's response to it— may cause us to be less surprised.

As has been suggested, Machen's best work was long behind him even when the first version of "Supernatural Horror in Literature" came to be written. The nine-volume Caerleon Edition of his *Works* (1923) was in this sense almost an epitaph. The last work Lovecraft takes note of is "The Shining Pyramid," a story first published in 1895, but which Lovecraft probably read in one of two competing volumes titled *The Shining Pyramid* (1924, 1925), one assembled by Vincent Starrett, the other compiled by Machen. After this date, Machen's publications largely consist of collections of his essays and journalism or reprints of his earlier work. The late weird novel *The Green Round* (1933) appeared just at the time Lovecraft was revising his essay for the *Fantasy Fan*, but in his reaction to it he strained to be polite:

> It is really extremely interesting—with some very potent reflections of that persistent sense of unreal worlds impinging on the real world which many imaginative persons possess. In the casualness & unexplainedness of the phenomena represented, it recalls some of Machen's queer prefaces—such as that to "The Three Impostors". Its faults are—mainly—a certain rambling diffuseness, & over-use of typical stylistic mannerisms. Also—the poltergeist manifestations tend to be somewhat hackneyed. Hardly one of Machen's greatest—but typically Machenian for all that.[18]

The case of Dunsany is of much greater interest. Lovecraft diligently read nearly every publication by the Anglo-Irish author subsequent to *Tales of Three Hemispheres* (1919), but discussed none of them in the revised "Supernatural Horror in Literature." He repeatedly chastised Dunsany for abandoning the prose-poetic manner of his early work, although he noted a partial return to this idiom in the superb novel *The King of Elfland's Daughter* (1924). But Dunsany himself was evolving creatively, and he had clearly said everything he had to say in that early manner; his novels, from *The Chronicles of Rodriguez* (1922) to *The Curse of the Wise Woman* (1933), all feature a greater infusion of the "real" world and its concerns, but still exhibit a delicate and ethereal weirdness. What is more, Lovecraft's own work was evolving in nearly the same

---

18. Lovecraft, Letter to August Derleth (March 29, [1934]); in *Essential Solitude: The Letters of H. P. Lovecraft and August Derleth*, ed. David E. Schultz and S. T. Joshi (New York: Hippocampus Press, 2008), 2.628.

manner, as he himself abandoned Dunsanian fantasy for the documentary realism of his later, longer tales. But he continued to express impatience with Dunsany's evolution, as he wrote very late in life to Fritz Leiber:

> As he gained in age and sophistication, he lost in freshness and simplicity. He was ashamed to be uncritically naïve, and began to step aside from his tales and visibly smile at them even as they unfolded. Instead of remaining what the true fantaisiste must be—a child in a child's world of dream—he became anxious to show that he was really an adult good-naturedly pretending to be a child in a child's world.[19]

I maintain that this is a seriously erroneous portrayal of the early Dunsany, which is hardly "naive" but is itself highly sophisticated in its implicit atheism and cynicism. Lovecraft (and, to be fair, many other readers) may have been duped by the surface naïveté of those early tales, which deliberately reflect what I have termed an "aesthetic animism"[20] that underscores the fundamental unity between human beings and the natural world—a unity that industrial civilization has broken and is on the verge of destroying. But Lovecraft could not get beyond Dunsany's evocation of pure fantasy, expressed in some of the most gorgeous prose-poetry in all English literature.

As for Blackwood, he too, like Machen, suffered a certain deflation of his inspiration following what could be called his "great half-decade" of writing (1908-14), when the unexpected popular success of *John Silence–Physician Extraordinary* (1908) allowed him to spend several years in Switzerland writing whatever he wished without concern for income or markets. This period culminated in *Incredible Adventures*, the last work Lovecraft discusses in his essay. After this date, Blackwood produced some uninspired story collections and a few novels of no great interest. Lovecraft owned *Julius LeVallon* (1916), but he only obtained his copy in 1933,[21] and it is not clear if he had read this work earlier. In late 1936 he received a copy of Blackwood's late collection *Shocks* (1935) as a Christmas present from August Derleth; indeed, he had the book with him when he went to the hospital in March 1937 during his terminal illness.[22] But he has left no account of his opinion of the contents of the book.

---

19. Lovecraft, Letter to Fritz Leiber (November 15, 1936); *Selected Letters* 5.354.

20. S. T. Joshi, *Lord Dunsany: Master of the Anglo-Irish Imagination* (Westport, CT: Greenwood Press, 1995), 19.

21. Letter to J. Vernon Shea (September 25, 1933), in *Letters to Vernon Shea, Carl F. Strauch, and Lee McBride White*, ed. S. T. Joshi and David E. Schultz (New York: Hippocampus Press, 2016), 167.

22. See *Essential Solitude* 2.764n2.

M. R. James wrote relatively little weird fiction subsequent to *A Warning to the Curious* (1925). Although Lovecraft celebrated the appearance of James's *Collected Ghost Stories* in 1931, he himself did not obtain the book, since he already owned James's four separate collections of ghost stories. The volume does include a few additional tales, but they are of little consequence.

Lovecraft's attitude toward James underwent a fairly significant—and downward—revision as his own work evolved from relatively conventional macabre tales such as "The Tomb" (1917) and "The Outsider" (1921) to the cosmic horror of "The Call of Cthulhu" (1926) and *At the Mountains of Madness* (1931). While defending him against the opinions of some colleagues (such as the young J. Vernon Shea) who apparently felt James was a bit tame and conventional in his weird scenarios, Lovecraft himself acknowledged James's weaknesses:

> About M. R. James—I think I can see what you mean, but can't classify him quite as low as you do. And if you can't see his utter, prodigious, & literally incalculable superiority to the W.T. [*Weird Tales*] plodders I must again urge you to give your sense of appreciation a radical analysis & overhauling. James has a sense of dramatic values & an eye for hideous intrusions upon the commonplace that none of the pulp groundlings could even approach if they tried all their pitiful lives. But I'll concede he isn't really in the Machen, Blackwood, & Dunsany class. He is the earthiest member of the "big four."[23]

Along with this revised evaluation of James came an increasing admiration for the work of Walter de la Mare (1873–1956). De la Mare, whose novel *The Return* (1910) probably influenced Lovecraft's *The Case of Charles Dexter Ward* (1927) and whose two story collections, *The Riddle and Other Stories* (1923) and *The Connoisseur and Other Stories* (1926), Lovecraft owned, wrote extraordinarily subtle weird tales that deeply probed the shifting psychological states of characters encountering the bizarre. For all Lovecraft's fundamental lack of interest in character-driven fiction ("Individuals and their fortunes within natural law move me very little. They are all momentary trifles bound from a common nothingness toward another common nothingness"[24]), he was keenly aware of the power and evocativeness of de la Mare's stories, even if some of them tended toward an almost impenetrable opacity.

De la Mare, indeed, almost missed being included in the original version of "Supernatural Horror in Literature" altogether. Lovecraft only came upon him after having largely finished the initial draft of his essay in the spring of

---

23. Lovecraft, Letter to J. Vernon Shea (February 5, 1932); *Letters to J. Vernon Shea* 90.

24. Lovecraft, Letter to E. Hoffmann Price (August 15, 1934); *Selected Letters* 5.19.

1926. Upon his return to Providence from New York on April 17, he conducted some further research on weird writers at the Providence Public Library; and it was then that he discovered de la Mare. Writing in late May to Frank Belknap Long, Lovecraft wrote: "I have not yet read his prose lucubrations: a thing which I really ought to do before giving my article a final form. I had been of opinion that Mr. D. shared the somewhat insipid whimsicality of Mr. [J. M.] Barrie, but 'tis easily possible that his fantasies have the sombre suggestiveness of Mr. Blackwood as well."[25] A few weeks later he wrote: "De la Mare can be exceedingly powerful when he chooses, and I only wish he'd choose oftener."[26] But Lovecraft's admiration of the British writer was sufficient for him to write several paragraphs about his work in chapter nine of his essay. With the passing of years his evaluation of de la Mare only increased, so that by 1934 he was referring to the "latest achievements of Blackwood or Machen or de la Mare or Dunsany"[27] as the pinnacles of contemporary weird fiction. Had Lovecraft written *Supernatural Horror in Literature* in 1934, de la Mare would likely have replaced James as one of the four "modern masters."

Contemporary Views of the Titans

Given the extent to which weird fiction in general remains a pariah to mainstream or academic criticism, it is difficult to state definitively whether Lovecraft's identification of Machen, Dunsany, Blackwood, and James as the titans of weird fiction in his day—the culmination of a literary tradition that began with the Gothic writers and proceeded through the revolutionary work of Edgar Allan Poe—has been confirmed by subsequent scholarship. The best we can say is that, gauged by these authors' current status among readers, publishers, and critics, Lovecraft's evaluation does indeed appear to be sound.

The chief reason for this—and the chief reason why an author like de la Mare has not attained a similar level of popularity among devotees of the weird—is that these four writers (and, of course, Lovecraft himself, who has now taken his place among them) devoted nearly all their fictional work to the weird, thereby allowing readers to sample volume after volume of their work. Many significant works of weird fiction were essentially "one-shot" ventures by authors whose chief fictional focus was elsewhere—a point embodied perhaps most notably by the endlessly anthologized story "The Monkey's Paw" (1902) by the British humorist W. W. Jacobs.

Machen is perhaps the most problematical in this regard, for his weird

---

25. Lovecraft, Letter to Frank Belknap Long (May 20, 1926); *Selected Letters* 2.53.

26. Lovecraft, Letter to Frank Belknap Long (June 11, 1926); *Selected Letters* 2.57.

27. Lovecraft, Letter to E. Hoffmann Price (August 15, 1934); *Selected Letters* 5.19.

work is largely confined to the episodic novel *The Three Impostors* (1895), the story collection *The House of Souls* (1906), the short novel *The Terror* (1917), and two late collections that appeared in 1936 but which are not highly regarded. But Philip Van Doren Stern's splendid compilation of Machen's *Tales of Horror and the Supernatural* (1948)—published in the United States by Knopf in 1948 (an extension of that publisher's campaign to introduce Machen to the American reading public, begun in the early 1920s)—has remained in print for most of the past seventy years and has been widely available in paperback in both the United States and the United Kingdom.

Criticism of Machen remains even today a kind of cottage industry among a relatively small band of devotees, many of them members of the Arthur Machen Society (it did not help that that society suffered an internal schism in the 1990s, leading to the formation of a competing group, Friends of Arthur Machen). Aside from Wesley D. Sweetser's exemplary but brief monograph, *Arthur Machen* (1964), for Twayne's English Authors Series, and a short biography by Mark Valentine (1996), most of the critical or scholarly work on Machen has been done in the small press. But his work continues to be reprinted, and my Penguin Classics edition of *The White People and Other Stories* (2011) featured a laudatory preface by filmmaker Guillermo del Toro.

Dunsany is problematical not because his work is not fantastic from beginning to end, but because his brand of imaginary-world fantasy has now become a virtually separate subgenre quite different—and inspiring a very different readership—from that of supernatural horror. The immense critical and popular esteem of Tolkien's *Lord of the Rings* trilogy (1954–55) and its numerous imitators and successors has led to the rediscovery of earlier work in the same vein that may have influenced Tolkien, ranging from William Morris to E. R. Eddison; Dunsany is chief among them. *The King of Elfland's Daughter* has come to be seen as the prototypical fantasy novel, and the current paperback edition contains an effusive introduction by Neil Gaiman.

Criticism of Dunsany has also been somewhat slow to appear, at least in academic venues; but in part this has to do with a curious prejudice among Irish readers and critics against an author who took, as it were, the "wrong" side in Ireland's quest for independence from England. As a loyalist who favored continuing political and cultural ties to England, Dunsany was virtually drummed out of Irish literature for decades as a kind of literary traitor. This prejudice now seems to be on the wane, and Dunsany's work is being embraced by at least some Irish scholars as a notable contribution to its national literature as well as a distinctive excursion into the weird.

Blackwood has been perhaps the least studied of the "modern masters," perhaps because the sheer extent of his work—thirteen novels along with more than 200 short stories and novelettes—makes a comprehensive analysis difficult. Alone among the Titans, Blackwood's work has not been extensively reprinted in the decades following his death, with only a few anthology chestnuts such as "The Willows" and "The Wendigo" being readily available. Mike Ashley has been leading a virtually solitary campaign for Blackwood's recognition, having compiled an exhaustive bibliography (1987) along with a detailed and sensitive biography (2001). Some of Blackwood's work is now being reprinted, but generally in expensive editions from small presses.

M. R. James has never lacked for popularity, in part because his work inspired a small cadre of disciples to write pastiches of his ghost stories. These disciples—among them E. G. Swain, R. H. Malden, and A. N. L. Munby—are not sufficiently original to have generated any devotees of their own; but James, by the mere fact that his work constituted a kind of culmination of the Victorian ghost story, inspired a more significant group of writers to evolve the more dynamic subgenre of the psychological ghost story, where the ghostly manifestations are portrayed as the product of an aberrant psyche, or at any rate cannot be definitively deemed to be purely supernatural. Such writers include Oliver Onions, Walter de la Mare, and L. P. Hartley; several of them are, in my judgment, superior in aesthetic accomplishment to James himself. But because none of these authors devoted themselves solely to the weird, and also because some of their work is a bit rarefied for popular consumption, they have not elicited the devotion of weird fiction readers and, consequently, not attracted uniform interest from critics and scholars for their strictly weird work.

But James himself, like Machen and Lovecraft, been the focus of attention by a wide array of devotees, chiefly in England. His *Collected Ghost Stories* has rarely been out of print in the last eighty or more years, and such small-press venues as *Ghosts & Scholars* have done significant scholarship on his life and work. An immense compilation, *A Pleasing Terror* (Ash-Tree Press, 2001), included not only the contents of James's four original collections of ghost stories, but also some fugitive tales as well as the children's fantasy *The Five Jars* (1922). Although now out of print, it was a landmark publication that exhibited the full range of James's work in weird fiction. Two very different biographies, one by Richard Pfaff (1980) and the other by Michael Cox (1983), focused, respectively, on James's scholarly work as an authority on medieval manuscripts and his work as a writer of ghost stories.

We must also deal with the curious fact that several of these writers—and many others whom Lovecraft discussed in his essay—are now experiencing a revival of critical and popular interest largely because Lovecraft himself discussed them. Enthusiasm for Lovecraft is today at such a fever pitch that many readers find themselves attracted both to his predecessors and to his successors. It is this phenomenon that has led dozens, perhaps hundreds, of contemporary writers to add to the pseudomythology underpinning many of Lovecraft's tales, now called the Cthulhu Mythos. Analogously, readers and critics have found consuming interest in the work of his predecessors and influences—and chief among them (aside from Poe) are the four Titans discussed here.

On the whole, then, Lovecraft's judgment regarding the literary superiority of Arthur Machen, Lord Dunsany, Algernon Blackwood, and M. R. James has been vindicated. The period 1880–1940 has come to be seen as a kind of "golden age" of weird fiction, and these writers have been recognized as its leading exponents. They all focused exclusively on the weird; their fictional work embodied not only a high level of aesthetic achievement, but was a potent expression of the distinct philosophical visions to which each author ascribed; their influence on subsequent weird fiction remains vital and significant. The only author missing from this list is Lovecraft himself, whose own tales in many ways formed a pinnacle of weird writing and set the stage for much of the best weird fiction to come. In his humility he would have been the last to believe that he deserved a place with such an eminent company, but the overwhelming judgment of readers and critics has emphatically established that he does.

Lovecraft and Zealia Bishop

The recent discovery of a sheaf of H. P. Lovecraft's unpublished, and previously unknown, letters to Zealia Brown Reed Bishop shed valuable light on a still little-known aspect of his life: his work as a "revisionist" or ghostwriter. While his efforts to revise the weird tales of such individuals as Adolphe de Castro, Hazel Heald, and Bishop herself (for whom Lovecraft ghostwrote three substantial tales—"The Curse of Yig," "The Mound," and "Medusa's Coil") are well known, Lovecraft's career as a reviser of all manner of other writing—from textbooks to poetry to novels—is still poorly understood, simply because of the lack of documentary evidence. This time-consuming and generally unprofitable work did, after all, occupy a substantial proportion of his time from at least 1922 to the end of his life, and it was the only "job" he ever had on a regular basis. He wrote and published original fiction too infrequently to bring in much of an income, and the drudgery of revision was all he had to fall back on to support himself.

That said, even these new letters, remarkably revelatory as they are, raise more questions than answers. It is illuminating to learn that Lovecraft had at least three different levels of revision, at differing rates of payment—"slight" revision (for which he charged 50¢ a page), "extensive" revision ($1.00 a page), and wholesale rewriting ($2.50 a page); the last was tantamount to original composition, since such works were customarily based only on a plot synopsis or outline, many of the details of which Lovecraft usually ignored in the process of composition. This is why "The Mound" and "Medusa's Coil" can virtually be considered works by Lovecraft alone: as we shall see, their synopses are so slight that virtually all the structural elements, character portrayals, and prose are his from beginning to end.

But Lovecraft's precise relations with Bishop remain a matter of uncertainty, chiefly because of the difficulty of reconciling some of the information found in these letters with what Bishop herself states in her memoir, "H. P. Lovecraft: A Pupil's View," published in *The Curse of Yig* (Arkham House, 1953), a volume that collects the three tales that Lovecraft ghostwrote for her. Although apparently written only fifteen years after Lovecraft's death, it contains a number of curious statements that fail to harmonize with the evidence found in Lovecraft's letters to her and others.

In the first place, Bishop states that she learned of Lovecraft's work as a reviser when she met Samuel Loveman in a bookstore he managed in Cleveland in 1928. But, as is obvious from the text of the letters, she was already writing to Lovecraft in the spring of 1927; moreover, Loveman had moved from Cleveland to New York no later than the fall of 1924.[1] The first mention of Loveman in the letters occurs on January 25, 1928, when Lovecraft speaks of "Samuel Loveman, once of Cleveland, to whom you wrote last spring." All I can conjecture is that Bishop, although apparently living in Cleveland in 1927, did not in fact meet Loveman face to face at that time; she may have gone to the bookstore where Loveman had once worked, been given his address, and written to him. He in turn presumably suggested that she get in touch with Lovecraft, as someone who could give her some assistance in fostering her budding career as a writer.

Bishop further confuses matters by stating in her memoir that "I was already qualified as a court reporter and selling short stories and articles as a means of supporting myself and young son while furthering my education in journalism at Columbia University."[2] This suggests that Bishop was living in New York at the time, but she was not: Lovecraft's letter of May 18, 1927, makes it clear that Bishop was still in Cleveland at this time, although about to move; and that she was only planning a visit to New York in the near future ("I will duly note your change of address when informed. Too bad Cleveland is uncongenial . . . If I am in New York during your visit I would surely be very much pleased to meet you").

The question of Bishop's one face-to-face meeting with Lovecraft is also a bit puzzling. She herself, in her memoir, states that he was "only thirty-five"[3] when the meeting took place in the apartment occupied by Frank Belknap Long and his parents; but this would place the meeting in 1925, which is of course impossible. In a letter to his aunt, Lillian D. Clark, Lovecraft notes that the meeting took place on May 29, 1928, when he was on an extended stay in Brooklyn while assisting his wife, Sonia, in setting up a new hat shop. He records the encounter with Bishop laconically: "Today—Monday—I rose at noon & went to Sonny's [i.e., Frank Belknap Long] to meet our client Mrs. Reed, who was in town Sun. & Mon. She seems quite prepossessing & intelligent."[4]

---

1. See S. T. Joshi, *I Am Providence: The Life and Times of H. P. Lovecraft* (New York: Hippocampus Press, 2010), 1.511.

2. "H. P. Lovecraft: A Pupil's View" (1953), in *Lovecraft Remembered*, ed. Peter Cannon (Sauk City, WI: Arkham House, 1998), 265.

3. "H. P. Lovecraft: A Pupil's View," 271.

4. H. P. Lovecraft to Lillian D. Clark, [29 May 1928] (ms. postcard, John Hay Library,

In any event, Bishop became one of Lovecraft's most persistent revision clients during the later 1920s and early 1930s, sending him story after story for analysis and touching up. And while it is of substantial interest to see how exhaustive Lovecraft's knowledge of current magazine markets was (see his letter of May 23, 1927), it is also plain that Lovecraft and Bishop had quite different views on the type of work she was writing and wished to write. Almost from the beginning Lovecraft encouraged Bishop to banish "superficial modern fiction" (letter of June 5, 1927) from her course of reading, even though it is evident that this is exactly the kind of fiction she wanted to read and write. Bishop herself betrays considerable resentment against Lovecraft for attempting to steer her in a direction she didn't wish to go:

> Being young and romantic, I wanted to follow my own impulse for fresh, youthful stories. Lovecraft was not convinced that his course was best. I was his protégé and he meant to bend my career to his direction. . . .
>
> Lovecraft's tutorial attitude was that of the master toward his protégé. Perhaps it could not have been otherwise. He either had no conception of a pupil's own direction and aims or he was not sympathetic to them, for he tried to direct his pupils into lines of development similar to his own. He lacked the catholicity of taste that the best teachers of writing must have. There is, for example, nothing wrong in writing confession or love stories if one knows what one is about and does his best.[5]

There is a good deal of truth in Bishop's statement; but Lovecraft was also correct in believing that even "confession or love stories" have to be well written and avoid trite and hackneyed tropes if they are to sell even to popular markets. In a later letter Lovecraft does admit that "I cannot enter into the spirit of commercial writing" (letter of February 24, 1928),[6] and another letter (undated, but probably written in April 1928) at last correctly identifies Bishop's chosen form of expression as "light, domestic fiction in the popular vein"; but it was precisely this kind of work that Lovecraft was least able to help Bishop with.

It is interesting to see how readily Lovecraft opens up to Bishop, ex-

---

Brown University, Providence, RI).

5. "H. P. Lovecraft: A Pupil's View," 267, 273–74.

6. This letter was written in response to comments made by one Thomas H. Uzzell, who was evidently working as a freelance writing tutor or instructor, after filling that same position at Columbia University (where Frank Belknap Long was one of his students). Uzzell (1884–?) was the author of *Narrative Technique: A Practical Course in Literary Psychology* (1923) and other handbooks on writing.

pounding on his travels; his other literary projects; his relations with Sonia, a woman to whom he remained married although they were no longer cohabiting (they would not begin divorce proceedings until early 1929); and other matters. His letter of February 13, 1928, written less than a year after he first came into contact with her and well before he met her in person, exhaustively discusses a wide range of issues, including his views on religion, politics, aesthetics, and even alcohol; it is clear, however, that Lovecraft only broached these topics in response to specific queries put to him by Bishop herself. (In this letter Lovecraft engagingly admits to not making a very good impression when he spoke to Bishop on the phone: "I was very sorry—and not a little surprised—to learn that my telephonic voice seemed in any way inhospitable!")

The Lovecraft-Bishop relationship takes an interesting turn in early 1928. A letter that apparently dates to late February provides a plot synopsis of "The Curse of Yig." Bishop's own account of the genesis of the story is, once again, quite different from what can be inferred from Lovecraft's letters. She states:

> The stories I sent him always came back so revised from their basic idea that I felt I was a complete failure as a writer. Disappointed and confused, I put aside everything that looked like a writer's tool and, with my son, set out for my sister's ranch in Oklahoma, a barren lonely place near the Texas border . . .
>
> There in Oklahoma, doubting more and more that I would ever become a writer, let alone a successful one, I sat one evening with a group of old Oklahoma settlers who had driven out to my sister's ranch. We sat around the kitchen fire and talked. Finally the conversation rambled on to folklore. Grandma Compton, my sister's mother-in-law, told a horror story about a couple who pioneered in Oklahoma not far from where we were. This story was a spark to me. I wrote a tale called "The Curse of Yig," in which snakes figured, wove it around some of my Aztec knowledge instilled in me by Lovecraft, and sent it off to him. He was delighted with this trend toward realism and horror, and fairly showered me with letters and instructions.[7]

There is reason to doubt numerous details of this account. There is no question that Bishop provided some kind of plot germ or outline for "The Curse of Yig"; but Lovecraft's undated letter (only leaf VI of which survives) makes it clear that the detailed synopsis of the story (appearing on the now-lost leaves IV and V of the letter) were of his own devising, and all that he asks of Bishop is for her to send these leaves back to him and supply "some more notes on points of local colour." In his letter of March 9 Lovecraft sends Bishop the completed story, which manifestly is largely of his own composition.

---

7. "H. P. Lovecraft: A Pupil's View," 268-69.

Lovecraft confirms this supposition in a letter to August Derleth:

> By the way—if you want to see a new story which is practically mine, read "The Curse of Yig" in the current W.T. Mrs. Reed is a client for whom Long & I have done oceans of work, & this story is about 75% mine. All I had to work on was a synopsis describing a couple of pioneers in a cabin with a nest of rattlesnakes beneath, the killing of the husband by snakes, the bursting of the corpse, & the madness of the wife, who was an eye-witness to the horror. There was no plot or motivation—no prologue or aftermath to the incident—so that one might say the story, as a story, is wholly my own. I invented the snake-god & the curse, the tragic wielding of the axe by the wife, the matter of the snake-victim's identity, & the asylum epilogue. Also, I worked up the geographic & other incidental colour—getting some data from the alleged authoress, who knows Oklahoma, but more from books.[8]

There are other problems with Bishop's account. She states that, after the story was written, it was sent out "not once, but many times" to various magazines but rejected, forcing her to shelve the story. Lovecraft then submitted the story to *Weird Tales*. It was, she claims, only when she personally visited editor Farnsworth Wright in Chicago at some unspecified date that he accepted the story—"four months later."[9] But this cannot be right. The story was written in early March and, by Lovecraft's account, already accepted by Wright by mid-May.[10] Bishop may be thinking of the long delay in the story's actual appearance in print (it was published only in the November 1929 issue).

It was around this time that Frank Belknap Long enters into Bishop's life. He and Lovecraft were beginning to work together on a revision service, as a now famous advertisement in the August 1928 issue of *Weird Tales* attests:

FRANK BELKNAP LONG, Jr.   H. P. LOVECRAFT

Critical and advisory service for writers of prose and verse; literary revision in all degrees of extensiveness. Address: Frank B. Long, Jr., 230 West 97th St., New York, New York City.[11]

---

8. H. P. Lovecraft to August Derleth, 6 October [1929]; *Essential Solitude: The Letters of H. P. Lovecraft and August Derleth*, ed. David E. Schultz and S. T. Joshi (New York: Hippocampus Press, 2008), 1.222.

9. "H. P. Lovecraft: A Pupil's View," 273.

10. H. P. Lovecraft to August Derleth, [19 or 26 May 1928]; *Essential Solitude* 1.146.

11. Cited in Joshi, *I Am Providence* 2.710.

Long appears to have worked on both weird and non-weird specimens by Bishop; indeed, at one point Lovecraft speaks of Long revising an entire novel she had written (letter of August 25, 1929). This appears to be a work that Bishop cites in her memoir as "a novel which dealt with a Catholic upbringing,"[12] since both Bishop and Lovecraft refer to its central character, Deon, in their discussions of the work. (In his letter of March 31, 1936, Lovecraft speaks of a novel by Bishop entitled *The Adopted Son*; whether this is the same novel is uncertain, but I suspect it is.) This novel clearly did not sell, nor did a rewriting of a mainstream story, "The Unchaining," as a weird tale (under the new title of "On the High Places"), which *Weird Tales* rejected.

In his letter of August 25, 1928, Lovecraft discusses a "weird tale of the Indian" that he is working on; there are further mentions of this in his letters of October 28, 1928, and January 22, 1929. One suspects that this is "The Mound"; but if so, it took Lovecraft quite some time to undertake the actual writing of the work, for it was only written in December 1929–January 1930. The story was completed by no later than January 14, and Bishop probably had no more input in it than in "The Curse of Yig." Indeed, in a note on one of the two surviving typescripts of the story, R. H. Barlow suggests as much as he records Bishop's synopsis: "There is an Indian mound near here, which is haunted by a headless ghost. Sometimes it is a woman."[13] Bishop introduces further confusion by stating that, at Lovecraft's suggestion, Long became involved in the writing of the tale ("At Lovecraft's gentle insistence, I left 'The Mound' with Frank Belknap Long, and it was Long who advised me and worked with me on that short novel").[14] In his memoir, *Howard Phillips Lovecraft: Dreamer on the Nightside* (1975), Long flatly denied that he had anything to do with the story;[15] and I believe it is safe to say that both the conception and composition of the tale are entirely Lovecraft's. As a curious postscript, Lovecraft urged Bishop to hire his Providence friend C. M. Eddy, Jr., to type the handwritten manuscript. Eddy was suffering extreme poverty at the time, and Lovecraft's accounts of how he tried to assist Eddy financially and in other ways make for poignant reading. Bishop in fact hired Eddy to type the story.

But the tale was far longer than it needed to be—at least, it was so long (more than 25,000 words) that acceptance by *Weird Tales* might be problematical. Sure enough, Wright rejected the story in short order. In an undated let-

---

12. "H. P. Lovecraft: A Pupil's View," 270.

13. Cited in Joshi, *I Am Providence* 2.745.

14. "H. P. Lovecraft: A Pupil's View," 271.

15. See my article, "Who Wrote 'The Mound?'", in *Lovecraft and a World in Transition: Collected Essays on H. P. Lovecraft* (New York: Hippocampus Press, 2014), 343–46.

ter to Bishop, Lovecraft expressed outrage, believing that Wright could have run the story as a two-part serial, and he encouraged her to submit it to other pulp magazines. Whether this was ever done is unclear; if it was, it was again rejected, and only appeared in abridged form in *Weird Tales* for November 1940.

It is unfortunate that letters discussing the composition of "Medusa's Coil" are apparently not extant. Lovecraft wrote this tale in the spring and summer of 1930. A synopsis of the story has recently come to light,[16] and it is clearly the work of Lovecraft. It features a general plot outline along with a five-part "Manner of Narration." One point in this document—"woman revealed as vampire, lamia, &c. &c.—& unmistakably (surprise to reader as in original text) a negress"—is highly intriguing. Does that mention of an "original text" suggest that there was an existing draft by Bishop that Lovecraft overhauled? If so, then there would be some reason to believe that the racist conclusion of the story—the revelation that the witch-woman Marceline Bedard is a negress, and that such a revelation is a horror far surpassing the horror of her supernatural powers—should be attributed to Bishop and not Lovecraft. In her memoir, Bishop makes note of "'Medusa's Coil,' which I had picked up as an idea from a Negress who did some housecleaning for me and expanded into a story similar in treatment to my earlier horror tale."[17] This remark is itself a little confusing, especially since "Medusa's Coil" is set in eastern Missouri and not Oklahoma; but we may infer that Bishop did provide a synopsis, and perhaps an actual draft, of the story to Lovecraft. But the story as written is without doubt entirely of his composition, at least as far as the prose is concerned. It too was rejected by *Weird Tales*, probably on account of length (or perhaps because it is just not a very good story). There was some talk between Lovecraft and Long of submitting it to *Ghost Stories*, an inferior pulp magazine that featured stories of the "true confession" type; but if it was sent there, it was also rejected. It finally appeared in *Weird Tales* for January 1939.

Bishop was not entirely a failure as a writer: in his letter of October 28, 1928, Lovecraft notes the sale of a story called "Red Blood," going on to suggest that Long had helped her with it. There are probably other Bishop tales in forgotten magazines of the period, and a few of them may betray Lovecraft's revisory hand, even if they are very far from the weird tales he is known to have worked on.

---

16. First published in *Collected Essays, Volume 5: Philosophy; Autobiography and Miscellany*, ed. S. T. Joshi (New York: Hippocampus Press, 2006), 243–44.

17. "H. P. Lovecraft: A Pupil's View," 271.

Zealia Bishop stayed in touch with Lovecraft almost to the end of his life, and she was at least contemplating giving him some additional revisory work as late as 1936 (to say nothing of paying off, in small increments, the debt she owed for past work). And although she states in her memoir that "I have carefully filed all his letters, postcards, and instructions,"[18] it is evident that a fair number of letters have now been lost. Nevertheless, what remains sheds a wealth of light on Lovecraft as a professional revisionist as well as a genial and considerate correspondent—one who seemed genuinely interested in his colleague and her family (one letter is charmingly written to her son, James) and happy to share with her his own evolving thoughts and beliefs. Barring the unexpected discovery of caches of letters to Adolphe de Castro, Hazel Heald, or other of his major revision clients, these letters may provide the best window we will ever have into the occupation that, for better or worse, Lovecraft made his own.

---

18. "H. P. Lovecraft: A Pupil's View," 268.

Lovecraft and "In Amundsen's Tent"

H. P. Lovecraft had been fascinated with the Antarctic since childhood, but the actual impetus for writing *At the Mountains of Madness* in early 1931 may have come from a succession of literary sources—M. P. Shiel's *The Purple Cloud* (1901), which Lovecraft read in a 1929 reprint and whose opening portions recount an expedition to the Arctic; John Taine's *The Greatest Adventure* (1929), another tale of prehistoric creatures unearthed in the snows of the Antarctic; and "In Amundsen's Tent" by John Martin Leahy (1886-1967), a story that was published in *Weird Tales* for January 1928.

Lovecraft commented on the story in a letter to August Derleth (December 13, 1927—the issue had appeared about a month before its cover date), remarking: "'In Amundsen's Tent' was *the* story of the issue, though the style is poor—as always with Leahy." The similarities between Leahy's tale and Lovecraft's are numerous. Leahy's tale is in essence a warning not to explore the Antarctic any further, lest subsequent explorers meet the fate of Robert Drumgold, whose diary forms the bulk of the text. Drumgold's account tells of an encounter with a nameless and tantalisingly undescribed entity that is suggested to have emerged from outer space, like Lovecraft's Old Ones; at one point the human protagonists even speculate that the entity is "hibernating," just as the Old Ones are in a state of cryogenic suspended animation. Dogs react with terror and loathing at the entity. Early in the tale Drumgold engages in a kind of cosmic speculation, wondering whether the earth or the universe is really "made for man": "May not there be other beings—yes, even on this very earth, of ours—more wonderful—yes, and more terrible too—than he?"

Certain crudities or deficiencies in Leahy's narrative might have inspired Lovecraft to see if he could do better. In particular, Leahy's story ends up being something of a tease, in that he refuses to describe the entity in the tent in any way aside from suggesting its extraterrestrial origin. Lovecraft, in the early stages of his quasi-science fiction phase, made sure to depict the Old Ones with meticulous precision. He avoids any sense of anticlimax in this clinical description because he withholds the true horror of the story—the protoplasmic shoggoth—until the end. And of course Lovecraft vastly expands on the cosmic implications of his narrative, supplying a detailed account of the origin of the Old Ones in the remotest reaches of the galaxy, their advent to earth, and their battles with other alien races, such as the "Cthulhu spawn" and the fungi from Yuggoth (from "The Whisperer in Darkness").

And yet, another story in *Weird Tales*—Katharine Metcalf Roof's "A Million Years After," published in the November 1930 issue—may also have had an influence on Lovecraft. This story dealt with the hatching of ancient dinosaur eggs. Lovecraft fumed when he saw the tale, not only because it won the cover design but because he had been badgering his friend Frank Belknap Long to write a story on this idea for years; Long had held off because he felt that H. G. Wells's "Æpyornis Island" had anticipated the idea. In mid-October Lovecraft wrote of the Roof tale:

> Rotten—cheap—puerile—yet winning prime distinction *because of the subject matter*. Now didn't Grandpa tell a bright young man just eight years ago this month to write a story like that? . . . Fie, Sir! Somebody else wasn't so afraid of the subject—and now a wretched mess of hash, just on the strength of its theme, gets the place of honour that Young Genoa might have had! . . . Why, damn it, boy, I've half a mind to write an egg story myself right now—though I fancy my primal ovoid would hatch out something infinitely more palaeogean and unrecognisable than the relatively commonplace dinosaur. (Letter to Frank Belknap Long, October 17, 1930)

Lovecraft seems to have followed through on his promise. But he may have felt that the actual use of a dinosaur egg was itself ruled out, so that the only other solution would be the freezing of alien bodies in the Arctic or Antarctic regions.

Many writers take a pre-existing idea and work with it, with the understanding that they might handle it better than their predecessors. Lovecraft may have been inspired by two *Weird Tales* stories to do just that in his Antarctic epic.

Why Michel Houellebecq Is Wrong about Lovecraft's Racism

The first published book by celebrated French novelist and poet Michel Houellebecq (b. 1958) was a little treatise entitled *H. P. Lovecaft: Contre le monde, contre la vie* (1991), translated into English in 2005 as *H. P. Lovecraft: Against the World, Against Life*. It has also been translated into Italian, German, and Spanish. It is a very odd piece of work. Its basic thrust is that Lovecraft was "full of rage,"[1] and that this rage—specifically manifested toward "the reality principle" (31), is what fuels the distinctive vision and ambiance in his fiction.

In all frankness, Houellebecq's conclusions are not based on sound research. Although it is evident that he read de Camp's biography (apparently in the French translation that appeared in 1988, when Houellebecq states that he wrote his treatise [see 240]), it is unclear whether he read any of Lovecraft's letters beyond those that appeared in the first (and only) volume of Francis Lacassin's translation of Lovecraft's letters (*Lettres* [1978]), containing letters only up to the year 1926. I assisted the translator of the English version of Houellebecq's treatise, Dorna Khazeni, and we were disconcerted to find that a number of his citations of passages from Lovecraft could not be located, including a strange passage (apparently from a Lovecraft story) about "certain ritual and particularly repugnant customs of the indigenous inhabitants of North Carolina" (75). The state of North Carolina is never mentioned in Lovecraft's fiction (including revisions). It would be unjust to suggest that Houellebecq simply invented these passages, since there seems no compelling reason for him to have done so; but at a minimum, his scholarship must be declared to be a tad careless.

Houellebecq heartily admires Lovecraft for what he believes to be Lovecraft's unique approach to literature; in particular, he declares that Lovecraft's work is "an antidote against *all forms* of realism" (29; my emphasis). Houel-

---

1. Michel Houellebecq, *H. P. Lovecraft: Against the World, Against Life*, tr. Dorna Khazeni (San Francisco: Believer Books, 2005), 109. Further references will occur in the text.

lebecq elaborates on what he means by this remarkable assertion. Seizing upon Lovecraft's early lament that "Adulthood is hell,"[2] as if this view remained uniform throughout Lovecraft's life (as it clearly did not), Houellebecq states: "Lovecraft, for his part, knew he had nothing to do with this world. [. . .] The world sickened him and he saw no reason to believe that by *looking at things better* they might appear differently" (31).

But Houellebecq has confused *indifference* and *hatred*. The one does not imply the other, and Lovecraft himself rejected such a conflation. Houellebecq concludes his treatise by asserting that, for Lovecraft, "the world was evil, intrinsically evil, even by its very essence" (117). This makes Lovecraft sound like Thomas Ligotti, who really is a pessimist and misanthrope. Lovecraft explicitly denied that he was one:

> Contrary to what you may assume, I am *not a pessimist* but an *indifferentist*—that is, I don't make the mistake of thinking that the resultant of the natural forces surrounding and governing organic life will have any connexion with the wishes or tastes of any part of that organic life-processes. Pessimists are just as illogical as optimists; insomuch as both envisage the aims of mankind as unified, and as having a direct relationship (either of frustration or of fulfilment) to the inevitable flow of terrestrial motivation and events. That is—both schools retain in a vestigial way the primitive concept of a conscious teleology—of a cosmos which gives a damn one way or the other about the especial wants and ultimate welfare of mosquitoes, rats, lice, dogs, men, horses, pterodactyls, trees, fungi, dodos, or other forms of biological energy.[3]

Nevertheless, Houellebecq clings to his view in defiance of all contrary evidence, because it serves as a vital basis for his view of Lovecraft's literary work. For Lovecraft, "hatred of life precedes all literature. He was to remain steadfast in this regard. The rejection of all forms of realism is a preliminary condition for entering his universe" (57). But what does Houellebecq really mean by "realism"? It soon becomes clear: "In his entire body of work, there is not a single allusion to two of the realities to which we generally ascribe great importance: sex and money. Truly not one reference" (57). Houellebecq must know this is preposterous nonsense. Bobby Derie has written an entire treatise on *Sex and the Cthulhu Mythos* (2014), with two substantial chapters,

---

2. Letter to the Gallomo, 3 September 1920; in *Letters to Alfred Galpin*, ed. S. T. Joshi and David E. Schultz (New York: Hippocampus Press, 2003), 95.

3. Letter to James F. Morton, [30 November] 1929; in *Letters to James F. Morton*, ed. David E. Schultz and S. T. Joshi (New York: Hippocampus Press, 2011), 186.

occupying 130 pages, on Lovecraft's own attitudes on sex and discussions or allusions to sex in his fiction. Here we can refer in passing to such things as the cosmic rape in "The Dunwich Horror," the obvious references to the Deep Ones' mating with humans in "The Shadow over Innsmouth," and the successive gender-swapping of Ephraim/Asenath Waite in "The Thing on the Doorstep." One can even cite *The Case of Charles Dexter Ward,* where the preternaturally aged Joseph Curwen probably committed marital rape on his unwilling wife, Eliza Tillinghast, in order to produce offspring—Ann Tillinghast, who became the direct descendant of Charles Dexter Ward. Allusions to money are less frequent and less significant in Lovecraft's stories, but this one from "The Shadow over Innsmouth" should suffice: "I had no car, but was travelling by train, trolley, and motor-coach, always seeking the cheapest possible route" (CF 3.160).

Let us be charitable to Houellebecq's exaggerations. Even if we grant that his references to "sex and money" are meant to allude more broadly to the social realism that dominated European fiction up to and beyond Lovecraft's day, two significant caveats need to be made. First, much the same analysis could be made of many of Lovecraft's predecessors in weird fiction, from Poe to Bierce to Machen to Dunsany to Blackwood; in this regard, Lovecraft's avoidance of "sex and money" are only a more extreme instance of a tendency that long dominated a genre that had very different foci. Some of these writers had a few more female characters than Lovecraft did, and some (notably Poe and Machen) did refer covertly to sex, usually of an aberrant sort (as in the suggestion of brother-sister incest in "The Fall of the House of Usher" or the sexual depravities of Helen Vaughan in "The Great God Pan"). But Lovecraft is not a notable outlier in this regard. It is significant that Houellebecq cites the work of Richard Matheson as a sharp contrast to Lovecraft (51–52). It was, indeed, precisely the contention of Matheson and other writers of his generation that Lovecraft and his cohorts in *Weird Tales* had ignored the "realism" of daily life and sought to return weird fiction to that level.

Well and good. But this brings me to my second caveat: there are other types of realism than merely the mundane realism of portraying ordinary human beings going about their daily affairs. When Houellebecq repeatedly states that Lovecraft rejected "all forms" of realism, he is plainly contradicting Lovecraft himself. Although Houellebecq reveals some familiarity with Lovecraft's commonplace book, he is apparently ignorant of the essay "Notes on Writing Weird Fiction" (1933), where Lovecraft states unequivocally:

> In writing a weird story I always try very carefully to achieve the right mood and atmosphere, and place the emphasis where it belongs. One cannot, except in immature pulp charlatan–fiction, present an account of im-

possible, improbable, or inconceivable phenomena as a commonplace narrative of objective acts and conventional emotions. Inconceivable events and conditions have a special handicap to overcome, and this can be accomplished only through the maintenance of a *careful realism* [my emphasis] in every phase of the story *except* [Lovecraft's emphasis] that touching on the one given marvel.[4]

The realism Lovecraft is here referring to may or may not be realism of character portrayal; but in his own work he certainly emphasizes meticulous realism of setting and landscape, to say nothing of realism in regard to the facts of science. Houellebecq even admires the "oneiric precision" (74) of the description of the Old Ones in *At the Mountains of Madness*, but fails to acknowledge that this is a "realism" just as compelling and just as vital to Lovecraft's purpose as the "utterly banal settings (supermarkets, gas stations . . .)" (51) found in Matheson's work.

But if Houellebecq is far off the mark in this aspect of his analysis of Lovecraft, he goes even further astray in regard to the most controverted aspect of Lovecraft's life and work—his racism. Because Houellebecq is convinced that the essence of Lovecraft's work is "Absolute hatred of the world in general, aggravated by an aversion to the modern world in particular" (57), and believes that Lovecraft himself is "misanthropic and slightly sinister" (99)—a view we have already seen to be largely false—he focuses on racism as some sort of secret key to understanding the totality of Lovecraft's literary work. He maintains that Lovecraft's difficult two years in New York—where, unlike in Providence, he was forced to rub shoulders with people of all different races in a bootless quest to secure income—were a kind of crucible that led him to his great burst of creativity when he returned to Providence for the final decade of his life.

Houellebecq trots out the now-familiar passages from Lovecraft's letters on this topic, notably the discussion of the "Italo-Semitico-Mongoloid"[5] denizens of the lower East Side (although this passage relates to Lovecraft's first trip to New York in April 1922). This passage is now, in Houellebecque's view, to be regarded as an all-purpose hermeneutic for the interpretation of the "great texts" of Lovecraft's later years: "His descriptions of the nightmare entities that populate the Cthulhu cycle spring directly from this hallucinatory vision" (107). What is the proof of this remarkable assertion? Houellebecq

---

4. *Collected Essays*, ed. S. T. Joshi (New York: Hippocampus Press, 2004–06), 2.177.

5. Letter to Frank Belknap Long, 21 March 1924; in *Selected Letters*, ed. August Derleth, Donald Wandrei, and James Turner (Sauk City, WI: Arkham House, 1965–76), 1.333–34.

offers . . . "The Horror at Red Hook" (1925). Well, yes—but, if I may lapse into common parlance, what else have ya got? How do the foreign-born people of the lower East Side bear any relation to the entities depicted in Lovecraft's later work—whether it be the crustacean fungi from Yuggoth in "The Whisperer in Darkness," or the barrel-shaped Old Ones in *At the Mountains of Madness*, or the Great Race in "The Shadow out of Time," or even the nebulous entities (assuming there is more than one) that come down in the meteorite in "The Colour out of Space" and corrupt both the landscape and the human denizens of the Gardner farmhouse? Any parallels are, as I have asserted elsewhere,[6] rather opaque. And this is apparently why Houellebecq simply doesn't even discuss the matter; he doesn't even cite the Deep Ones of "The Shadow over Innsmouth," which of all the "great texts" of Lovecraft's last decade of writing could be plausibly assumed to be founded on racist presuppositions (in this case, the dangers of miscegenation).

Houellebecq does claim that the various cultists who worship the Great Old Ones are "almost always half-breeds, mulattos, of mixed blood, among the basest of species" (109). Even this description is not accurate in its details and seems largely derived from the portrayal of the Cthulhu cultists in "The Call of Cthulhu." The sinister Mr. Noyes in "The Whisperer in Darkness," who is clearly allied with the fungi from Yuggoth, is unimpeachably Caucasian and well-bred. Otherwise, however, Houellebecq simply *asserts* the ubiquity of the racial motif in Lovecraft's fiction without making any attempt to establish it with compelling evidence—or evidence of any sort.

It may be helpful to contrast Houellebecq's discussion of this topic—and especially of the effect of Lovecraft's two years in New York upon the rest of his life and work—with the comments of someone who *actually knew Lovecraft* and could speak much more authoritatively on the matter. In his celebrated memoir, *In Memoriam: Howard Phillips Lovecraft* (1941), W. Paul Cook speaks eloquently of how Lovecraft became a very different human being after New York:

> But Lovecraft never became thoroughly humanized, he never became the man we love to recall, until his New York experience. To the very end of his days he hated New York with a consuming passion. I mean the city itself, not the many good friends he had there. But it took the privations, trials and testing fires of New York to bring his best to the surface. And it took personal contact with those cultured, clever, sophisticated New York amateurs and

---

6. See (see "Charles Baxter on Lovecraft," *Lovecraft Annual* No. 9 (2015): 120–21.

semi-amateurs to make him look out and not in, to broaden him so that he could cultivate an artistic tolerance, if not entirely altering his viewpoint.[7]

This sounds a lot more like the Lovecraft that we see in the letters of his last decade of life—and, more pertinently, in his literary work of that period.

Houellebecq's characterisation of Lovecraft's racism is part and parcel of his view that Lovecraft was an "obsolete reactionary" (115)—but again, he must know that this is false. Even de Camp's biography makes plain Lovecraft's late conversion to moderate (non-Marxist) socialism, and his later letters are full of condemnations of his own earlier conservatism in the political and economic sphere. But this fact would constitute a serious qualification of the conclusions Houellebecq has already arrived at, and therefore it is simply ignored. Here as in other facets of his book, it becomes clear that Houellebecq has evolved a specific view of Lovecraft, derived from early readings (he first read Lovecraft in French translation at the age of sixteen) and augmented by highly selective absorption of other texts, and he has by accident or design dispensed with evidence that would contradict that view.

It is, on the face of it, implausible to think that a young French enthusiast who may or may not have read much of Lovecraft's work in English, who does not claim to be a literary scholar, and who clearly has his own agenda in portraying Lovecraft as he did.[8] could have come up with a magic formula for understanding Lovecraft's work—that it is all based on "racial hatred"—that has eluded the hundreds of other critics, in English and in other languages, who have assessed the Providence writer's work. Houellebecq is not shy about his purported breakthrough. In his preface to the 1999 French edition of his book he declares that he experienced two surprises when first reading Lovecraft—one was his "absolute materialism," and the "other great cause of my surprise was his obsessive racism; never in the reading of his descriptions of nightmare creatures could I have divined that their source was to be found in *real* human beings" (24). Here again he simply asserts the point, apparently believing that it has been proven in the body of his treatise; but it hasn't. Elsewhere he remarks, without the least trace of irony, that "The role of this racial hatred in Lovecraft's body of work has often been underestimated" (108). Just so! But this circumstance does not incline Houellebecq to raise doubts about his own conclusions.

Houellebecq's views in his rather sophomoric treatise have had a lamen-

---

7. *Ave atque Vale: Reminiscences of H. P. Lovecraft*, ed. S. T. Joshi and David E. Schultz (West Warwick, RI: Necronomicon Press, 2018), 42.

8. See Todd Spaulding, "Lovecraft and Houellebecq: Two Against the World," *Lovecraft Annual* No. 9 (2015): 182–213.

tably wide influence on other critics who have harped on the same theme. China Miéville has maintained that the "depth and viciousness of Lovecraft's racism is [sic] known to me . . . It goes further, in my opinion, than 'merely' being a racist—I follow Michel Houellebecq . . . in thinking that Lovecraft's oeuvre, his work itself, is inspired by deeply structured with race hatred."[9] Needless to say, Miéville himself provides no evidence for this assertion, believing that Houellebecq has done the job for him; but he hasn't. Charles Baxter, in his extremely hostile review of Leslie S. Klinger's *The New Annotated H. P. Lovecraft* (*New York Review of Books*, 18 December 2014), claims that Lovecraft was a "pathological racist"[10] and goes on to maintain that racism was central to Lovecraft's literary work; he does not specifically cite Houellebecq as a source for this view, nor does he argue for his view with anything approaching convincing evidence.

There is some amusement in noting that Houellebecq himself stated, in his 1999 preface, that "it seems to me that I wrote this book as a sort of first novel. A novel with a single character (H. P. Lovecraft himself)—a novel that was constrained in that all the facts it conveyed and all the texts it cited had to be exact, but a sort of novel nonetheless" (23). We have seen that Houellebecq's citation of Lovecraft's texts are far from "exact," but otherwise he is sadly accurate in stating that his work really is a kind of novel. It should be emphasized that his view of Lovecraft is on the whole a positive one, and he has great admiration for Lovecraft as a prose stylist and as one who contributed something genuinely new to the literature of the world; even his discussion of Lovecraft's racism is largely free of the rancor and bitter hostility that we have seen in a number of other commentators on this subject. But even so, the sad fact is that Michel Houellebecq has promulgated a scurrilous falsehood—based on inadequate evidence and a jaundiced view of what he wants Lovecraft's work to represent—that has infected the work of critics and scholars far more hostile to Lovecraft than he is.

---

9. Quoted in S. T. Joshi, *Lovecraft and Weird Fiction: Selected Blog Posts, 2009–2017* (Seattle: Sarnath Press, 2017), 83–84.

10. See Joshi, "Charles Baxter on Lovecraft" 109.

Lovecraft and "Adept's Gambit"

The publication of the original version of "Adept's Gambit" by Fritz Leiber (1910–1992) is a literary event worth noting for more than one reason, not the least of which is that it is probably the first major prose work by a writer who would go on to become one of the leading figures of fantasy, horror, and science fiction literature in the twentieth century. But the fascination of this version of "Adept's Gambit" is augmented by what it tells us about Leiber's relations with his earliest mentor, H. P. Lovecraft.

For Lovecraft read "Adept's Gambit" in late 1936, just a few months before his untimely death on March 15, 1937, and commented on it at length. However, an examination of that letter (printed here as an appendix to the Leiber story) establishes that the version of "Adept's Gambit" published here is, in fact, not the first draft that Leiber must have written earlier in 1936, but one that has already taken account of some of Lovecraft's strictures regarding historical anachronisms, stylistic infelicities, and other apparent flaws in the text.

Interest in the Leiber story—or, rather, this version of it—was strengthened by Lovecraft's several passing comments that Leiber had dropped references to the ersatz myth-cycle that Lovecraft had created in the stories of his final decade of writing, now called the Cthulhu Mythos. Could "Adept's Gambit" be Leiber's first pastiche of Lovecraft? He did not in fact write a full-fledged pastiche of the Cthulhu Mythos until the late story "The Terror from the Depths" (1976), assuming that we can exclude such a whimsy as "To Arkham and the Stars" (1966) or several other stories, some as early as 1942, in which Lovecraft's tales could be said to have served as an imaginative springboard.

A reading of this early version of "Adept's Gambit" will dispel any suggestion that Leiber was attempting to imitate Lovecraft. What we have, in the way of references to Lovecraft's myth-cycle, is a succession of oaths or expostulations by various characters, including one, "By Cthulhu!" in which, in his original typescript, Leiber has in fact misspelled the name of Lovecraft's octopoid entity. There are other passing references to Shub-Niggurath and Yog-Sothoth, and one reference to the *Book of Eibon*, a tome of elder lore invented by Clark Ashton Smith, but that is the extent of it. Lovecraft is quite right in saying that the dominant influences on Leiber's story were such fantasists as

Lord Dunsany, James Branch Cabell, and James Stephens. Lovecraft might have added Robert E. Howard, for "Adept's Gambit" is the first of a whole series of adventures by Fafhrd and the Grey (later Gray) Mouser, written over the entire course of his career, in which Leiber adapted, updated, and humanized the literary subgenre of sword-and-sorcery, which Howard could be said to have initiated with his stories of Conan the Cimmerian, King Kull, and other superheroes.

The differences between this version of "Adept's Gambit" and the one first published in *Night's Black Agents* (1947) are, on a surface level, easy to detect. The central female character, here named Elsbeth, was renamed Ahura; her brother, the adept of the title, is here called Isaiah ben Elshaz but later named Anra Devadoris. Overall, the narrative has been shortened from 37,500 words to about 34,000; Leiber here may have taken to heart Lovecraft's advice to condense the rather flippant opening section and focus on the increasingly grim and compelling tale of Elsbeth, her brother, and Fafhrd and the Grey Mouser's encounter with the Old Man without a Beard in the Castle Called Mist.

Interestingly, the phrase "Elder Gods" appears in both texts. The term has gained notoriety among readers and critics of Lovecraft. It never appears in Lovecraft's own work; August Derleth, Lovecraft's most fervent disciple, coined it in order to create a set of "good" gods to counter what he believed to be the "evil" gods of the Cthulhu Mythos—Cthulhu, Yog-Sothoth, Nyarlathotep, and the like. In so doing, Derleth created exactly the naïve good-vs.-evil scenario that Lovecraft expressly eschewed in his own work. Leiber's use of the term "Elder Gods" may nonetheless owe something to his reading of Lovecraft. The phrase "Elder Things" appears in *At the Mountains of Madness* (1931), which Leiber surely read when it was serialized in *Astounding Stories* (February–April 1936); it refers to the barrel-shaped intergalactic entities found by explorers in Antarctica. In "The Strange High House in the Mist" (1926) the phrase "Elder Ones" appears, in a context not entirely dissimilar to that of "Adept's Gambit." The phrase recurs in *The Dream-Quest of Unknown Kadath* (1926–27), but Leiber could not have read this work when he wrote "Adept's Gambit," as Lovecraft's short novel remained unpublished until 1943.

Some conjectures can be made as to what the earliest version of "Adept's Gambit" might have been like if we read Lovecraft's detailed comments on the version he read. He pointed out numerous anachronisms and misspellings of ancient historical terms; for example, he noted that Hittites could not have existed at the time the story is evidently set (probably the 3rd century B.C.E.), and that Philistines were "less & less heard from as the Hellenistic age advances." Sure enough, there are no mentions of Hittites or Philistines in this draft of "Adept's Gambit." Lovecraft also comments on the apparent error of writing "Cilesia," a non-existent country; he conjectures that Leiber had the ancient realm of Cilicia in mind, and this term shows up in this draft. Other comments by Lovecraft show that Leiber took to heart many of Lovecraft's strictures in regard to historical details of this sort.

What Leiber did not change, in this or the later, published text of "Adept's Gambit" is the very fact that the tale is set in the ancient world of Hellenistic Greece and the Middle East. In later adventures of Fafhrd and the Gray Mouser, Leiber wisely invented the setting—either Nehwon ("nowhen" backwards) or Lankhmar, a city that has elements that evoke classical antiquity but which is fundamentally a product of Leiber's imagination. Indeed, in the published draft of "Adept's Gambit" Leiber has in some senses augmented the historical references, disregarding Lovecraft's advice to downplay them. As his Fafhrd and Gray Mouser cycle evolved, he then had to account for why and how his adventurers had managed to get themselves thrust into a specific historical period, doing so in the later story "The Wrong Branch" (1968).

Leiber's revisions of this draft of "Adept's Gambit" apparently were completed in early 1946.[1] In the late essay "The Profession of Science Fiction" (1977), Leiber provides valuable clues as to his purpose in writing the story:

> I had a supernatural-terror story plot-device somewhat resembling that of Poe's "The Fall of the House of Usher," which enabled me to say something about my sexual curiosities and inhibitions. A brother and sister are mutually telepathic, but his will is stronger. He is avidly curious about life but dreads direct human contact. So he forces her into a life of prostitution and sexual debauchery which he experiences vicariously through her. The contrast between their life-ways grows until he is living in a tomb while experiencing erotic delights telepathically through her. How to involve the Mouser and Fafhrd in this tale? He wants to have telepathic experiences through them as well. . . . (Incidentally, I don't believe I could have written this analysis of the story *then*.)[2]

Bruce Byfield points out that this very interpretation of the story shows that Leiber had accepted Lovecraft's analysis of "The Fall of the House of Usher" in "Supernatural Horror in Literature" (1927)—that it "displays an aabnormally linked trinity of entities at the end of a long and isolated history—a brother, his twin sister, and their incredibly ancient house all

---

1. See Bruce Byfield, *Witches of the Mind: A Critical Study of Fritz Leiber* (West Warwick, RI: Necronomicon Press, 1991), 15.

2. Cited in Byfield, 15.

sharing a single soul and meeting one common dissolution at the same moment."[3] Leiber was probably aware of this analysis; he may have read it in the original publication of Lovecraft's essay in the *Recluse* (1927), and almost certainly read the revised serialization in the *Fantasy Fan* (1933–35). It is of interest that the puritanical Lovecraft says nothing about the sexual suggestions and implications of "Adept's Gambit," including a vivid description of Elsbeth's witnessing her own mother descend into prostitition.

Leiber wisely preserved this early draft of "Adept's Gambit"; he eventually passed it on to Jack L. Chalker.[4] While the later version is unquestionably more polished, there is much reason to appreciate the expansiveness and richness of this earlier, longer text. The many fans of both Fritz Leiber and H. P. Lovecraft have waited too long for its appearance, but they need wait no longer.

3. *The Annotated Supernatural Horror in Literature*, ed. S. T. Joshi (New York: Hippocampus Press, 2nd ed. 2012), 61–62.

4. The title page of the story bears the following inscription in Leiber's handwriting: "With best wishes to Jack Chalker from Fafhrd, the Mouser, and Fritz Leiber." I am grateful to John Pelan for providing me with a copy of the text.

Solar Pons Meets Cthulhu:
Detective Elements in Derleth's Mythos Tales

August Derleth could well be called the inveterate imitator. Save in his (admittedly brilliant) regional writing, Derleth appeared content to do nothing but produce pastiches of those authors who most appealed to him—although in some cases the result was unwitting parody or caricature. The two best-known objects of Derleth's imitation are, of course, H. P. Lovecraft—represented by Derleth's innumerable and interminable "posthumous collaborations" (to which only his own demise put an end) and additions to Lovecraft's myth-cycle—and Sir Arthur Conan Doyle—represented by Derleth's seven volumes of tales (one a novel) dealing with Solar Pons and his assistant, Dr. Lyndon Parker. It should, then, not be surprising that Derleth would take the opportunity to mingle Lovecraftian elements in the so-called Pontine canon, and Pontine (or, more broadly, detective) elements in his "Cthulhu Mythos" tales. Such is indeed the case, although this mingling occurs to a much greater degree than has hitherto been realised.

Derleth began writing the Solar Pons tales well before he started his Mythos stories and novels: the first Pons work, "The Adventure of the Black Narcissus," was written in the fall of 1928, when Derleth had just graduated from the University of Wisconsin—he was nineteen years old.[1] (Conan Doyle himself was, incidentally, still alive—he would not die until 1930.) The tale appeared in the detective pulp *Dragnet* for February 1929. Already, however, in March 1927 Derleth was writing to Lovecraft about Conan Doyle and was even then thinking of starting a series of pastiches; Lovecraft writes to him: "Good luck with your continuations—& may the mantle of greatness fall upon you!"[2] When the "Black Narcissus" tale appeared in *Dragnet*, Derleth urged Lovecraft to write to the editor and praise the tale, so that the latter would be

---

1. See Derleth's "Afterword" to *The Casebook of Solar Pons* (New York: Pinnacle, 1975), 273.

2. Lovecraft to Derleth, 26 March 1927; *Essential Solitude: The Letters of H. P. Lovecraft to August Derleth,* ed. David E. Schultz and S. T. Joshi (New York: Hippocampus Press, 2008), 1.77.

willing to use more of Derleth's work. Lovecraft amiably complied, and his letter was duly published in the letter column in the issue for April 1929. The concluding sentence reads: "I sincerely hope that Mr. Derleth is a permanent member of your writing staff, for his 'Solar Pons' seems eminently qualified to take rank with the standard detectives of fiction."[3]

But the Solar Pons tales were not Derleth's only excursions into the mystery genre. In the early 1930s he churned out several (abysmally wretched) novels involving a Judge Peck, most of them set in his native Wisconsin. Lovecraft read several of these (*The Man on All Fours*, *The Sign of Fear*,[4] *Three Who Died*); remarking of the first: "[I] guessed the solution on p. 32."[5] Lovecraft well knew that these detective stories of Derleth's were "all mere pot-boiling";[6] what he didn't know was that most of Derleth's entire output would be pot-boiling.

But the Solar Pons tales are the more amusing for their actual inclusion of Lovecraftian elements. We learn that Pons was himself author of two rather peculiar works: *An Inquiry into the Nan-Natal Ruins of Ponape* and *An Examination of the Cthulhu Cult and Others* (1931).[7] I have not been able to locate the tale or tales where these titles are cited—perhaps they are only mentioned in Derleth's little study of Pons, *A Praed Street Dossier* (Mycroft and Moran, 1968), which I have not been able to consult. But what is still more interesting is that in "The Adventure of the Six Silver Spiders" (1950) Pons encounters a book catalogue in which the *Necronomicon*, the *Cultes des Goules* of the Comte d'Erlette, Prinn's *De Vermis Mysteriis*, and the *Liber Ivonis* are cited! (One interesting datum is that Derleth provides a date and place—Madrid, 1647—for the reputed Spanish printing of Olaus Wormius's Latin translation of the *Necronomicon*, although in "History of the 'Necronomicon'" Lovecraft says that the Spanish edition was "without identifying marks, and located as to time and place by internal typographical evidence only.") The clever Pons, however, realises that the catalogue is a hoax and that "All these books have a precarious existence only in the writings of certain minor [!] authors of Amer-

---

3. Letter to the editor, *Dragnet* 2, No. 3 (April 1929): 372.

4. The title is, of course, a blatant plagiarism of Conan Doyle's Holmes novels *The Sign of Four* and *The Valley of Fear*.

5. Letters to J. Vernon Shea, 10 February 1935; *Letters to J. Vernon Shea, Carl F. Strauch, and Lee McBride White* (New York: Hippocampus Press, 2016), 242.

6. Ibid., 275.

7. See Luther Norris's "Foreword" to *The Memoirs of Solar Pons* (New York: Pinnacle, 1975), ix, and Anthony Boucher's "Introduction" to *The Reminiscences of Solar Pons* (New York: Pinnacle, 1975), 2–3.

ican origin, all apparently followers, in a remote sense, of the work of Edgar Allan Poe."[8] The catalogue turns out to be merely a ruse, and these Lovecraftian elements do not figure in the rest of the tale. There is, however, one further and exceedingly subtle Lovecraftian echo in the story. Parker tells of one of Solar Pons's frequent utterances: "There is a sense of adventurous expectancy about a London fog."[9] This is nothing less than a reminiscence of a celebrated remark made by Lovecraft in one of his letters: "What has haunted me for nearly 40 years is *a strange sense of adventurous expectancy connected with landscape & architecture & sky-effects.*"[10] This quotation actually derives from a letter to Derleth, and the phrase "adventurous expectancy" becomes a catchword in Lovecraft, occurring in letters and stories alike. It can only, then, be wondered in how many other Pons tales such Lovecraftian reminiscences can be found.

But if Lovecraft is seen to mingle with Pons, then Pons can equally well be said to mingle with Lovecraft—or, rather, with Derleth's pastiches of Lovecraft. The two most striking occurrences are found in the two novels, *The Lurker at the Threshold* (1945) and *The Trail of Cthulhu* (1962).

In *The Lurker at the Threshold* we are presented with an exact counterpart for the Holmes-Watson and Pons-Parker duo, in the figures of Dr. Seneca Lapham and Winfield Phillips, the narrator of Part III of *Lurker*. The whole concluding section of the novel exactly duplicates the scenario formed by Conan Doyle and taken up by Derleth in the Pontine canon: "The client seeks, the detective helps, the detective examines the scene of the crime, the detective investigates and, finally, the detective exposes the criminal and brings the culprit to book."[11] In this case the client is Stephen Bates, who duly consults Lapham on the campus of Miskatonic University, is queried by Lapham in strict Holmesian fashion as to the nature of the case, and who leaves a bundle of papers (his own account of his experiences and those of his cousin Ambrose Dewart) for Lapham to examine. After Bates leaves, Lapham proceeds to debate the matter with the Watsonian Phillips, who acts as the "straight man" and allows Lapham to pontificate in a very Holmesian and Pontine manner ("Faith comes readily without any evidence whatever, and very hard in the face of evidence that should not be there").[12] Lapham, in-

---

8. "The Adventure of the Six Silver Spiders," in *the Memoirs of Solar Pons*, 126.

9. Ibid., 131.

10. *Essential Solitude* 1.237; emphasis Lovecraft's.

11. Luther Norris, "Foreword" to *The Memoirs of Solar Pons*, viii–ix.

12. *The Lurker at the Threshold*, in *The Watchers out of Time and Others* (Sauk City, WI: Arkham House, 1974), 117.

deed, frequently remarks that the whole affair at Billington's Wood is a "mystery" and a "puzzle,"[13] and in the course of the discussion he "advance[s] an hypothesis"[14] to explain the whole matter. Most remarkably, Lapham manages to elucidate the entire mystery merely by inference and the examination of the evidence presented to him by Bates—he has not yet even gone to the "scene of the crime"! This is oddly reminiscent of John Dickson Carr's novel *The Arabian Nights Murder* (1936), where Dr. Gideon Fell, after merely listening (for an entire night) to the accounts of three detectives who have successively been put in charge of a case, solves the whole matter in the comfort of his easy chair. It is, of course, unlikely that Derleth had the Carr novel in mind when writing *The Lurker at the Threshold*, but the very similarity underscores the detective elements in the work. Lapham in the end does in fact go to Billington's Wood and, by killing Dewart (who is possessed by his ancestor Billington), ends the horror and prevents Yog-Sothoth from re-entering the world of man.

The Trail of Cthulhu is less strictly Holmesian or Pontine, and Dr. Laban Shrewsbury seems less a pure detective than a "psychic detective" in the manner of Hodgson's Carnacki or Blackwood's John Silence. Lovecraft's remark about the volume *John Silence–Physician Extraordinary* is illuminating: it is "a book of five related tales, through which a single character runs his triumphant course. Marred only by traces of the popular and conventional detective-story atmosphere—for Dr. Silence is one of those benevolent geniuses who employ their remarkable powers to aid worthy fellow-men in difficulty—these narratives contain some of the author's best work."[15] So, too, *Trail* is a series of five connected tales in which the presence of Shrewsbury can always be felt, although in the second and third narratives he is nominally absent (presumably because he is off on Celaeno in the Hyades, an especially favoured place of repose for him). Like Pons, Shrewsbury is the author of several curious volumes—*An Investigation into the Myth-Patterns of Latterday Primitives with Especial Reference to the R'lyeh Text* and *Cthulhu in the Necronomicon*.[16] And like Sherlock Holmes, who appeared to have died at the end of *The Memoirs of Sherlock Holmes* but who came back to life in *The Return of Sherlock Holmes* due to popular clamour, Shrewsbury is believed to have perished at the end of the first episode,[17] but is ultimately resurrected (although it might well be said that this

---

13. Ibid., 120, 126.

14. Ibid., 127.

15. "Supernatural Horror in Literature" (1927), in *The Annotated Supernatural Horror in Literature*, ed. S. T. Joshi (New York: Hippocampus Press, 2nd ed. 2012), 89.

16. *The Trail of Cthulhu* (New York: Ballantine, 1971), 30.

17. Ibid., 45.

is *against* popular clamour; I for one would have been perfectly happy to countenance Shrewsbury's death). The fifth episode of *Trail* takes place near Ponape—we can hardly fail to recall Pons's treatise on the subject.

The Holmes-Watson or Pons-Parker parallel does not hold quite as good in *Trail*, although each episode is narrated by a young man who is ultimately initiated into the mysteries of the Elder Gods by Shrewsbury. The similarity is more with John Silence, since Shrewsbury, "in his pursuit of Cthulhu, [is] intent upon saving the world he knows from enslavement to a ghastly era of aeon-old evil completely beyond the comprehension of mankind!"[18] (You tell 'em, Augie.) Derleth professed to enjoy the John Silence tales,[19] and it is likely that, given his addiction to pastiche, he has in *The Trail of Cthulhu* attempted to render the highest form of flattery to both Lovecraft and Blackwood.

It may well be remarked that Lovecraft himself was not above using elements of the detective story in his own work: "The Lurking Fear," "The Shunned House," "The Call of Cthulhu," *The Case of Charles Dexter Ward*, and others all involve characters who gradually piece together disparate bits of information and ultimately encounter the horror as a result. Mystery may indeed be a key element in a horror tale, since it provides the element of the unknown that produces the "fear of the unknown" which Lovecraft knew to be the foundation of fantastic writing.

But it must be said that Lovecraft employed his mystery or detective elements in a far subtler manner than Derleth. Derleth's "Cthulhu Mythos" tales are not merely atrociously bad attempts to imitate Lovecraft's style and themes, but their inclusion of a very conventional detective element only augments their dismal wretchedness. The Solar Pons tales, conversely, are really enjoyable bits of pastiche, and the intermittent Lovecraftian elements found in at least a few of them create that tongue-in-cheek humour adding to the sense of "affectionate spoofing"[20] which Vincent Starrett rightly detected in the Pontine canon. The Pons tales deserve to survive, whereas it should probably be a blessing both to Lovecraftdom and to Derleth's reputation if his Mythos tales obtained the permanent inhumation which they so richly deserve.

---

18. Ibid.

19. Cf. Lovecraft to Derleth, 25 December 1926: "I am not surprised that you found 'John Silence' interesting" (*Essential Solitude* 1.57).

20. Vincent Starrett, "In Re: Solar Pons," in *Regarding Sherlock Holmes: The Adventures of Solar Pons* (New York: Pinnacle, 1974), n.p.

IV. The Moderns

Shirley Jackson and Weird Fiction

Shirley Jackson (1916-1965) was an American novelist and short story writer who utilized the supernatural in numerous works, notably *The Haunting of Hill House* (Viking, 1959). In a career that spanned little more than two decades and included six novels (only one of them truly supernatural, however), dozens of short stories, and two scintillating works about her four children, Jackson produced a substantial body of work that is insuffiently appreciated both as a contribution to American literature and as a contribution to supernatural fiction.

Jackson began her career by writing short stories, chiefly for the *New Yorker*, in the early 1940s. Not long thereafter, however, she also began writing stories about her family (she would eventually have four children with her husband, the literary critic Stanley Edgar Hyman), most (but not all) of which were collected in two delightful volumes, *Life among the Savages* (Farrar, Straus, 1953) and *Raising Demons* (Farrar, Straus, 1957). By a comparison of these two bodies of work, it becomes clear that one of the central themes in Jackson's work is the perversion of domestic felicity by mental instability, psychological cruelty, and isolation. There is, to be sure, a certain element of fantasy even in her domestic accounts, since she deliberately ignored or downplayed the tensions in her own family life (her husband, for instance, was a notorious philanderer, and she herself was a social and intellectual outcast when her husband was teaching at Bennington College in Vermont). But in her fiction, familial conflicts reach such a stage that they generate sadness, loneliness, and even horror.

"The House" (*Woman's Day*, May 1952) exemplifies the skill with which Jackson can insinuate the supernatural into an otherwise innocuous-seeming domestic narrative. In this account of a family moving into a ramshackle old house in New England. As the tale develops, the house seems almost to be alive, and a conversation with an old lady suggests that she may be well over a century and a half old. But when this story was incorporated into *Life among the Savages*, the suggestions of the supernatural were excised and the tale becomes harmlessly genial. Another domestic scenario—the act of hiring or using a maid—is made the focus of several stories, and in one instance the supernatural comes into play. "Family Magician" (*Woman's Home Companion*,

September 1949) is a humorous tale in which a maid named Mallie uses magic to fulfill her duties. It is apparently Jackson's first explicitly supernatural story.

Many of Jackson's early stories were gathered in *The Lottery* (Farrar, Straus, 1949), but the collection betrays some signs of hasty assemblage, as it is very heterogeneous and somewhat uneven. It was meant to capitalize on the notoriety of "The Lottery," which created a sensation when it appeared in the *New Yorker* (26 June 1948). This celebrated tale is of course not supernatural in the conventional sense; indeed, the horror is engendered precisely because the incidents it relates—a lottery held every year among the townspeople, the one chosen then being stoned to death, evidently as a means of ensuring a good harvest—might occur anywhere. In another sense, however, the story might be considered an alternate-world fantasy: lotteries of this sort have never existed, but Jackson suggests that they are being held in many other communities aside from the one in which the tale is set.

Other tales in *The Lottery* suggest the supernatural, if only because of the bizarre behavior of their protagonists. One of the most delicate is "The Daemon Lover" (*Woman's Home Companion*, February 1949), which introduces a whole series of tales in which a character named James Harris, the Daemon Lover, figures or is alluded to. In this story a rather neurotic young woman named Margaret expects Harris to show up at her apartment one day to marry her. When he does not show up at the appointed time (leading the reader to wonder whether he exists at all or is merely a wish-fulfillment fantasy on Margaret's part), Margaret goes out to look for him; after a time she is led successively to various locations by people who claim to have seen Harris, and in the end she comes to the door of another apartment and thinks she hears his voice within. The tale ends on a properly inconclusive note, and the reader is faced with several disturbing alternatives: Has Margaret imagined the entire series of incidents? Or worse, have strangers deliberately misled her out of some twisted sadistic impulse? Another tale in *The Lottery*, "The Intoxicated," reveals a rather tiresome party at which a man ends up talking with the teenage daughter of his hostess, who is convinced that the world is about to end. Once again we are left in doubt as to whether the girl is either truly clairvoyant, or insane, or merely poking some malicious fun at the guest. Another tale, "'All She Said Was "Yes"'" (*Vogue*, 1 November 1962), is more explicitly a tale of clairvoyance in its depiction of a girl who knows that her parents will die in a boating accident and is not shocked but merely saddened when the inevitable outcome occurs.

Strangely, Jackson herself did not assemble another story collection after *The Lottery*, although she wrote a substantial number of stories in the 1950s and 1960s. Possibly her attention had shifted to novel-writing. In any case, one masterful story, "The Lovely House" (in *New World Writing: Second Mentor Selection* [New American Library, 1952]), remained uncollected until after her death, when it was included (under the title "A Visit") in the posthumous volume *Come Along with Me* (Viking, 1968). This delicate and subtle story again features a young woman named Margaret, who comes to the home of her college friend, Carla, for a visit. (The story was evidently inspired by a visit to Jackson's house in Westport, Connecticut, by the poet Dylan Thomas.) In the course of the narrative we are led to believe that Margaret will no longer be able to leave the house, because her spirit has been captured by Carla's mother, who is weaving a tapestry and has now incorporated a figure resembling Margaret into it.

Jackson's novels are all of interest, but only three can be said to be horrific, and of these only one, the celebrated *Haunting of Hill House*, is explicitly supernatural; it is, indeed, one of the finest haunted house novels ever written, and its atmosphere of mingled pathos and terror is almost unparalleled. Her first two novels, *The Road through the Wall* (Farrar, Straus, 1948) and *Hangsaman* (Farrar, Straus, 1951), are mainstream novels of character and society, although the latter engenders a compelling atmosphere of weirdness by its use of stream-of-consciousness, which at times produces a bizarrely hallucinatory effect. *The Bird's Nest* (Farrar, Straus, 1954) is a novel about split personality, as a young woman named Elizabeth Richmond appears to have four separate personalities, one of whom, Bess, is a frightening megalomaniac. But the narration is crude and lacking in subtlety. *The Sundial* (Farrar, Straus, 1958) is nearly unclassifiable: this account of the Halloran family, ruled by a matriarch, Oriana Halloran, that is convinced that the rest of the world will imminently be destroyed and only their house preserved, gains hypnotic power by its suggestion that the family member who devised the prediction—Aunt Fanny, who claimed to have gained it from the spirit of her dead father—will actually come true. The novel is ferociously satirical in its dissection of the psychological failings of each member of the household, and is perhaps the pinnacle of the artistic misanthropy that Jackson displayed in a number of her works. This misanthropy is not only exhibited in such a short story as "One Ordinary Day, with Peanuts" (*F&SF*, January 1955)—in which a couple chooses, purely by whim, to be alternately benevolent and malicious to the people they encounter in the course of their day—but in Jackson's final novel, *We Have Always Lived in the Castle* (Viking, 1962), a non-supernatural tale mystery tale in which a woman and her cousin, Constance and Merricat Blackwood, are the victims of social ostracism because of a murder committed years before—a murder that proves to have been committed by Merricat.

The incomplete novel *Come Along with Me* might have become a work of the supernatural, as it features a woman who leaves her past behind and adopts the name Angela Motorman. She admits that she "dabbles in the supernatural," and at the end of the fragment she holds a séance. Nothing is known about Jackson's plans for the development of this novel.

The Haunting of Hill House concerns the efforts of Dr. John Montague, an investigator of "supernatural phenomena," to probe the secrets of Hill House (whose exact location is never specified), with the aid of three other persons who have exhibited sensitivity to the occult: Eleanor Vance, a woman named only Theodora, and Luke Sanderson. The focus is on Eleanor, who has led a dismal and lonely life up to that point but seems transformed into a vibrant, carefree personality when in Hill House. Although Theodora initially befriends Eleanor, she is disturbed by Eleanor's increasingly odd behavior and thereafter develops a relationship with Luke, earning Eleanor's jealousy. A succession of supernatural phenomena—a cold spot in the hallway; knocking heard intermittently at night on various guests' doors; some doglike creature seen on the grounds—plagues the house. Montague comes to believe that Eleanor should leave the house because it is upsetting her, but she refuses; in a final gesture of defiance she drives off in her car and smashes it into a tree in the yard, killing herself; her act echoes that of the last occupant of Hill House, who died in this fashion eighteen years before.

The key to the novel appears to be the Shakespearean tag "Journeys end in lovers meeting," repeated frequently throughout the text. We are led to believe that Eleanor has in fact met her lover—the house itself, which does not want her to leave. And yet, the various supernatural manifestations in the novel do not appear to be well coordinated, and come to seem random and unmotivated. Nevertheless, *The Haunting of Hill House* develops a powerful atmosphere fusing weirdness with pathos, so that it becomes simultaneously a tale of the supernatural and an incisive study of character. Jackson wrote a lecture about the novel, "Experience and Fiction" (included in *Come Along with Me* [Viking, 1968]), in which she states that she herself believed in the supernatural and did considerable research in writing the work, including reading papers by the Society for Psychical Research.

The Haunting of Hill House has served as the basis for two films, Robert Wise's powerful and atmospheric *The Haunting* (1963), and a tawdry, special-effects-laden remake, *The Haunting* (1999), directed by Jan De Bont.

Jackson's work is widely various, especially in the short story. She has written charmingly witty tales of her own experiences ("My Life with R. H. Macy" [*New Republic*, December 22, 1941]), grim tales of psychological horror ("The Renegade" [*Harper's*, November 1948], "The Summer People" [*Charm*,

September 1950]), even a curious tale of science fiction ("Bulletin" [*Fantasy and Science Fiction*, March 1954]). Many of her short stories remain uncollected; some of them are now been gathered in *Just an Ordinary Day* (Bantam, 1997), edited by two of her children, Laurence Jackson Hyman and Sarah Hyman Stewart; the volume also contains some unpublished fiction, but little of it is of any distinction. Because of the unclassifiable nature of much of her work, Jackson has not received the study and analysis she deserves, nor does she occupy as high a place in the canon of American literature or in that of supernatural literature as the high quality of her work merits. At her best, she produced some of the finest supernatural work of any author in the second half of the twentieth century.

On Rod Serling's
"Clean Kills and Other Trophies"

Rod Serling's television series *Night Gallery* (1970–73) tends to be regarded as something of an embarrassment, even among Serling devotees. In a documentary that accompanied the boxed DVD set of the complete *Twilight Zone*, "Rod Serling: Submitted for Your Approval" (originally shown on PBS's *American Masters* series), the three-year-long run of *Night Gallery* was covered in a matter of seconds, as an utterly forgettable episode in Serling's later career.

In some senses, this disdain is warranted. *Night Gallery* was clearly not the groundbreaking, even revolutionary show that *The Twilight Zone* was; and because Serling did not have full editorial control over the series, he felt unable to stamp it with his unique moral vision. As he noted to Universal Studios: "I wanted a series with distinction, with episodes that said something; I have no interest in a series which is purely and uniquely suspenseful but totally uncommentative on anything."

But on the upside, *Night Gallery* did present some vivid and memorable episodes (in living color, no less), including adaptations of several classic weird tales—H. P. Lovecraft's "Cool Air" and "Pickman's Model," stories by August Derleth and Basil Copper, and an unforgettable adaptation of Conrad Aiken's "Silent Snow, Secret Snow."

But it is one of Serling's own teleplays—"Clean Kills and Other Trophies"—that I wish to discuss here. In particular, it is worth comparing it with the short story that Serling subsequently wrote based upon the teleplay. Serling wrote two slim volumes of *Night Gallery* stories (1971, 1972), paralleling the three equally slim *Twilight Zone* books he had written earlier (1960–62). As we compare the teleplay to the story, we see how radically Serling could revise the basic thrust of an episode to create a very different moral and psychological effect.

"Clean Kills and Other Trophies" aired on January 6, 1971, featured a bluff, dogmatic, and intolerant elderly man, Colonel Archie Dittman, Sr. (Raymond Massey), an enthusiast of big-game hunting—and, by extension, a proponent of a vicious "survival of the fittest" morality—who holds his apparently spineless and cowardly son, Archie Jr., in extreme contempt. Accordingly, he makes a curious stipulation before Archie Jr. can secure the millions of dollars that would come to him from a trust upon his twenty-first birthday: he must kill an animal with a gun. Archie Jr. (Barry Brown) seems resigned to carrying out the demand, although the family lawyer, Jeffrey Pierce (Tom Troupe), objects. Archie Jr. accompanies his father on a hunting trip and manages to kill a deer—although it is not a "clean kill," because the animal was shot in the lungs and lingered for hours before dying. A surprise twist occurs when the Colonel's African manservant, Tom Mboya (Herbert Jefferson Jr.), subsequently summons his tribal gods, who apparently behead the Colonel so that Tom can mount the head on the wall of a vast room in the house containing the heads or bodies of the many other animals the Colonel has killed over a lifetime.

The episode is moderately effective because of the taut conflict between the Colonel and Pierce, and because of the brooding presence of Tom Mboya, who appears on the surface civilized but continues to be under the sway of the "savage" gods of Africa.

What Serling did in writing the story was to cut the figure of Tom Mboya out of the scenario altogether. In the teleplay, Tom at one point prevents Archie Jr. from recklessly shooting his own father on the stairs of his house (not out of sympathy for the Colonel, as we learn later, but only so that he himself can gain his supernatural revenge on him). This scene is eliminated entirely—or, rather, is transferred to the end of the story, where Archie Jr. kills his father with the very gun he used to shoot the deer. Archie Jr. tells Pierce (who, in contrast to the teleplay, had accompanied the two men on the hunt) that it was "An altogether clean kill, Mr. Pierce. A damned clean kill."

Serling was shrewd in eliminating the Tom Mboya character. The central conflict in the scenario is that between the Colonel and his son, and the figure of Tom proves to be a somewhat distracting character. The logic of the story requires that Archie Jr. be the one who causes the Colonel's death, as a way of both physically and morally declaring his independence from him and asserting his own individuality. Also, the teleplay's O. Henry-like supernatural ending is a trifle contrived (as well as being telegraphed well before it is revealed to the viewer); in the story Serling drops it and produces a chilling tale of psychological terror and suspense where the son's vengeance on the father is carried out without any adventitious use of the supernatural.

The story, of course, also allows for numerous characteristic rhetorical flourishes that make Serling's short fiction a pleasure to read. Whereas in the teleplay the Colonel's intolerance and overt racism are conveyed by his condescending treatment of Tom Mboya (and this, in fact, may be the central reason why that character exists at all) and in other relatively innocuous remarks, in the story Serling does not hesitate to put the pejorative word "nigger" into the Colonel's mouth on several occasions, as an unmistakable marker of the Colonel's vicious prejudice. Later in the story, the Colonel refers to his son as "a nutless, faggoty, simpering little son of a bitch who dishonors me"—another remark that Serling could probably not have gotten away with on a show on broadcast television.

In the story the Colonel waxes eloquent about his impressive gun collection—in such a way that one comes to believe that this obsession with guns verges on the pathological. And Serling writes pungently of Archie Jr. after the Colonel lays down his stipulation about killing an animal: "A birthright was being stripped from him like an animal pelt." (Both the teleplay and the story have the Colonel state: "Didn't Adam Smith have a theory about overpopulation?" This is of course an error, for it was Thomas Malthus who made such a theory in his *Essay on the Principle of Population* [1798]. It is not clear whether this is the Colonel's error or Serling's.)

The story "Clean Kills and Other Trophies" is one of Serling's best—featuring crisply realized characters, a prose style laced with sardonic touches, and, most importantly, a firm moral vision that condemns the savagery of the "kill or be killed" (im)morality advocated by the Colonel. Serling was plagued with doubts about his abilities as a short story writer; but his entire output, and this story in particular, shows that he easily deserves a high rank among the weird fiction writers of his time.

Ramsey Campbell and Weird Fiction

Ramsey Campbell (b. 1946), British author of supernatural novels and tales, is perhaps the leading figure in weird fiction since H. P. Lovecraft. Campbell, who has spent most of his life in or around the city of Liverpool, has established his reputation with more than a score of novels (predominantly supernatural, although some are in the domain of psychological suspense) and hundreds of short stories that span the entire range of the supernatural from "cosmic" narratives to intimate tales of personal conflict to grim accounts of horrors in the decadent urban landscape. With a prose style of unexcelled fluidity and quiet power, an ability to draw character in a few deft strokes, and a seemingly inexhaustible fertility of imagination, Campbell begs comparison with Poe, Blackwood, and Lovecraft as the preeminent author of supernatural horror in all literary history.

Campbell's upbringing was of a sort to incline him toward the dark, cheerless work that is his trademark. Shortly after his birth, his parents became estranged; as Catholics they could not divorce, and so an awkward arrangement was established whereby Campbell's father lived in the upstairs part of their house, with Campbell and his mother living downstairs. Campbell rarely saw his father, who became a shadowy presence more often heard than seen. His attendance at a Catholic primary school, with its customary doses of corporal punishment, did not help matters. Years later, Campbell's mother degenerated into paranoia and madness, rendering his own life a living hell. Campbell has related the events of his upbringing with rare candor in the introduction to the Scream/Press edition of *The Face That Must Die* (1983).

Campbell early developed a taste for horror by reading British and American pulp magazines before the age of ten. He had already begun writing by then: a fragmentary "science thriller," "Black Fingers from Space," dates to the age of seven (it is included in the introduction to *The Height of the Scream* [Arkham House, 1976]), and in 1957 Campbell produced an entire small collection of horror stories, *Ghostly Tales* (published in *Crypt of Cthulhu* No. 50 [Michaelmas 1987]), and actually sent it to a publisher.

Not long thereafter, Campbell encountered the work of H. P. Lovecraft, and almost immediately began producing pastiches of the American writer.

Most of the contents of his first collection, *The Inhabitant of the Lake and Less Welcome Tenants* (Arkham House, 1964), published under the name J. Ramsey Campbell, had been written by the age of sixteen, although Campbell received valuable advice from Arkham House's proprietor, August Derleth, who read Campbell's early tales and recommended that he devise an English equivalent of Lovecraft's imaginary New England topography. Campbell did so, inventing the towns of Severnford, Goatswood, Temphill, and others in the Severn Valley. It can charitably be remarked that the tales in Campbell's first volume, published when he was eighteen, are at least written with a verve and enthusiasm lacking in many other writers' "additions" to Lovecraft's pseudomythology.

Immediately after writing these tales, Campbell violently repudiated Lovecraft and sought to establish his own voice in the field. He did so with remarkable dispatch: some of the first drafts of the tales that would comprise the landmark story collection *Demons by Daylight* (Arkham House, 1973) date to as early as 1963. Moreover, Campbell was able to harness his interest in Lovecraft with his new focus on the horrors of urban life, of sexuality, and other contemporary issues. "Cold Print" (written in 1966–67; in *Tales of the Cthulhu Mythos*, ed. August Derleth [Arkham House, 1969]) is an atmospheric tale in which the Lovecraftian topos of the "forbidden book" is tied to violent pornography. Campbell probably reached the culmination of his neo-Lovecraftian style with "The Franklyn Paragraphs." His collected Lovecraftian tales can be found in *Cold Print* (Headline, 1993).

Demons by Daylight could be said to have almost single-handedly ushered in a new era in weird fiction by its dreamlike, hallucinatory prose and its frank focus on contemporary issues of sexuality, gender, drugs, and identity.

Campbell has admitted that the volume was conceived as a unity, although he does not explicitly say what that unity is; it seems more a matter of mood rather than theme or subject matter. The matter is complicated by the fact that the published volume does not contain the stories Campbell had initially selected; of its 14 stories, one ("The Lost") was a last-minute substitution for two stories, "The Cellars" (in *Travellers by Night*, ed. August Derleth [Arkham House, 1967]) and "Reply Guaranteed" (in *Tandem Horror 2*, ed. Richard Davis [Tandem, 1968]), that were omitted for various reasons. Only one story—"The Stocking" (in *Tandem Horror 2*)—had been previously published.

Demons by Daylight is divided into three parts. The first, "Nightmares," features such stories as "Potential" (in which a young man at a gathering of hippies appears to turn into a god) and "The End of a Summer's Day" (in which a neurotic young woman seems to find her fiancé replaced by an old blind man). In the second section, "Errol Undercliffe: A Tribute," Campbell creates the figure of Errol Undercliffe, a writer from the invented town of Brichester who has disappeared. "The Franklyn Paragraphs," a complex tale that tells of his disappearance, is perhaps Campbell's finest adaptation of Lovecraft's theme of the "forbidden book," focusing on the volume *We Pass from View* by Roland Franklyn. "The Interloper" purports to be a story by Undercliffe, and draws upon Campbell's schooldays in telling of the hideous transformation of a school official and his pursuit of two hapless schoolboys.

The final section, titled "Relationships," is the longest and most substantial. Perhaps the greatest tale is "Concussion," an ambiguous narrative suggesting that a young woman, Anne, has traveled back in time as a result of a concussion received on a bus and, for the week in which she was in the hospital, carried on a love affair with a bashful loner, Kirk Morris. Several other tales are more explicitly sexual, notably "The Second Staircase," a nightmarish account of a man who appears to turn into a woman. "The Sentinels" tells of the horrors to be found in a megalithic site, while "The Guy" is a poignant tale of inadvertent tragedy and class conflict among teenage boys.

Most of the stories in the volume were written between 1966 and 1968; it should have been published around 1971, but August Derleth's death delayed the volume for two years. It received a laudatory review by T. E. D. Klein,[1] which Campbell found encouraging. He has written a new introduction to the Carroll & Graf (1990) edition.

After the publication of his second volume, Campbell—who had married Jenny Chandler, daughter of the science fiction writer A. Bertram Chandler, in 1971 and worked successively for the Inland Revenue and the Liverpool Public Library system—decided to become a professional writer. He not only began writing short stories at a rapid pace (27 were written in 1974 alone), but he came to the realization that he must write a novel if he wished to become an established figure in the field. The result was *The Doll Who Ate His Mother* (Bobbs-Merrill, 1976), an enjoyable if undistinguished work that uneasily mingles supernatural and psychological horror. Relating the search for an apparent serial killer and cannibal, Christopher Kelly, Campbell introduces a cult leader named John Strong who has seemingly supernatural powers and who exercised them over Kelly's mother when she was pregnant with him. The supernatural features of the novel seem extraneous to the overall development, and Campbell has also felt the need to abandon the distinctively dreamlike or hallucinatory prose that made his short stories of the period so memorable.

---

1. "Ramsey Campbell: An Appreciation," *Nyctalops* No. 13 [May 1977]; 19–25; rpt. in *Discovering Modern Horror Fiction II,* ed. Darrell Schweitzer (Starmont House, 1988), 88–102.

Campbell's next novel was, however, unequivocally non-supernatural; and a grimmer work than *The Face That Must Die*, about the serial killer John Horridge, would be difficult to find. In many ways it remains Campbell's most compelling novel. But its cheerlessness made it difficult to sell, and it appeared only in a truncated edition (Star, 1979); it appeared in complete form four years later (Scream/Press, 1983). Campbell's next two novels, *The Parasite* (Millington, 1980 [as *To Wake the Dead*]; Macmillan, 1980) and *The Nameless* (Fontana, 1981), are routine supernatural thrillers of the sort that Stephen King and his imitators were writing. Campbell's early novelistic career comes to a close with the entertaining if pulpish *The Claw* (Futura, 1983), written under the transparent pseudonym "Jay Ramsay," and the brilliantly complex *Incarnate* (Macmillan, 1983), perhaps his most accomplished novel.

Although *Incarnate* interweaves at least five significant narrative voices, its chief protagonist is Molly Wolfe, a television producer who is one of a group of people who had participated in an experiment on precognitive dreams run by Stuart Hay and Guilda Kent. Years later, Molly and the other participants— Joyce Churchill, the head of a small home for the elderly; Helen Verney, a woman attempting to reconstruct her life after the breakup of her marriage; Danny Swain, a working-class youth full of rage and resentment; Freda Beeching, a woman whose friend Doreen is shattered by the death of her husband— all begin to have bizarre dreams. These dreams—which are so real that the dreamers have trouble distinguishing them from reality—focus around a mysterious figure named Sage, who appears in various guises in the different dreams (including the figure of a little girl, Eve, befriended by Helen Verney's daughter, Susan). It seems that Sage is attempting to control human dreams as a means of replacing the real world with the dream world. As Guilda Kent—now in an insane asylum—states ominously, "Dreaming isn't a state of mind . . . it's a state of being." The conclusion of the novel grippingly displays the five protagonists desperately attempting to control the spreading of the dream-world as it insidiously replaces the real world of London. In its crisp character portrayal, immense complexity, and fluidity of prose, it perhaps ranks as Campbell's most distinguished novel.

But it was Campbell's short stories of the 1974–83 period that cemented his reputation as a writer who could raise supernatural fiction to the level of high art, and a significant means of social, political, and cultural commentary. Although *The Height of the Scream* cannot rank with *Demons by Daylight*, his next collection, *Dark Companions* (Macmillan, 1982), features many intense and gripping tales. In these volumes we see Campbell radically updating many of the traditional tropes and modes of supernatural fiction: the haunted house ("Napier Court" [in August Derleth, *Dark Things* (Arkham House,

1971)]), the reanimated corpse ("Mackintosh Willy" [in *Shadows 2*, ed. Charles L. Grant (Doubleday, 1979)]), the werewolf ("Night Beat" [*Haunt of Horror*, June 1973]), the double ("The Scar" [*Startling Mystery Stories*, Summer 1969]). "The Little Voice" (in *Shadows*, ed. Charles L. Grant [Doubleday, 1978]) is a poignant ghost story: the voice in the next house that the lonely schoolteacher Edith hears—which utters only the sounds *la, la, la*—may well be the ghost of the baby Edith had aborted years before. It would, however, be unjust to Campbell to suggest that all he has done is to revise conventional Gothic themes. A tale such as "Broadcast" (in *New Writings in Horror and the Supernatural*, ed. David Sutton [Sphere, 1971]), in which a radio broadcaster finds his voice, and perhaps even his very essence, drained away by the microphone, is a story that could only have been written in the 20th century.

"The Depths" (*Dark Companions*), a chilling tale in which a writer finds that if he does not write down the loathsome dreams that plague him, the events in the dreams will occur in real life, is a paradigm for the paranoiac tale of urban horror that Campbell has made his own. All the detritus of city life—plastic bags ("In the Bag" [in *Cold Fear*, ed. Hugh Lamb (W. H. Allen, 1977)]), garbage ("Litter" [in *Vampires, Werewolves and Other Monsters*, ed. Roger Elwood (Curtis, 1974)]), cigarette smoke ("Ash" [in *The Taste of Fear*, ed. Hugh Lamb (Taplinger, 1976)]), an old raincoat ("Old Clothes" [in *Midnight*, ed. Charles L. Grant (Tor, 1985)])—can serve as the foci of horror. The reanimated derelict in "Mackintosh Willy" is a symbol for the scorn and disrespect that poverty engenders in the middle class.

Campbell's second phase of novel-writing begins with *Obsession* (Macmillan, 1985), a deft but slight novel that suggests the supernatural in its apparent depiction of old wishes coming true, but proves to be non-supernatural. *The Hungry Moon* (Macmillan, 1986) is a powerful work, set in rural England and focusing upon an American evangelist, Godwin Mann (modeled upon Billy Graham), who seeks to inflict his narrow and intolerant Christianity upon the townsfolk but ends up unwittingly evoking a monster from the depths of a cave, with the result that the town and the surrounding area are engulfed in blackness. Although the metaphor is transparent (darkness symbolizing the ignorance of religious fundamentalism), the treatment is skillful. Campbell continues this "cosmic" vein in one of his most challenging novels, *Midnight Sun* (Macdonald, 1990), in which Ben Sterling is increasingly attracted by an immensely powerful ice-entity who, if ushered in by Sterling, would overwhelm the earth; although this transformation is presented as more awesome than horrific, Sterling in the end rejects the entity for the love of his wife and family. This change of heart is not entirely convincing, but the suppleness of the novel's prose and its cosmic scope (Campbell makes an avowed nod to the work of Machen, Blackwood, and more recent writers of "visionary" horror) give it a high place in Campbell's output. Two other novels of the period—*The Influence* (Macmillan, 1988), about an elderly woman's thirst to extend her life beyond normal bounds, and *Ancient Images* (Legend/Century, 1989), about a horror film from the 1930s that hints at bizarre supernatural manifestations in the rural landscape—are slighter. *The Count of Eleven* (Macdonald, 1991), a *comic* serial killer novel, is one of Campbell's most distinctive works—simultaneously a send-up of the endless succession of hackneyed serial killer novels then being produced and a surprisingly poignant portrayal of the hapless protagonist, Jack Orchard, who takes to killing as a final means of providing for his family. Almost unclassifiable is the novelette *Needing Ghosts* (Legend/Century, 1990), a nightmarish fantasy in which the writer Simon Mottershead appears to have fallen into his own Kafkaesque fictional universe. There is some debate as to what actually happens in this tale, other critics believing that the events of the tale are the dreams of the dead Mottershead. Perhaps, like *The Turn of the Screw*, no single interpretation of even the bare events can be termed definitive.

Campbell's novels of the 1990s continued to be strong and showed him at his most assured. The subtle novel *The Long Lost* (Headline, 1993) resurrects the old trope of the sin-eater—the stranger who must eat cakes placed upon a corpse and thereby take away the deceased's sins. Campbell has updated the idea in the figure of Gwendolen Owain, who seems to be a long-lost relative of David and Joelle Owain, but who is in fact a sin-eater hundreds of years old. She seeks to rid herself of her accumulated sins by distributing cakes to the Owains and their friends, with the result that each of them begins to exhibit "sins" or psychological flaws that lead to their death or destruction. In a particularly harrowing tableau, Richard Vale, in despair over his inability to support his family, lures his wife and children into spending a lovely day by the river and then feeding them poisoned hot chocolate. Although his wife and children die, Richard himself has not taken enough poison, so he first slits his throat with a broken piece of glass and then hurls himself in front of a bus.

Three other novels of this period are powerful but non-supernatural. *The One Safe Place* (1995) is perhaps Campbell's grimmest portrayal of urban horror and class conflict, telling of how a middle-class family becomes insidiously involved with a criminal lower-class clan. *The Last Voice They Hear* (Tor, 1998) and *Silent Children* (Tor, 1999) are linked in depicting the victimization of children, but, although written in impeccable prose, are only intermittently compelling. But Campbell's supreme triumph of this period is *The House on Nazareth Hill* (Headline, 1996; Tor, 1997 [as *Nazareth Hill*]), one of the greatest haunted house novels ever written.

The House on Nazareth Hill is remarkable for having only two significant characters: Oswald Priestly and his daughter Amy. As a child Amy had inadvertently fallen into a deserted house on a hill named Nazarill (short for Nazareth Hill), which she termed "the spider house." Years later, as a teenager, she rebels against her father's strict discipline (her mother had died some years before). The house on Nazareth Hill has become a set of apartments, and she and her father have moved in there; but shortly thereafter she and other tenants appear to witness a succession of terrifying supernatural incidents. Amy learns that the site had previously been a cruelly-run mental institution run in the 18th century. Relations between Amy and her father deteriorate rapidly, and it becomes clear that he has been possessed by the spirit of the place's brutal hospital staff. Amy, locked in her room by her father, then sees a hideous, bony figure who proves to be one of the "Partington witches"—women falsely accused of witchcraft and locked up in the institution. The novel rushes to a tragic and cataclysmic conclusion.

In this novel, Campbell has united the supernatural with searing domestic conflict, along with the display of psychosis that marked much of his earlier work. Tightly constructed, with a succession of chilling set-pieces, *The House on Nazareth Hill* lays claim to being the finest haunted house novel ever written.

Campbell's short stories of the 1980s and 1990s exhibit a great diversity of style, mood, and theme, in contrast to the perhaps excessively claustrophobic analysis of urban paranoia found in many of the tales of the 1970s. His stories of this period were gathered in two strong volumes, *Waking Nightmares* (Tor, 1991) and *Strange Things and Stranger Places* (Tor, 1993), and range from "In the Trees" (in *Night Visions 3*, ed. George R. R. Martin [Dark Harvest, 1986]), a chilling tale of the horror of Nature, to "Wrapped Up" (*Fantasy Tales*, Spring 1981), a half-comic, half-grotesque account of religious fanaticism. Later stories exhibit a fascination with the complexities of language. "The Word" (in *Revelations*, ed. Douglas E. Winter [HarperPrism, 1997]) is prototypical—a bizarre and disturbing tale fusing ruminations on the power of words and on the effect of fundamentalist religion. "Boiled Alive" (*Interzone*, Winter 1986–87) hints at the baleful effect of films and the media in general, especially their capacity to replace the "real" world.

Ramsey Campbell continues to produce work of high merit. His story collection *Ghosts and Grisly Things* (Pumpkin Books, 1998) contains many powerful tales, from "The Alternative" (in *Darklands Two*, ed. Nicholas Royle [New English Library, 1994]), an anguished tale of class conflict, to "Going Under" (in *Dark Love*, ed. Nancy A. Collins, Edward E. Kramer, and Martin H.

Greenberg [Penguin/Roc, 1995]), in which the cellular telephone is made an object of terror. A still more recent collection is *Told by the Dead* (PS Publishing, 2003). The novel *Pact of the Fathers* (Tor, 2001) is non-supernatural in relating a hideous secret society of fathers who advance their careers through the sacrifice of their first-born children. *The Darkest Part of the Wood* (PS Publishing, 2002) returns to the fictional realm of Brichester, drawing upon the Lovecraftian notion of the "forbidden book" in depicting the baleful effects of a 17th-century mage's journal upon a contemporary family. *The Overnight* (PS Publishing, 2003) chillingly speaks of nebulous horrors that cluster around an innocuous-seeming shopping plaza, victimizing the employees of a bookstore.

Campbell has, throughout his career, experimented in a variety of modes and styles. He has produced some striking works of science fiction, notably *Slow* (Footsteps Press, 1986) and *Medusa* (Footsteps Press, 1987). In the 1970s he was asked to complete some fragmentary tales by Robert E. Howard, and in the course of so doing wrote several tales of sword-and-sorcery, now collected in *Far Away and Never* (Necronomicon Press, 1996). A distinctive collection of horror tales mingling sex and the supernatural is *Scared Stiff* (Scream/Press, 1986). He has written three novelizations of horror films, *The Bride of Frankenstein* (Berkley Medallion, 1977; rev. Universal Books, 1978), *The Wolfman* (Berkley Medallion, 1977), and *Dracula's Daughter* (Berkley Medallion, 1977), written under the house name "Carl Dreadstone." Campbell has also written a substantial quantity of nonfiction, in the form of reviews, essays, and other commentary. He was a columnist for the *British Fantasy Society Bulletin* (1974–77), *Fantasy Review* (1984–86), and *Necrofile* (1991–99), and many reissues of his novels bear introductions or afterwords. Some of this material has now been gathered in *Ramsey Campbell, Probably*, ed. S. T. Joshi (PS Publishing, 2002). Campbell is one of the most articulate spokesmen for the dignity and seriousness of the tale of supernatural horror, and his comments on horror films are also of interest. He has edited an array of anthologies of horror fiction, notably *New Tales of the Cthulhu Mythos* (Arkham House, 1980) and *Uncanny Banquet* (Little, Brown, 1992). His best tales have been gathered in two omnibus editions, *Dark Feasts* (Robinson, 1987) and *Alone with the Horrors* (Arkham House, 1991).

Campbell has received the British Fantasy award for "In the Bag" (1978) and *To Wake the Dead* (1981), and the World Fantasy award for "The Chimney" (1978), "Mackintosh Willy" (1980), and *Alone with the Horrors* (1991).

With a body of work as variegated as Campbell's, it is difficult to find any single overarching theme that can encompass the whole or even a large portion of it. Suffice it to say that Campbell, more skillfully than any other contemporary writer, has utilized supernatural (and non-supernatural) horror to probe complex questions of identity, sexuality, crime, violence, marital and familial conflict, and other issues in such a way as to make weird fiction a relevant form of social commentary, while at the same time exhibiting the imaginative breadth, deft plot construction, and emotive power that make his work so pleasurable to read. And the continuing vigor of his recent work suggests that he has by no means finished saying what he has to say on the topics he chooses to address.

Brian McNaughton:
The Care and Feeding of Ghouls

When I read Brian McNaughton's "Meryphillia" in *Lovecraft's Legacy*, I found it a breath of fresh air; for it was not merely one of the two or three fine stories in an otherwise lacklustre anthology, but it was perhaps the *only* story in the book that showed actual originality. Here, for once, was not a self-proclaimed "disciple" of Lovecraft paying dubious homage by merely writing a half-baked ripoff of one of his mentor's own tales. Reading that story again in McNaughton's collection *The Throne of Bones*, in the company of its fellows (many of which are still finer specimens of horrific art), I come to wonder whether "Meryphillia" was even conceived as a "Lovecraft pastiche," or a pastiche of any kind.

For Brian McNaughton seems to have mastered one of the most difficult of literary arts: to draw upon the classics of the field without losing his own voice.

Like few modern writers in our realm, McNaughton has drunk deep in the well of literary horror and absorbed what he has read. To say that one can find echoes of Lovecraft, Clark Ashton Smith, Lord Dunsany, Robert E. Howard, and perhaps other writers in his work is not to say that he is in any way dependent upon them; rather, they seem merely to have provided him with suggestive hints on how to say the things he himself has to say.

Perhaps Clark Ashton Smith, with his delightful mixing of morbidity and humour and his evocative use of language, is the chief influence on McNaughton; but let me say bluntly that, in my humble opinion, McNaughton is a better prose writer than Smith. Smith's true greatness is as a poet. He is one of the great poets of our lamentable century, and would be so recognised if modern poets had not suffered a kind of collective insanity and decided that bad prose is superior to poetry. But what has been said of Smith's prose fiction certainly brings to mind the principal qualities of McNaughton's. Recall Ray Bradbury: "Take one step across the threshold of his stories, and you plunge into color, sound, taste, smell, and texture—into language." Or remember the precocious Donald Wandrei, who in his teens wrote what may still be one of the finest appreciations of Smith in "The Emperor of

Dreams" (*Overland Monthly*, December 1926); Wandrei was of course writing about Smith's poetry, since Smith had not yet begun the extensive writing of fiction; but his words uncannily anticipate the fiction of both Smith and McNaughton:

> He has constructed entire worlds of his own and filled them with creations of his own fancy. And his beauty has thus crossed the boundary between that which is mortal and that which is immortal, and has become the beauty of strange stars and distant lands, of jewels and cypresses and moons, of flaming suns and comets, of marble palaces, of fabled realms and wonders, of gods, and daemons, and sorcery.

The world that McNaughton has created in this book is the world of the ghoul; and who knows but that *The Throne of Bones* will become the standard textbook for the care and feeding of ghouls just as *Dracula* has become that for vampires? The ghoul entered Western literature chiefly through William Beckford's Arabian extravaganza, *Vathek* (1786); and it was the learned Samuel Henley who—aside from pilfering Beckford's French original and sneaking into print an English version a year before the French edition emerged—wrote highly learned notes to *Vathek* that H. P. Lovecraft absorbed when writing of ghouls himself in "The Hound" and other tales. Here is Henley on ghouls:

> Goul or *ghul*, in Arabic, signifies any terrifying object which deprives people of the use of their senses; hence it became the appellative of that species of monster which was supposed to haunt forests, cemeteries, and other lonely places, and believed not only to tear in pieces the living, but to dig up and devour the dead.

From this nucleus, and from elaborations upon it in Bierce, Lovecraft, Smith, and others, McNaughton has built up an entire ghoulish universe—a universe, to be sure, full of danger and terror, but one that we perhaps wistfully wish we occupied rather than this prosy sphere of ours where the only ghouls are pathetic specimens of the Jeffrey Dahmer type.

But McNaughton has drawn upon far more than merely the masterworks of horror for his conceptions. As I read this book I was startled to note how easily I could have imagined myself in the classical world—perhaps that long twilight of the Roman Empire, with barbarians at the gates, whose twisted decadence is so perfectly captured in Petronius' *Satyricon*. The influence of Graeco-Roman antiquity upon McNaughton would make an interesting essay. Those "Fomorian Guards" he speaks of: how can we not recall the Praetorian Guards, that cohort which began as members of the staff of Roman generals during the Republic but which later became the Emperor's private army and caused much mischief in the later Empire? When we read the name of Akilleus Bloodglutter, how many of us know that Akilleus is nothing more than a literal transcription from the Greek of that hero of the *Iliad* whom most of us know more familiarly under the name of Achilles? And perhaps it also takes a classicist not to be fazed by McNaughton's casual tossing in of recondite words like "psittacine nugacities," a charming Graeco-Latin hybrid (from *psittakos*, parrot, and *nugae*, trivialities).

An essay, indeed, ought to be written on the general influence of classicism on weird writers. It was Lord Dunsany who, in speaking of his failed attempts to learn Greek and the possible influence of that experience upon the creation of his worlds of fantasy, wrote that it

> left me with a curious longing for the mighty lore of the Greeks, of which I had had glimpses like a child seeing wonderful flowers through the shut gates of a garden; and it may have been the retirement of the Greek gods from my vision after I left Eton that eventually drove me to satisfy some such longing by making gods unto myself.

Lovecraft read far more widely in ancient literature than Dunsany (although he too was very deficient in Greek, as his thoroughly botched derivation of the word *Necronomicon* attests), but he goes on to say that he himself derived his myth-pattern—what we now call the "Cthulhu Mythos"—chiefly from Dunsany. In other words, he too sensed that Dunsany's pantheon of gods in Pegāna draw upon classical myth, and his own myth-cycle would do the same. Clark Ashton Smith's knowledge of the classics—not to mention his knowledge of such classically influenced poets as Shelley, Keats, and Swinburne—is evident on every page of both his fiction and his poetry. I have no doubt that McNaughton has his share of classical learning as well, whether gained directly from the ancients or from their modern disciples.

Then there are McNaughton's names. They are a wonder, for, bizarre as many of them are, they all seem uncannily right for the universe he has created. Lovecraft remarked of Dunsany: "His system of original personal and place names, with roots drawn from classical, Oriental, and other sources, is a marvel of versatile inventiveness and poetic discrimination""; and I can think of no better description of McNaughton's nomenclature. Sythiphore, Chalcedor, Paridolia, Zephryn Phrein, Lord Nephreiniel of Omphiliot—these names seem not so much invented as found in some remote corner of the collective imagination to which only McNaughton has had access. They are not the products of whim, but are logically formed on the basis of a language as rigidly governed by the rules of grammar and syntax as the classical tongues themselves.

But beyond the surface glitter of McNaughton's work—its controlled exoticism of language, its many nods to distinguished predecessors in the field, its flamboyant mixture of sex, satire, and morbidity—there is the incessant rumination on that most inexhaustible theme in the human imagination: Death and that "undiscovered country" that may lie beyond. And it is here that McNaughton draws upon that immemorial classic of our field, Edgar Poe, who knew more than he or any man should have known of Death:

> Our—out are the lights—out all!
>   And, over each quivering form,
> The curtain, a funeral pall,
>   Comes down with the rush of a storm.
> While the angels, all pallid and wan,
>   Uprising, unveiling, affirm
> That the play is the tragedy, "Man,"
>   And its hero the Conqueror Worm.

It is that Worm that is the true hero of *The Throne of Bones*.

W. H. Pugmire: Lovecraftian and Prose Poet

Few writers in the field of weird fiction were as beloved as Wilum Hopfrog Pugmire (1951–2019). A kind, gentle soul, he melded a number of seemingly disparate characteristics: he was anabashedly gay, he was a fixture in Seattle's punk rock scene, and he was one who remained faithful to the Mormon faith in which he had been born in spite of his church's decades-long banishment of him because of his sexual orientation.

Pugmire had come upon the works of H. P. Lovecraft while on missionary work in Ireland in the early 1970s. There, at the height of Ireland's "troubles," he somehow managed to dodge bullets and bombs and found solace and inspiration in the tales of Lovecraft, Robert Bloch, and other weird writers. But his literary tastes extended far beyond the weird, and he counted Shakespeare, Oscar Wilde, and Henry James among his literary favorites. He was profoundly interested in the theory and practice of poetry, from Dante to Gerard Manley Hopkins, and he also made a profound study of Judaism.

All these diverse qualities are reflected, in one form or another, in Pugmire's weird fiction—but chiefly his devotion to Lovecraft. Even though he frequently referred to himself self-deprecatingly as nothing but a "Lovecraft fanboy," his work is as far from mechanical pastiche as could be imagined. His study of Lovecraft was profound: he absorbed not only his weird tales, but his essays, poetry, and letters, as well as the smallest particulars of his life.

Pugmire's greatest tribute to Lovecraft was in fashioning a parallel landscape of terror and strangeness. Lovecraft had vivified his native New England with a constellation of imaginary towns—Arkham, Kingsport, Dunwich, Innsmouth—in which he infused a lifetime's interest in New England history, culture, and architecture. Pugmire similarly brought to life the primeval forests and imposing mountains of the Pacific Northwest in the creation of his mythical Sesqua Valley, enlivened by such redoubtable figures as the "beast," Simon Gregory Williams, and the poet William Davis Manly.

But Pugmire wasn't content with merely adapting Lovecraft's topography to his own native realm. He may not have been as attuned to "the cosmic quality" as Lovecraft was, but he had a sure sense of the weirdness that arises out of human beings' encounters with the bizarre. He shattered the stereotype of the woman-scorning gay man by featuring a number of vividly realized female characters in his tales, ranging from "The Hands That Reek and Smoke" to "Pickman's Lazarus."

Pugmire is the prose-poet of the horror/fantasy field; he may be the best prose-poet we have. The very titles of his most representative stories are weirdly evocative—who but Wilum could have devised such titles as "The Zanies of Sorrow" or "The Phantom of Beguilement" or "Bloom of Sacrifice"? There is a hint of the archaic, a soupçon of unearthliness, in these titles, and the stories themselves transport us to a realm of deliberate artificiality and poetic strangeness. The mundane realism that drags down so much of the work of Stephen King and his would-be imitators to the level of clumsy hackdom is entirely absent in Pugmire's work. When we read his tales we realise from the start that we are entering a realm of pure literature, where the words and gestures of the characters are self-consciously literary in the best sense—and they transport every reader to an imaginative realm that has nothing of banal reality about it.

The development of Pugmire's literary palette, from *Tales of Sesqua Valley* (1997) to *Dreams of Lovecraftian Horror* (1999) to *Tales of Love and Death* (2001) to *Sesqua Valley and Other Haunts* (2003) to *The Fungal Stain* (2006) to the revised *Sesqua Valley and Other Haunts* (2008) to *The Tangled Muse* (2010), is little short of miraculous. Wilum himself is far too humble in stating that he is merely an imitator of Lovecraft. He is one of that rare breed of pastichists who paradoxically find their own identity most keenly when seeming to imitate their literary idols. Pugmire enters—body, soul, mind, and imagination—into the Lovecraftian cosmos and makes it his own. But it is a careless reader indeed who fails to detect the elements of originality that escape from his pen even when he seems to be most faithfully reflecting the style, themes, and even the very language of his mentors. I am not merely referring to the powerful, at times even grim, moments of sexual explicitness in some of the narratives—moments that would make the puritanical Lovecraft lapse into a merciful faint. I refer more broadly to a keenness of psychological insight—drawn, perhaps, from a deep introspection into his own complex personality—that allows him to probe the disturbed mentalities of some of his characters in ways that Lovecraft could only have dreamed about. Characterisation was the weakest feature of Lovecraft's literary art, but Wilum Pugmire views his multiplicity of characters with a sympathetic understanding that illuminates them from within.

One thing that Wilum has learned from Lovecraft is that the employment of recurring characters and settings in successive tales allows those tales to build upon one another so that they become more than the sum of their parts. Just as Lovecraft fashioned an imaginatively rich New England topography through constant references to—and constant portrayals of—such towns as

Arkham, Innsmouth, and Kingsport, so Pugmire has painted a verbal portrait of a Sesqua Valley that, even to those who have no first-hand knowledge of the Pacific Northwest, gains a vitality that in many ways causes it to become the main "character" of the narratives in which it is featured. With each successive tale, the valley becomes a bit more real and a bit more weird, and those hapless souls who enter it from outside are never the same. And those recurring figures who dwell in the valley, like Simon Gregory Williams, are lovingly shaped like clay sculptures from story to story, until they too seem as real as the deep woods and craggy mountains surrounding them.

The meticulousness with which Pugmire handles prose has already been suggested. Sentences such as "They came to me in midnight rain, during an hour of wondrous lunacy" are, as Lovecraft said of some of Poe's tales, "assuredly poems in every sense of the word save the metrical one." But there is more to it than this. The seemingly jarring juxtaposition of antique and modern diction that we find, say, in "Inhabitants of Wraithwood" is deliberate and calculated; for it suggests the unwitting infiltration of a contemporary character into a nebulously archaic fantasy realm, and in the process it allows us—those contemporary readers who find ourselves overwhelmed with the modernity of iPods and Blackberrys—to drift insensibly into the fantastic past as well. Pugmire realises, as did Poe, Wilde, and Lovecraft, that the creation of an atmosphere of shimmering unreality is effected entirely by language; and he knows that a single false note can destroy a story's mood as surely as an inapposite word falling from a character's lips or a clumsy transition from scene to scene.

What infuses Pugmire's work from first to last is an appreciation of the distinctively *sensuous* quality inherent in words. It could be plausibly argued that every one of his tales is a kind of prose-poem, as the author assembles each word, phrase, and sentence with the goal of invoking the music inherent in the mellifluous collocation of sound and meaning. He would enthusiastically endorse the statement of another great prose-poet, Clark Ashton Smith, who once said:

> An atmosphere of remoteness, vastness, mystery and exoticism is more naturally evoked by a style with an admixture of Latinity, lending itself to more varied and sonorous rhythms, as well as to subtler shades, tints and nuances of meaning—all of which, of course, are wasted or worse than wasted on the average reader, even if presumably literate.

That final comment is truer today than when it was written, as we are now deluged with shoddy and even ungrammatical prose by would-be authors whose closest approach to prose-poetry lies in reeling off a litany of brand names.

It is this sensitivity to language that makes Pugmire the perfect author to render Lovecraft's evocative *Fungi from Yuggoth* sonnets into prose, as he did in that tour de force, *Some Unknown Gulf of Night* (2011), reprinted here in its entirety. Consider the opening of one segment (XIX):

> I hear the faint far ringing of a deep-toned bell as I carry you up the black mountain in this midnight wind. I have heard the call before, in deepest dreaming; but I do not imagine that I am dreaming now, this witching hour, for I feel too bitterly the sharpness of the trumpeting tempest; and I feel too sharply a pain in my ankles as I traverse toward the apex of the spectral peak with my burden in my arms.

We can see at once that this is far more than a mere rewriting of the opening lines of the corresponding sonnet ("The Bells") in Lovecraft's poem cycle:

> Year after year I heard that faint, far ringing
> Of deep-toned bells on the black midnight wind;
> Peals from no steeple I could ever find,
> But strange, as if across some great void winging.

Pugmire has recognised that each of these sonnets is a miniature story, and he has teased out the narratives submerged in them—perhaps not the way Lovecraft himself would have done, but in a way that holds the reader far beyond the mere succession of pretty words.

Indeed, Pugmire doesn't get enough credit for his skill in story construction. The items in this book range from the most fleeting of prose-poems ("Artifice," at 200 words) to novelettes of more than 12,000 words ("Gathered Dust"). Each work is filled with distinctive settings, characters, and elements of strangeness and terror to carry the reader along from beginning to end. Some tales end with powerfully bizarre dénouements; others conclude with pensive and brooding quietness, hinting at marvels under the surface.

But nearly every tale pays homage to one or more of the elements of plot or theme or imagery that make Lovecraft's work so fascinating. And yet, even those stories that purport to be merely rewritings or updatings of Lovecraft's own tales—"The Horror on Tempest Hill," a re-imagining of "The Lurking Fear"; "The Imps of Innsmouth," a riff on "The Shadow over Innsmouth"; "Pickman's Lazarus," a new take on "Pickman's Model"—always offer something new and original.

Pugmire is fully aware that Lovecraft's most novel contribution is a kind of cosmic regionalism: the fictitious towns of Arkham, Innsmouth, Kingsport, and Dunwich are merely the stepping-stones to their denizens' wanderings throughout a universe of awe and terror. While he is comfortable utilising these towns in his own work (as in the Arkham of "Gathered Dust" or "Underneath an Arkham Moon"), early on he realised that something new—but analogous to Lovecraft's fantastic New England—was needed. So, just as Ramsey Campbell drew upon his own English heritage in conceiving an imaginary constellation of cities in the Severn Valley, Pugmire has made superb use of his lifelong acquaintance with the untenanted wilderness of the Pacific Northwest in fashioning his Sesqua Valley. The inhabitants of this domain—whether it be the redoubtable sorcerer Simon Gregory Williams or the poet William Davis Manly or the hapless visitors who innocently stumble into the valley to meet their variegated fates—all tread in the shadow of the looming twin peaks of Mount Sesta, covered by evergreens whose centuried antiquity casts silent derision upon our transient tenancy of this earth.

Even the details of Lovecraft's life, as well as the cadre of distinctive individuals he knew in Providence, New York, and elsewhere, serve as fodder for Pugmire's creative imagination, as in "Letters from an Old Gent" and "Smooth Artifact of Bone." Piquant character names evoke smiles of recognition in the devoted Lovecraftian: "An Ecstasy of Fear" introduces us to Sarah Paget-Lowe (reminiscent of the pseudonym Henry Paget-Lowe that Lovecraft used for some of his poems) and also to "the young poet, Akiva Loveman," echoing the name of the poet Samuel Loveman.

But transcending all these tips of the hat to facets and passages in Lovecraft's work, there is the overriding atmosphere inherent in every one of Pugmire's tales, long and short. Beyond his "crystalline singing prose" (that memorable phrase that Lovecraft applied to the work of Lord Dunsany), beyond the many moments of terror, gruesomeness, whimsy, and melancholy, there is an utterly captivating atmosphere of *antiquity* that sets Pugmire's work apart from all other writers working today. In an era when authors seem determined to make use of the myriad tokens of abrasive modernity—cell phones, the Internet, GPS tracking—it is vastly refreshing to drift insensibly into the past in these tales. About a century ago, W. H. P. Faunce, president of Brown University, complained that people of his era were "too desperately contemporary." That criticism could be levelled even more to the majority of people of our own day, who are so overwhelmed with imagination-crippling gadgets that they scarcely have the time or leisure to reflect on the countless ages that have gone by. But Lovecraft's resounding pronouncement—"The past is *real*. It is *all there is*"—cannot be gainsaid, and it takes a writer like Wilum Hopfrog Pugmire, imbued with the sensibility of prior centuries, to remind us of what we have lost in our mad rush to be up-to-date. Perhaps it is this feature that most clearly links him to the writers from whom he continues to draw inspiration.

One of the transcendent events of Pugmire's life was his trip to Providence in 2007. After decades of admiring his literary mentor, he was now walking in Lovecraft's footsteps in the city of his birth. The visit led to a rejuvenation of Pugmire's imagination—at the exact time when a new cadre of writers, editors, and publishers were transforming the realm of Lovecraft-inspired fiction by probing more searchingly into the essence of Lovecraft's philosophy of the weird. Pugmire happily contributed to many of the magazines and anthologies that featured Lovecraftian fiction, and his appearance in these venues carried the assurance of at least one contribution that was certain to reflect the core of Lovecraft's aesthetic rather than the mere externals of his literary creation.

In his later years Pugmire teamed up with David Barker and Jeffrey Thomas on novels and tales that continued to expand on his fusion of Lovecraftian elements with those drawn from his own life and temperament. He had earlier faced some criticism that his tales were largely mood-pieces with minimal narrative drive, even though this attention to mood was Lovecraft's own chief desideratum as a weird writer ("Atmosphere is the all-important thing, for the final criterion of authenticity is not the dovetailing of a plot but the creation of a given sensation"), and even though he evolved a prose idiom whose fluidity, musicality, and evocativeness was rivalled by few contemporary writers. Indeed, it could be said that Pugmire's vignettes and prose poems (some of which are included here) are among the most powerful of his works. But with the aid of Barker he produced two short novels (*The Revenant of Rebecca Pascal*, 2014; *Witches in Dreamland*, 2018), while with both Barker (*In the Gulfs of Dream and Other Lovecraftian Tales*, 2015) and Thomas (*Encounters with Enoch Coffin*, 2013) he produced scintillating tales, both solo and in collaboration, that added to his standing as one of the leading lights of contemporary Lovecraftian and weird fiction.

But Pugmire didn't need to rely on others to achieve his goals. In his hundreds of tales, long and short, he fashioned a legacy of accomplishment that will be difficult to surpass. And, belatedly, his work is reaching a worldwide audience. A German edition of his tales (*Der dunkle Fremde*, 2018) appeared less than a year before his passing, and Spanish and Russian editions are forthcoming. There will also be further efforts to gather his fugitive tales, as well as his poetry, essays, and literary commentary.

Shy and humble as he may have been; unwilling as he was to engage in self-promotion or (to his eternal credit) to engage in the bitter feuding that has created so much needless antagonism in recent years, Wilum Pugmire stands as a man devoted to the essential act of writing as "self-expression," in the exact spirit that H. P. Lovecraft intended when he coined that expression. It is this, along with his undoubted and multifaceted talents, that will allow his work to remain a literary treasure for the foreseeable future.

Caitlín R. Kiernan and the Mythos

Caitlín R. Kiernan has a surprising number of commonalities with H. P. Lovecraft, and so it should not come as a surprise that, for more than twenty years, she has used the older writer's stories—and, more generally, the motifs, imagery, and even the prose idiom that fuel his work—as springboards for her own profoundly original and evocative tales that probe in ever-increasing depth and detail the anxieties and complexities of being human in an indifferent and perhaps malign cosmos.

The first and most significant element that links these writers is science. But Lovecraft was a mere amateur in numerous scientific fields, notably astronomy and chemistry: his lack of formal education beyond the high-school level blighted his plans to become a professional astronomer, so that he was forced to rely on his freelance writing and "revision" for his paltry income rather than resting in comfort on a professor's salary. Kiernan, in contrast, did postgraduate work in paleontology; indeed, an early story, "Valentia," cites the *Journal of Vertebrate Paleontology*, an actual scholarly journal where some of Kiernan's own papers were published. But readers of weird fiction are lucky that both writers chose to make careers as fiction writers rather than confining themselves to the cloistered halls of academia. Both have evinced marked interest in other such disciplines as archaeology, anthropology, and astrophysics, with the result that, in both cases, there is a dynamic fusion of weird fiction with science fiction that lends texture and nuance to their writings.

"Valentia," set in Ireland, the land of Kiernan's birth, is a tale of archaeological horror that draws upon the Lovecraftian notion of horrors too dreadful for the human mind to endure. In this story, the discovery of footprints of entities millions of years older than the dinosaurs strongly brings to mind Lovecraft's greatest tale of cosmic menace, *At the Mountains of Madness*, where similar footprints herald the actual emergence of creatures that have come to Earth from the remotest depths of space and time. The theme is elaborated upon in a more light-hearted fashion in "The Drowned Geologist (1898)," where the geologist in question meets none other than Sherlock Holmes in the English town of Whitby—but also encounters evidence of "dark and ancient powers, the whim of inhuman beings of inconceivable antiquity and malignancy."

Cosmicism is the focus of "Tidal Forces," where a woman suffers a strange injury—a hole in her side that grows inexorably, revealing an impenetrable blackness within the wound—that may have something to do with Lovecraft's "blind idiot god" Azathoth (never mentioned by name in the text). This tale is a remarkable fusion of the cosmic and the human, as typified by a single memorable line: "I think there are galaxies trapped within her eyes." Two stories, "John Four" and "Black Ships Seen South of Heaven," are bleak ruminations on what life on earth might be like after the Old Ones have taken over.

Then there is "A Mountain Walked," whose title refers to one of the most poignant utterances in Lovecraft's tales (it is said of Cthulhu that "A mountain walked or stumbled"). This gripping story of palaeogean terror is told by means of the diary entries of an explorer in Wyoming. Like Lovecraft, Kiernan relies on the physical tokens of the past to weave a sense of cosmic terror; this is why the *artefact* plays such a key role in the stories of both writers. In Kiernan's "The Bone's Prayer," a woman finds a strange piece of soapstone on a beach—and when a friend puts it into a particularly sensitive part of her anatomy, she is strangely changed. The tale features delicate but remote references to both *At the Mountains of Madness* and "The Shadow over Innsmouth."

Lovecraft transformed his native realm of New England into a land of terror and strangeness. As he wrote in "The Picture in the House," it is there that "the dark elements of strength, solitude, grotesqueness, and ignorance combine to form the perfection of the hideous." Kiernan follows Lovecraft's lead in such tales as "At the Gate of Deeper Slumber," a retelling and elaboration upon "The Haunter of the Dark," which found a source of terror in the decaying (and now destroyed) St. John's Catholic Church, in the Federal Hill section of Providence, Rhode Island. But we must turn to *The Red Tree* (2009) for her most searching investigation of the wonders and terrors abiding in the soil of New England. That novel is not explicitly Lovecraftian, but it remains a triumph in its evocation of the dark history and topography of that ancient region.

It is perhaps not surprising that "The Shadow over Innsmouth," a chilling evocation of the sinister history of New England, is a particular favourite of Kiernan's; for its suggestions of *metamorphosis* and *transformation*—both in body and in mind and soul—understandably resonate in Kiernan's heart. One of her earliest Lovecraftian tales, "From Cabinet 34, Drawer 6," cleverly links Innsmouth with the horror film industry, suggesting that the producers of *Creature from the Black Lagoon* derived their inspiration from the hybrid creatures in the decaying seaport. From here we move on to such tales as "Fish Bride," "On the Reef," and "The Transition of Elizabeth Haskings." That last story is a poignant account of a female Innsmouth resident whose gradual and painful metamorphosis into a Deep One is witnessed by a deeply sympathetic gay man who tends to her until the final transformation. And we can hardly pass over "The Cats of River Street (1925)," set in the hot summer that saw the Scopes trial in Tennessee, cited by name in the story. This touching narrative about the various cats in Innsmouth, living amongst a diverse array of humans and hybrids, tells of how they "hold the line," fighting against the incursion of the Deep Ones at every full moon. Lovecraft, with his own deep and abiding love of felines, would have found this tale especially moving.

The Innsmouth theme is shifted to the West Coast in "Houses under the Sea," set in John Steinbeck country—the coastal town of Salinas, California. What is it that led Jacova Angevine to form a cult that worships Dagon and then lead her followers to commit mass suicide by drowning? One can only guess. The four tales in the "Dandridge Cycle" form a kind of ghostly family saga, relating the construction in 1890 of a dubious house on the California coast by one Machen (!) Dandridge, an apparent worshipper of Dagon. The Lovecraftian element in some of these stories is somewhat remote, but Kiernan repeatedly underscores a key Lovecraftian motif: the suggestion of a dark and secret history behind the surface events in the historical record.

The ghoul theme is one of great fascination to Kiernan. (Drawing upon Lovecraft's own source for the conception, Samuel Henley's notes to William Beckford's *Vathek*, she properly refers to these rubbery, corpse-eating creatures as ghūls.) We begin with "Pickman's Other Model (1929)," where Lovecraft's most famous ghoul, the painter Richard Upton Pickman, is the focus, even though he never actually appears in the narrative. This story, with its deliberately old-fashioned prose and manner of narration, using Lovecraft's patented method of the documentary style, paradoxically reveals Kiernan's own sophistication—her awareness of the ambiguities inherent in the historical record and the mysteries that may lurk beyond and behind bland newspaper reports and film reviews.

Even before Kiernan moved to Lovecraft's Providence from Birmingham, Alabama, in 2008, that New England city was a source of pervasive interest to her. "So Runs the World Away," published in 2001, reveals ghouls in the heart of that centuried city—and this tale cleverly links the ghoul theme (found chiefly in "Pickman's Model" and *The Dream-Quest of Unknown Kadath*) with a throwaway line in "The Shunned House" that refers to an actual case of vampirism in Exeter, Rhode Island, in 1892. The story, indeed, largely takes place in the stately, five-story house at 135 Benefit Street that inspired

Lovecraft's haunted-house tale, as does "The Dead and Moonstruck," where ghouls charmingly behave like rambunctious children. In "The Thousand-and-Third Tale of Scheherazade," a man in Providence tells the tale (possibly derived from the work of the mad Arab, Abd-al-Hazred) of a little girl who was taken in by an elderly female ghoul. Kiernan's most exhaustive working out of the ghoul motif occurs, of course, in her richly textured novel *A Daughter of Hounds* (2007).

The ghoul motif is intimately linked, in Lovecraft, with the dreamworld, since the ghouls—including Pickman himself—make regular trips from the dreamworld (which apparently lies underneath our own, accessed by openings in the earth in remote and hidden places) to the waking world. Kiernan is one of the few writers who has successfully elaborated upon Lovecraft's dreamland stories. Here we begin with "The Peril of Liberated Objects, or the Voyeur's Seduction," where a woman in the waking world has somehow come into possession of a red book (consisting only of images, not words) that originated in dreamland. "The Alchemist's Daughter," a tale set in Ulthar that shows us the daughter of an alchemist who becomes one herself and comes upon a dragon's egg that may hold that secret of immortality. Here Kiernan dares to imitate the very prose of Lovecraft's dreamland stories (a prose style that is itself derived from the tales of Lord Dunsany)—a dangerous practice, but one that Kiernan accomplishes with elegance and aplomb.

Several stories explicitly unite the ghoul and the dreamland stories. "Love Is Forbidden, We Croak and Howl" is a touching story of love between a male ghoul and a sixteen-year-old female denizen of Innsmouth. In "Pushing the Sky Away (Death of a Blasphemer)," which features explicit references to Dunsany's own cosmic mythology, we learn of the centuries-long war between the ghouls and the Djinn. "Pickman's Madonna" and "The Peddler's Tale" exhibit a pair of twins, Isaac and Isobel, whose incestuous offspring may lead the ghouls to a reconquest of the waking world. It is here that Kiernan's own prodigal evocation of fantastic names reaches its height:

> They weren't about to cast aside their veneration of Great Amylostereum or Mother Paecilomyces, Camponotus the Tireless Maw or eyeless, all-seeing Claviceps, in exchange for one god who'd not even seen fit to send his martyr down to the Lower Dream Lands. . . . They brought into being the Maghor Rostrum (patron of the starving and toothless), Mortifien the Crypt Mason, Mistress Praxedes the Many-Limbed (midwife to the transformed who once were only women and men), bat-winged Pteropidion, the maimed bride Saint Lilit (invoked for the endurance of exile and pain).

This is only one instance among many in this book—and in Kiernan's work generally—where language itself is paramount in the creation of weird atmosphere. Caitlín R. Kiernan is far and away the best prose stylist in contemporary weird fiction, and in this too she follows her mentor Lovecraft, whose own mastery of poetic prose is unexcelled. Our breath is taken away when we read passages like this:

> There is a sense of spectral whirling through liquid gulfs of infinity, of dizzying rides through reeling universes on a comet's tail, and of hysterical plunges from the pit to the moon and from the moon back again to the pit, all livened by a cachinnating chorus of the distorted, hilarious elder gods and the green, bat-winged mocking imps of Tartarus. ("The Call of Cthulhu")

Likewise, such specimens as "The Peril of Liberated Objects" and "On the Reef" are sonorous poems in every sense but the metrical one. But Kiernan's prose is more supple and variegated than Lovecraft's: she can express anything. Her tone varies from bleak pessimism to pungent humour, from the cosmic to the human; she can portray character in a few deftly chosen images, and she can seamlessly fuse the disparate genres of weird fiction, fantasy, and science fiction into an indefinable amalgam that is *sui generis*. Kiernan has learned much from Lovecraft, but she could teach him a thing or two about expressing the bewildering diversity of human thoughts and emotions on paper.

Some Younger Weird Writers

Michael Aronovitz

In a prefatory note to *Deathbird Stories* (1975), Harlan Ellison wrote: "It is suggested that the reader not attempt to read this book at one sitting. The emotional content of these stories, taken without break, may be extremely upsetting." Without attempting to compare a relative novice to a literary legend, I would repeat Ellison's caveat in regard to Michael Aronovitz's *Seven Deadly Pleasures* (2009). In fact, I would go on to add that it might be advisable to read only one of the stories in this book at a sitting, perhaps one a day.

The emergence of a writer like Michael Aronovitz is a highly interesting literary phenomenon. As we come close to the end of this first decade of the twenty-first century, the horror "boom" that began, more or less, with the simultaneous appearance on the bestseller lists in 1971 of William Peter Blatty's *The Exorcist* and Thomas Tryon's *The Other* has been over for close to twenty years. Stephen King and Anne Rice still make the bestseller lists, but the former remains there for shorter and shorter periods and the latter scarcely seems to be writing horror at all. The best writers in the field appear to have retreated to the small press, for it is only those presses that can take a chance that a Thomas Ligotti, a Caitlín R. Kiernan, or a Jonathan Thomas will be able to find an audience without generating that blockbuster (usually a bloated and gore-filled novel) which commercial houses appear to require of their genre writers. And so, when Michael Aronovitz submitted these stories to me—first one or two, then the entire volume—I could see at once that here was a writer who deserved his audience but whose intense, gripping, and emotionally wrenching tales would be sure to scare off—in the wrong sense of the term—any commercial publisher he approached.

What is impressive about Aronovitz's tales is their range of tone, mood, and substance. To be sure, such stories as "How Bria Died," "The Legend of the Slither-Shifter," and "Toll Booth" shows the author to be unusually attuned to the angst of teenagers—as is fitting for a high school teacher. But to turn from the dramatic tensity of "How Bria Died"—one of the most terrifying supernatural tales I have read in many years—to the sardonic humour of "The Clever Mask" is to wonder how a single author could be responsible for such wildly diverse specimens. And the philosophical depth that Aronovitz shows in stories like "Quest for Sadness" and "The Exterminator" makes one realise that he is far more than a mere shudder-coiner; rather, he follows the best traditions of supernatural fiction in making us ponder our tenuous position in the universe by means of terror and wonder. And the story "Passive Passenger" confronts us with the quasi-science fictional horror of the computer and the Internet.

This collection's capstone is "Toll Booth," a 40,000-word novella that seamlessly accomplishes many things at once. It is simultaneously a poignant tale of teenagers' ability—or inability—to face a moral dilemma, an almost unbearable tale of physical gruesomeness that any splatterpunk writer would be proud of, and a subtle tale of supernatural haunting in the unlikeliest of places—a highway toll booth. From Le Fanu to Lovecraft to Ramsey Campbell to T. E. D. Klein, the novella has been the chosen venue of many masters of the supernatural to fuse the intensity of the short story with the character development usually possible only in the novel, and in "Toll Booth" Aronovitz has fully realised the aesthetic possibilities of this hybrid literary mode.

It would be unjust to consider Michael Aronovitz a novice, for some of his stories have appeared either in print on online more than fifteen years ago. His surehandedness in prose, in character portrayal, and in the pacing and development of the short story also mark him as a veteran.

The ghost story is perhaps the oldest form of weird literature, but we have come a long way from the old-time Gothic novels, where ghosts did little but appear in their shrouds clanking chains and uttering obscure prophecies. Today's ghosts, if they are to be convincing and compelling, must be *active* in ways that the more genteel ghosts of the past could not bring themselves to be.

This is exactly the kind of ghost we find in Michael Aronovitz's hypnotic novel *Alice Walks* (2013).

The fact that most of the main characters in this book—its narrator, Michael Fitzsimmons; the ghost, Alice Arthur; and Michael's friends, Will and Nick—are teenagers shouldn't deceive us into thinking this is a "young adult novel." To be sure, Aronovitz uncannily conveys the highs and lows of teenage life throughout *Alice Walks*, but there is much more here than you will find in your average novel aimed at young adults—and much more than in the average horror novel.

In the first place, there is Aronovitz's mesmerising prose style—a style that can take your breath away, even when, as here, it is narrated in the voice of a not notably intellectual teenager. But more than that, there is Aronovitz's deep understanding of human life and human emotions—the emotions of a boy struggling to understand why his parents' marriage seems to be unraveling; the emotions of a mother who does everything she can to hold her family together and finds that it seems insufficient; and, most keenly of all, the emotions of a father whose past derelictions have cast a baleful shadow over the present and future of his entire household. Even if there was no element of supernatural terror in *Alice Walks*, it would deserve to be read as a plangent document of a family's inexorable descent into heartbreak and tragedy.

But luckily for us, there is terror in abundance here. What strikes me about *Alice Walks* is the exquisitely, excruciatingly slow and gradual way in which the horror builds and builds to a spectacular climax. What starts out as a lark, when teenage boys heedlessly probe the grave of a recently deceased girl, turns into something far more terrifying than they know how to deal with, and it is this sense of the insidious, all-engulfing nature of the ghost that is Alice Arthur that is the most impressive thing about *Alice Walks*.

Michael Aronovitz is nothing if not prolific: he will soon issue a second story collection, and he has written several other novels that will see print in due course of time. I have little doubt that he will rapidly gain wide recognition as a leading contemporary writer of weird fiction, and that the following he has already attracted will continue to grow as each of his successive books appears. And in that process *Alice Walks* will occupy a vital place.

Clint Smith

It was, I believe, in 2009 that Clint Smith sent me his story "Benthos." Finding it a remarkably powerful weird tale, I expressed approbation but at that time could not think of any publication in which it could appear. Soon thereafter, Jerad Walters of Centipede Press asked to edit an annual magazine, the *Weird Fiction Review*, devoted both to original fiction and to articles about weird fiction. I could not think of a better vehicle for the publication of "Benthos" than this, and it duly appeared in the first issue of 2010.

Then, curiously, I heard no more from Clint. Could he be, I thought occasionally, just a one-shot wonder? I will confess that my own canvassing of contemporary weird fiction—in magazines, website, and other venues—is not exactly wide-ranging, so I was unaware that Clint was in fact placing his stories in any number of other journals, print and online. Then, about a year ago, Clint submitted to me his first collection, *Ghouljaw and Other Stories* (2014). I was thrilled. While in no sense do I credit myself with being Clint's "discoverer" (the title story of the collection had already appeared in 2009), I was delighted to be able to offer an entire volume of his work to the reading public.

Clint Smith's virtues as a writer are easy to detect: a fluid, mellifluous prose style that conceals its artistry by its seeming effortlessness; a power and originality in weird conceptions that grasp readers by the throat; a sensitivity to emotional pain, domestic trauma, and interpersonal conflict that mainstream writers would envy. Every story bears the mark of his distinctive literary style: you could not possibly mistake one of his stories for someone else's work.

I know little of Clint's literary influences: the pungent twist on Poe's "The Tell-Tale Heart" that he effects in "The Tell-Tale Offal" says no more than that he has taken to heart Poe's dictum on the "unity of effect" in the crafting of a short story. Clint's work is bracingly modern, but with a sense of the heavy hand of the past weighing upon the present (most evident, perhaps, in "Like Father, Like . . ."). Also like Poe (but like many others too, ranging from Ambrose Bierce to Laird Barron), Clint knows how to dance elegantly on the borderline of supernatural and psychological horror; indeed, his best stories fuse these ordinarily disparate veins of weird fiction. "Benthos" seems on the surface to be a cheerless story of drug taking, easy sex, and gang violence, but a supernatural undercurrent raises its head at the most unexpected moment. "What Happens in Hell Stays in Hell" uses the war in Afghanistan as a grim backdrop to unthinkable horrors unleashed in the parched sands of the Middle East.

I have no doubt that Clint Smith will be heard from in the future as a leading practitioner of the modern weird tale. The stories in this collection testify not only to his literary potential but to his already significant accomplishments. His subsequent tales (and, let us hope, novels) can only enhance his standing.

David Hambling

In the decades-long history of pastiches of or elaborations on the tales of H. P. Lovecraft, one of the most interesting phases was what might be called the "British invasion" of the 1960s, precisely paralleling the British invasion of American rock music led by The Beatles and other bands. In our realm, such writers as Ramsey Campbell, Brian Lumley, and Colin Wilson led the charge. Campbell, at the tender age of fifteen, submitted his earliest Lovecraftian tales to Arkham House's August Derleth, who quickly resolved to publish them in a book; *The Inhabitant of the Lake and Less Welcome Tenants* (1964) appeared when Campbell was eighteen, although these early tales could hardly have presaged the titan who would emerge in the following decades—a titan whose collected weird writing may now surpass Lovecraft's own in overall substance and merit. Lumley, a decade older than Campbell, began publishing his Lovecraftian work in the later 1960s, and by the 1970s was writing fast-paced adventure novels such as *The Burrowers Beneath* (1974) and *The Transition of Titus Crow* (1975). Wilson, a respected philosopher, had spoken harshly of Lovecraft in *The Strength to Dream* (1961), and was challenged by Derleth to write his own Lovecraftian tale; he did so with *The Mind Parasites* (1967) and other works. In later years, such distinguished British writers as Neil Gaiman, Brian Stableford, Nicholas Royle, and David Langford have contributed to the ever-growing universe of Lovecraftian fiction.

We can now add David Hambling to that list. A well-known journalist who has written for the *Guardian* and the *Economist*, Hambling has produced, in *The Dulwich Horror and Others* (2015), some of the most distinctive and intellectually challenging neo-Lovecraftian stories in recent decades. In a sense, Hambling fuses the best elements of his British predecessors—Campbell's deep knowledge of Lovecraft, Lumley's thrilling narrative pace, Wilson's philosophical depth. Along the way, Hambling makes more than a few tips of the hat to such other writers as Arthur Machen, Raymond Chandler, T. S. Eliot, Joseph Conrad, Bertrand Russell, and a number of others.

Let it not be thought, however, that Hambling's work is a mere echo of his predecessors. These tales are not simple pastiches; they are genuine and provocative elaborations of the themes, motifs, concepts, and imagery found in some of Lovecraft's greatest tales, from "The Shadow over Innsmouth" to "The Whisperer in Darkness," from "The Dunwich Horror" to "The Shadow out of Time." Hambling's journalistic experience has no doubt contributed to the acuity of his character portrayal, and his profound knowledge of science and philosophy allows him to hint at Lovecraftian cosmicism while simultaneously conveying the emotional plangency of human beings brought face to face with their own insignificance.

And just as Ramsey Campbell took Derleth's advice and fashioned a British analogue for Lovecraft's constellation of imaginary New England cities, devising the distinctive Severn Valley towns of Brichester, Severnford, and Goatswood, so Hambling has enlivened the South London suburb of Norwood with a series of narratives that stretch from the later nineteenth century to the present day. It is certainly convenient for Hambling that the town of Dulwich—so close in spelling to Lovecraft's central Massachusetts village of Dunwich—is in the general area. The tale that opens this book, "The Dulwich Horror of 1927," is not only a takeoff of "The Dunwich Horror," but it deliberately alters the spelling of Lovecraft's baleful Whateley family, since Hambling knows that the spelling Whatley is more typical of British usage.

These tales constitute David Hambling's initial foray into the realm of Lovecraftian fiction. The fertility of imagination, the crisp character delineations, and the smooth-flowing prose that we find in these seven tales leave us wishing for more of the same, and Hambling will no doubt oblige in the coming years. For now, we can sit back and relish a brace of stories that not only evoke the shade of the dreamer from Providence, but which that dreamer himself would have enjoyed to the full.

Curtis M. Lawson

The fusion of music and weirdness has been a slim but consistent thread in literary history. H. P. Lovecraft's "The Music of Erich Zann" (1922) is perhaps the best-known example today, but there are many others, ranging from J. Meade Falkner's *The Lost Stradivarius* (1895) to Algernon Blackwood's *The Human Chord* (1910). E. T. A. Hoffmann (1776–1822) was both a composer and an author of weird fiction, his work was the basis—partial or complete—of such musical works as Tchaikovsky's *The Nutcracker*, Offenbach's *Tales of Hoffmann*, and Wagner's *Tannhäuser* and *Die Meistersinger*. Hoffmann wrote an opera based upon *Undine*, the short novel published in 1811 by his friend Friedrich Heinrich Karl, baron de La Motte-Fouqué; but it does not appear as if he incorporated musical elements into his own weird tales. From a very different perspective, rock bands of all sorts have drawn inspiration from Lovecraft and other authors of supernatural fiction, in ways both hackneyed and creative.

Now Curtis M. Lawson has, in *Black Heart Boys' Choir* (2019), created a hypnotic tale of music and terror that can take rank with any of its predecessors. The supreme difficulty of writing about music is, of course, the utter divergence of the two media; perhaps the divergence is a bit less extreme in the case of vocal music, since such works are manifestly designed to appeal both to the musical and to the verbal imagination. Even so, as any music critic can tell you, trying to describe the effects of a musical composition by means of words is often a hopeless task. And yet, Lawson has created a striking narrative that brings to life the latent terror of a piece of music that may have the potential to tear apart the fabric of creation.

But there is a great deal more going on in Lawson's narrative than the horror of a possibly supernatural musical composition. His portrayal of high school life, with its inevitable cliques, bullying, and personal traumas (academic, sexual, and otherwise), is both grim and poignant, and many will be able to relate to his depiction of a cadre of loners and outsiders who seek the ultimate revenge on their rivals. The central figure in the text, Lucien Beaumont, reveals the many sides of his conflicted personality through his own words, carrying the reader on in appalled fascination as he advances (or descends) into psychosis.

I myself sing in a community choir—the Northwest Chorale, in Seattle—and have composed both instrumental and vocal music, so I received a particularly powerful jolt from *Black Heart Boys' Choir*. But no knowledge of music is needed to appreciate this skilful novel; all one needs is an awareness of the torments that beset many youths in this land, and an appreciation of the spectacular violence of which they are capable.

Some Modern Weird Poets

Ann K. Schwader

The emergence, over the past two or three decades, of Ann K. Schwader as perhaps the leading weird poet of our time has been steady and sure. From *The Worms Remember* (2001) to *Architectures of Night* (2003) to *In the Yaddith Time* (2007) to *Wild Hunt for the Stars* (2011), Schwader has exhibited a mastery of poetic technique and an imaginative richness that have placed her at the pinnacle of her field. *Twisted in Dream: The Collected Weird Poetry of Ann K. Schwader* (2011) seemed a fitting capstone to her achievement; but she is not content to rest on her laurels, as triumphantly demonstrated in her new collection, *Dark Energies* (2015).

It is a good time to be a poet of fantasy, terror, and the supernatural. No one can deny that a genuine renaissance in this long-neglected subgenre is taking place. During the heyday of *Weird Tales* in the 1920s and 1930s, poets such as Clark Ashton Smith, H. P. Lovecraft, Robert E. Howard, Donald Wandrei, and Frank Belknap Long made lasting contributions to the form; but in the succeeding decades, only such relatively lonely figures as Joseph Payne Brennan and Stanley McNail added to it. In recent decades, however, we have seen such poets as Leigh Blackmore, Wade German, Michael Fantina, Fred Phillips, and Charles Lovecraft (who skilfully fills the double role of poet and publisher) come to the fore. Several publishers regularly issue substantial books of weird poetry, and magazines such as *Spectral Realms* are exclusively devoted to the form.

What sets Schwader's work apart from that of her contemporaries is not merely her impeccable poetic technique—she has demonstrated conclusively that formal verse is far and away superior to free verse in the capturing of concentrated images of horror and strangeness—but in a kind of cosmic pessimism that makes her poems far more than mere exercises in shudder-coining. The imperishable lines from "A Voyage(r) Too Far"—"Humanity, / Beyond the fragile light that marks our star, / May prove no more than fireflies in a jar / Against the mindless void"—captures the essence of that vision. Possibly it is a vision partly derived from the work of Smith or Lovecraft; but it is too heartfelt, and expressed in too personal and intense a manner, to be merely the product of literary influence.

This is not to deny that there are literary influences on Schwader's poetry. This book contains numerous poems that derive from—or, perhaps more accurately, engage in a vibrant and constructive imaginative dialogue with—the writings of Smith, Lovecraft, Robert W. Chambers, Edgar Allan Poe, and so many other leading writers of weird fiction. How far Schwader is from mechanical pastiche can be seen in a poem like "Climate of Fear," an extraordinarily compact encapsulation of the essence of Lovecraft's Antarctic novella *At the Mountains of Madness*. Lovecraft, indeed, many be a dominant influence, or, at any rate, a dominant figure with whom Schwader wishes to engage: "Keziah" is a moving sonnet cycle that focuses on the central figure in "The Dreams in the Witch House," probing the depths of that cosmic witch's mind and psyche in a way that Lovecraft himself could not bring himself to do. And even such recent writers as the late lamented W. H. Pugmire and Adam Niswader come in for poignant poetical tributes.

It would be an error to think that cosmic terror is the sole focus of Schwader's poetry. Her imaginative palette is remarkably wide, and such a poem as "Giving Up the Ghost," with its striking opening line ("It's habit-forming, being haunted"), exhibits a grim whimsicality that other poems in this book build upon. And in terms of form, we find here a brace of exquisite prose-poems (with an admixture of haiku-like poetic fragments) that make it abundantly clear that Schwader can do far more than write flawless sonnets and quatrains. (Indeed, her prose fiction is now gaining an ever-increasing following, as her recent volume *Dark Equinox and Other Tales of Lovecraftian Horror* [2015] demonstrates.)

We have certainly not heard the last of Ann K. Schwader, and this volume can only leave readers thirsting for more poetic jewels from her pen. What further work will emerge in the coming years and decades it is impossible to predict; but it is safe to say that every poem will embody the technical perfection, the meticulous care in word-choice, the imaginative range, and the brooding sense of humanity's fragile and transient place in the universe that we find throughout this book. It is, as I say, a good time to be a weird poet; but it is an even better time to be a reader of weird poetry.

Kyla Lee Ward

I have never read a book quite like *The Macabre Modern* (2019). Kyla Lee Ward, building upon the promise of her first poetry collection, *The Land of Bad Dreams* (2011), has weaved together a compelling tapestry of poetry, fiction, and nonfiction, all unified by the theme of the *danse macabre* (the dance of death). Ward shows that this single theme is capable of infinite variety, and this book features a striking diversity of emotional resonance while nonetheless retaining a thematic and structural unity.

In the opening section, where Death holds a dialogue with a succession of hapless mortals who will all, in due course of time, come under his sway, Ward seems to channel the keen-edged wit and satire of Ambrose Bierce, who similarly saw in Death the ultimate arbiter of human destiny. But what is generally lacking in Bierce's work but present in Ward's is a sense of empathy with those human beings—whether high-born or low-born, rich or poor, successful or otherwise—who must all shuffle off this mortal coil when their time approaches. The dismal fate of the Office Worker, having spent a lifetime in futile busywork ("So many dreams, / all buried now, beneath the reams / of copying"), is etched in a few plangent lines.

The learned essay on the history of the *danse macabre* fittingly occupies a central place in this volume, leading to an array of longer poems that return in different ways to the book's overall theme. Whereas, in her essay, Ward explores the history of the *danse macabre* from its origins in the Middle Ages up to the present day (including some surprising appearances in contemporary films and song lyrics), the poems reach back much farther in time. The horrors of ancient Egypt ("Boat of a Million Years," "The Tomb Robber's Complaint") and Rome ("Libitina's Garden") are on display; and in "Vanth— A Myth Derived" Ward performs a tour de force in rooting her work in the culture of the Etruscans, that shadowy and obscure civilisation that preceded Rome on the Italian peninsula and were ultimately conquered by the latter. "Buried in Jade" evokes death in a Chinese setting.

Ward is at her best in such long poems as "The Necromancer's Question" and "Lucubration," the latter first published in a volume of poems inspired by two of the greatest weird poems in literary history, George Sterling's "A Wine of Wizardry" and Clark Ashton Smith's *The Hashish-Eater*. "Lucubration" is anything but a mechanical pastiche, its sonorous iambic pentameter lines echoing its impressive predecessors but reflecting Ward's own poetic sensibility. And we can hardly overlook "The Loquacious Cadaver," a vignette of succulent graveyard humour that shows Ward as deft in prose as in verse.

With each new work she produces, Kyla Lee Ward—who, like William Blake and Clark Ashton Smith, has chosen to illustrate her own work—makes clear why she should be regarded as one of the preeminent exemplars of contemporary weird poetry. *The Macabre Modern and Other Morbidities* is a book to be savoured unhurriedly and with due contemplation of its essential message: that Death is omnipresent and inescapable, and that its surface terrors may also hold some faint hope of relief for the weary creatures who will inexorably succumb to it.

Wade German

The Canadian poet Wade German has definitively established himself as one of the premier weird poets of our time, joining Ann K. Schwader, Kyla Lee Ward, and a few others in that lofty rank. And yet, until the appearance of this latest volume, he had published only a single collection of poems, *Dreams from a Black Nebula* (Hippocampus Press, 2014). His new book, *The Ladies of the Everlasting Lichen and Other Relics* (2019), relatively slim as it is, goes far in confirming German's high standing as a poet, and it is a shame that the book's minuscule print run and high price might severely limit its readership.

German's poety is characterised by meticulous attention to the formal meters he employs (most notably the sonnet, but also the quatrain and other stanzaic forms, the triolet, and even the compressed verse drama, of which we have several shining examples in the present book). He can evoke terror with a single line or even a single word; and yet, his poems are far from mere shudder-coining, becoming thought-provoking meditations on the fragility of our tenure on this pain-wracked globe.

Poets do not need to establish any kind of overriding theme or motif in a collection, but I detect two such motifs in this book. The first is religion—or, perhaps more accurately, the perversion of religion, or the establishment of a dark religion of death, decay, and terror as a grim parody of the conventional religions of the earth, which seek to provide an antidote (spurious, in my mind) to the "thousand natural shocks that flesh is heir to."

One of the most evocative of German's poems in this book is "Ride of the Witchfinder," a magnificent sonnet on the eternal punishment meted out to a persecutor of witches. It deserves quotation in full:

> I slew them all, and watched their corpses burn
> In flames that rose by forces not my own,
> Then witnessed all their evil ashes blown
> By winds that voiced the vows of their return.
> And as I rode, the very sky went black,
> Subverting day to never-ending night
> As nails of horror hammered in my sight—
> Black magic vengeance followed in my tracks.
>
> And so I ride as one who flees from sin,
> Pursued by shadow-things that curse and scream
> Across a world become a dead god's dream,
> Abominated, bare, my soul worn thin—
> Three hundred years, and on and on I ride
> Through endless hells—and Hell's no place to hide.

Other poems elaborate upon the (anti-)religious theme. I cannot tell if "Out of Endor" has any specific connection with the Old Testament account of the Witch of Endor, who summoned up the shade of Samuel; but the baleful first stanza of the poem is memorable:

> The horned red moon has risen clear,
> And evening augurs heresies;
> The rites and rituals commence—
> And demon principalities
> Grow silent momently to hear
> Our song of strange malevolence.

"Ecclesiastical Triptych" is more forthright subversion of Christian myth, and its third section provides the title for the book; that section's repeated use of "lichen" in multiple different contexts provides a haunting ritornello to a memorable poetic sequence. Also explicitly biblical is "Methusaleh"; but here, that ancient figure's nine hundred-odd years on this planet have turned him into a misanthrope who loathes the moral and physical corruption of the human race.

The second major motif in this book is German's skillful riffs on the long history of weird fiction and poetry. "The Driver of the Dragon's Coach" is set in the realm of Stoker's *Dracula*; "The Secret Prayer of Victor Frankenstein" betrays its source in its very title; "Naotalba's Song" purports to be a segment from the play *The King in Yellow*. More significantly, "Lore" is a 100-line poem that elaborates upon Lovecraft's theme of the forbidden book, and its concluding lines effectively convey Lovecraft's cosmicism:

> An apostate, I keep the eldritch lore,
> The revelation of an elder faith—
> Our world is but an altar in the void
> Where souls shall be devoured and destroyed.

"Beddoes: Marginalia in a Cadaveric Atlas" is presumably an expansion of Thomas Lovell Beddoes's *Death's Jest-Book* (1850), taking the form of a short verse drama. 'The Ghosts of Hyperborea" is a nod to Clark Ashton Smith. And we can hardly bypass "The Tomb of Wilum Hopfrog Pugmire," a moving elegy that seeks to capture the essence of that late author's imaginative realm.

Other poems in the book do not fit easily into the two rubrics outlined above, but they are no less vital and dynamic. "Wraiths" features a memorable passage where metaphor is used to telling effect: "We are as exiles who exist / Like lovers long-since left behind / In mausoleums of your mind . . ."

The book concludes with three long poems featuring figures from Greek myth. Historically, weird poets have not drawn frequently on this body of myth, since its major features appear to convey an atmosphere of light-hearted paganism; but there are plenty of dark corners in Greek myth that a poet of German's skill can exploit.

"Scylla and Charybdis" is a meditation on those two baleful creatures whom Odysseus encountered in his voyages, as recounted in Homer's *Odyssey*. The eponymous figure of the poem "Eurynomos" is much more obscure, and German helpfully provides an epigraph from Pausanias, who writes that Eurynomos" is "one of the spirits of the Underworld, who devours the flesh of corpses, leaving only bones." This sounds highly promising; and German's poem insidiously morphs from a catalogue of body horror and decay to a chilling indictment of human frailty, moral and physical. The book concludes with "Gorgonum Chaos," a poetic dialogue between Stheno and Euryale, the sisters of Medusa, who lament the demise of their sibling at the hands of Perseus and curse the goddess Athena for encouraging that valiant hero.

The production of this book calls for especial praise. The typeface is suitably archaic, the paper stiff and heavy, and scattered throughout the book are peculiar illustrations taken from what I take to be an 1825 book on black and white magic. This is a book to savour in small doses; each poem is evocative and striking in its own way, and the lengthier poems are Golgothas of horror and grue that will long linger in the mind. It can only be hoped that the poems in the book will one day reach a wider audience.

Acknowledgments

"Algernon Blackwood and John Silence," introduction to Blackwood's *The Complete John Silence Stories* (Dover, 1998).

"Arthur Machen and Weird Fiction," "The Criticism of Weird Fiction," "The Haunted House," "Ramsey Campbell and Weird Fiction," "Shirley Jackson and Weird Fiction," "The Supernatural in Greek and Latin Literature," first published as entries in *Supernatural Literature of the World: An Encyclopedia*, ed. S. T. Joshi and Stefan Dziemianowicz (Greenwood Press, 2005).

"Brian McNaughton: The Care and Feeding of Ghouls," afterword to McNaughton's *The Throne of Bones* (Terminal Fright, 1997).

"Caitlín R. Kiernan and the Mythos," introduction to Kiernan's *Houses Under the Sea: Mythos Tales* (Centipede Press, 2018).

"The Canon of Weird Fiction," *Necrofile* No. 19 (Winter 1996): 23–25.

"Carl Jacobi: The Life of a Pulpsmith," introductions to Jacobi's *Mive and Others* (Weird House, 2020) and *Witches in the Cornfield* (Weird House, 2020).

"Clark Ashton Smith's Juvenilia," introductions to Smith's *The Black Diamonds* (Hippocampus Press, 2002) and *The Sword of Zagan* (Hippocampus Press, 2004).

"The Ghost Story, 1870–1920," in *American History through Literature 1870–1920*, ed. Tom Quirk and Gary Scharnhorst (Thomson Gale, 2006; as "Ghost Stories").

"H. B. Drake's *The Shadowy Thing*," afterword to Drake's *The Shadowy Thing* (Hippocampus Press, 2010).

"The Life and Career of Ambrose Bierce," introduction to *A Sole Survivor: Bits of Autobiography*, ed. S. T. Joshi and David E. Schultz (University of Tennessee Press, 1998).

"Lovecraft and 'Adept's Gambit,'" introduction to Leiber's *Adept's Gambit: The Original Version* (Arcane Wisdom, 2014).

"Lovecraft and 'In Amundsen's Tent,'" in Lovecraft's *At the Mountains of Madness* (PS Publishing, 2015).

"Lovecraft and the Gothic," in *Gothic Writers: A Critical and Bibliographical Guide*, ed. Douglass H. Thomson, Jack G. Voller, and Frederick S. Frank (Greenwood Press, 2001).

"Lovecraft and the Titans: A Critical Legacy," in *New Directions in Supernatural Horror in Literature: The Critical Influence of H. P. Lovecraft*, ed. Sean Moreland (Palgrave Macmillan, 2018).

"Lovecraft and Zealia Bishop," introduction to *The Spirit of Revision: Lovecraft's Letters to Zealia Brown Reed Bishop*, ed. Sean Branney and Andrew Leman (H. P. Lovecraft Historical Society, 2015).

"May Sinclair: The Spiritual Ghost Story," introduction to *If the Dead Knew: The Weird Fiction of May Sinclair* (Hippocampus Press, 2020).

"On Rod Serling's 'Clean Kills and Other Trophies,'" in *Another Dimension Anthology*, ed. Angel McCoy (Wily Writers, 2016).

"Poe and Lovecraft," foreword to *The Lovecraftian Poe: Essays on Influence, Reception, Interpretation and Transformation*, ed. Sean Moreland (Lehigh University Press, 2017).

"Solar Pons Meets Cthulhu: Detective Elements in Derleth's Mythos Tales," *Crypt of Cthulhu* No. 6 (St John's Eve 1982).

"Some Modern Weird Poets," afterword to Kyla Lee Ward's *Macabre Modern and Other Morbidities* (P'rea Press, 2019); preface to Ann K. Schwader's *Dark Energies* (P'rea Press, 2015); review of Wade German's *The Ladies of the Everlasting Lichen and Other Relics*, *Spectral Realms* No. 12 (Winter 2020).

"Some Younger Weird Writers," introduction to Michael Aronovitz's *Seven Deadly Pleasures* (Hippocampus Press, 2009), afterword to Aronovitz's *Alice Walks* (Centipede Press, 2013); introduction to Clint Smith's *Ghouljaw and Other Stories* (Hippocampus Press, 2014); foreword to David Hambling's *The*

Dulwich Horror and Others (PS Publishing, 2015); foreword to Curtis M. Lawson's *Black Heart Boy's Choir* (Wyrd Horror, 2019).

"The Theory and Practice of Satirical Criticism," *Dead Reckonings* No. 23 (Spring 2018): 98–102.

"W. H. Pugmire: Lovecraftian and Prose Poet," introductions to Pugmire's *The Tangled Muse* (Centipede Press, 2010), *An Ecstasy of Fear* (Centipede Press, 2019), and *An Imp of Aether* (Hippocampus Press, 2019).

"Weird Fiction and Ordinary People," *Necrofile* No. 6 (Fall 1992): 20–22.

"The Weird Work of M. P. Shiel," introduction to *The House of Sounds and Others* (Hippocampus Press, 2005).

"The Weird Work of Robert Hichens," introductions to Hichens's *The Return of the Soul* (Midnight House, 2001) and *The Dweller on the Threshold* (Sarnath Press, 2017).

"Why Michel Houellebecq Is Wrong about Lovecraft's Racism," *Lovecraft Annual* No. 12 (2018).

"Women and the Ghost Story," introduction to *The Cold Embrace: Weird Stories by Women* (Dover, 2016).

Index